BACKFIRE

BACKFIRE

CARLY FIORINA'S HIGH-STAKES BATTLE FOR THE SOUL OF HEWLETT-PACKARD

PETER BURROWS

WILEY

John Wiley & Sons, Inc.

For Wendy and Ari

Contents

Acknowledgments

It's fitting that the first words in this book are a thank you to Kim Girard. I hired her in May 2002, with the intention of getting some research and editing help. Instead, Kim, an accomplished business writer in her own right, devoted herself wholly to the project. Her reporting, writing, editorial shaping, and support were invaluable. I could not have met my deadline without her help.

Most of the reporting for this book was collected while I was covering HP for *BusinessWeek*, where I have worked since 1993. I am indebted to Editor-in-Chief Steve Shepard for giving me the time and support to write this book, and to Assistant Managing Editor Kathy Rebello, who has helped me immeasurably over the years in honing my skills as a journalist and my coverage of the company. Also, much thanks to my colleagues on the tech beat, who have contributed great reporting and insights over the years, particularly Andrew Park, Jim Kerstetter, Jay Greene, Joan Hamilton, Robert Hof, Ira Sager, Steve Hamm, Peter Elstrom, Andy Reinhardt, and David Rocks. Also, thanks to John Byrne for providing words of wisdom for a first-time author.

There are countless sources to thank. Walter Hewlett spent many hours with me, at a time when he would have preferred to be moving past a very difficult portion of his life. Given the Hewlett family's preference for privacy, I am grateful to Esther Hewlett and to Eleanor and Jean-Paul Gimon for their willingness to speak with me. Dozens of current and former employees and executives at HP have spent many hours with me, many of them on a background basis. While opinions vary widely on many topics, it is the passion and commitment that HP's employees show toward their company that in large part led me to want to write the book in the first place. In particular, former HP CEOs John Young and Lew Platt and former executives including Al Bagley, Rick Belluzzo, Doug Chance, Nick Earle, Paul Ely, Phil Faraci, Bob Frankenberg, Dave Kirby, Jim Mackey, Dean Morton, Carl Snyder, and

Bill Terry provided invaluable background and insights. Agilent Technologies' public relations director Karen Lewis, HP's former archivist, helped me focus on key parts of HP's history. Jeff Christian and Rich Hagberg, among others provided details about the CEO search that brought Fiorina to HP. Walter Hewlett's advisors, particularly Steve Neal, Laurie Hoagland, Tully Friedman, and Spencer Fleischer, gave freely of their time, as did Todd Glass at Joele Frank, Wilkinson Brimmer Katcher. Much thanks also to Michael Busselen, Linda Himelstein, and Marc Dubroff for their input on drafts and their constant support. Naheed Attari provided fact checking, copy editing, and a cool head as the deadline approached. Finally, thanks to my agent, Martha Millard; to the folks at John Wiley & Sons, including Linda Witzling, Jesica Church, and Michelle Patterson; and to my editor at Wiley, Airié Stuart, for her sage counsel and help in crafting the narrative.

Most of all, endless thanks to my wife Wendy for her patience, and for gallantly dealing with a headline-addled husband when she could have used extra help chasing our two-year-old son. I am a lucky man to have such a wonderful wife.

PROLOGUE

One last obstacle stood between Walter B. Hewlett and a peaceful Labor Day weekend at the family cabin in the Sierra Nevada Mountains. The date was August 31, 2001. At around 1:45 P.M., the son of Hewlett-Packard's cofounder pulled out of the long driveway to his house on leafy Addison Avenue in Palo Alto, California. He turned right, driving past homes of understated wealth in the corner of the university town where he grew up. If he'd gone straight for just a few blocks, he would have passed a stone plaque in the front yard of a run-down two-family house, which declares the spot a California historical landmark: "The Birthplace of Silicon Valley," it reads. In the unassuming one-car garage out back, his father, William R. "Bill" Hewlett, and "Uncle Dave" Packard had founded their legendary company in 1938.

On this day, taking a trip down memory lane was the furthest thing on the younger Hewlett's mind. There was far more important business to attend to. He turned his electric-powered car, a General Motors EV1, in the direction of HP's world headquarters on Page Mill Road. He'd made the three-mile trip hundreds of times over the years, to attend board meetings or spend an afternoon with engineers learning about some promising new technology. He traveled down the Oregon Expressway, where his dad had been bitten by a rattlesnake when Hewlett was a kid. He paid no notice as he passed Agilent Technologies, an HP spin-off that stood on the site of the first company-owned headquarters, where he and his father used to go on weekends to find production scraps for him to use in school projects. The past was all around him, as usual.

This day, he was focused on the future. HP was less than a mile ahead on the left, but he wasn't going that far. On the other side of the busy El Camino Real, he turned into the sprawling seven-building campus of Wilson Sonsini Goodrich & Rosati, Silicon Valley's preeminent law firm. Larry Sonsini, Silicon Valley's most famous lawyer, had chaperoned some of the biggest deals in tech industry history from the safety of his boardroom. At 2 o'clock that afternoon, Sonsini would lead HP's board through a review of the final merger agreement by which HP would buy Compaq Computer Corporation. It was to be a blockbuster, $25-billion transaction, more than twice the size of the biggest deal previously attempted in the computer business and the single most important deal in HP's 63-year history. It would be a point of no return—a massive infusion of new people and new ways that would change the company forever.

Hewlett says he never considered leaking news of the deal to the press, but life certainly would have been easier if the world had known. All summer, he'd agonized about the transaction, which he was certain would be disastrous for the company. Other than his wife, he'd told no one—not his fellow scion and childhood friend David Woodley Packard, not his colleagues on the Agilent board, and not the trustees of the William and Flora Hewlett Foundation, the huge family charity that stood to lose billions if his fears proved correct.

He first heard about the proposed merger at a board meeting in May. HP's nine directors had just finished their normal quarterly two-day session, when the company's larger-than-life chief executive and chair Carly Fiorina had asked them to stay put, says Hewlett. Fiorina, easily the world's most powerful female executive as head of America's twenty-eighth-largest firm,[1] was usually too polished to betray any pride in her own business instincts. But Hewlett sensed a haughtiness as she announced the news. "Eighteen months ago, I figured out that Compaq would come to us and ask to be bought," Hewlett recalls her saying. "Well, guess what. It has happened."

Fiorina laid out the basics of how the marriage would work, claims Hewlett. The company would still be called Hewlett-Packard, would be based in Palo Alto, and Compaq CEO Michael D. Capellas would report to her. She outlined the strategic thinking behind the merger. While the two computer companies were struggling overall, they had strengths that would fit seamlessly together like a zipper. Compaq was strong in PCs used by office workers,

2

while HP was the leader in home PCs. Though Compaq's high-end computer business was a financial mess, it had some products that could lift HP from also-ran to leader in the critical business of selling the sophisticated gear corporations use to run their operations. Together, HP and Compaq would have a huge share in almost every computing market worth mentioning, and the merger would enable them to slash billions in costs—a surefire way to lift profits for awhile.

Fiorina needed to have the board's permission to continue with talks. "We have to decide whether to pursue this or not," she said. Working counterclockwise around the table, all seven of Hewlett's other colleagues—Boeing Corporation CEO Phil Condit, former HP executive Dick Hackborn, and former Reagan aide George "Jay" Keyworth among them—gave her the okay to proceed. Then she got to Hewlett.

"No, this is not a good idea," Hewlett claims he told her. "It would take us in exactly the wrong direction."

It was as if no one heard his protest, he says.

"Well, it looks like we have a consensus on this," Fiorina said breezily after a short interchange, according to Hewlett. "Let's take the next step."

What happened at the board meetings that followed in the summer is subject to dispute. Some HP directors say Hewlett expressed vague concerns, but nothing solid. Hewlett contends that he repeatedly objected to the deal. As the weeks passed, he began to suspect that the board was trying to marginalize his influence. Take the board meeting on July 19 and 20. He had missed the first day of the two-day session, as he had for the previous few years, to play his cello in a concert at Bohemian Grove, an exclusive retreat north of San Francisco. It turned out that the board spent the entire day discussing the Compaq deal in detail. "No one made any attempt to say, 'You've got to be there. This will be the critical day,'" he says.

When Hewlett arrived the next morning, his fellow board members were clearly miffed by his truancy. His isolation grew clearer when Fiorina sprung another quickie poll: "Do you believe this company can continue to pursue the strategy it's embarked on without a major, scene-changing step, such as buying Compaq?" Again, all the other board members agreed that drastic action was required, except for Hewlett. "I don't know why you guys want to make a crisis out of this," he said. "What's the rush?" While none of his colleagues said anything rude, "There were lots of white eyeballs looking at the ceiling," says a board member. "There was a tremendous amount of frustration."

Since then, negotiations had continued, despite his concerns. Just the week before, on August 25, Hewlett had made his final, most considered argument against the deal. He'd been up at the Hewlett family's five-house compound in Lake Tahoe with a bunch of musical friends, for a weekend of playing Mozart quartets and Brahms concertos. He ducked out for the teleconference with the board, and laid out his chief concerns. Buying Compaq would make HP so big that it could not possibly match the double-digit growth rates it had enjoyed over the decades—and investors don't pay a lot for slow-growing behemoths, he argued.[2] He also feared the deal would put a stake into the unique corporate culture "Bill and Dave" had nurtured over the years. The famous "HP Way" was built on teamwork and a tight social contract between management and employees. But this deal threatened to sever that bond with at least 15,000 layoffs, and subject HP's communal ethos to Houston-based Compaq's far more confrontational, cutthroat ways. And so much had to go right for the deal to be successful. What if antitrust regulators forced HP to sell off businesses to prevent it from monopolizing certain markets? What if competitors such as Dell or IBM stole more business than the board expected while the companies focused on merging their operations? "If everything doesn't go exactly right, this won't be the deal you think it will be," Hewlett recalls saying. "I beg you to reconsider. Please don't do this."

Should he have done more to prevent the deal? Some corporate governance experts say yes, he should have threatened the board members right then with a nasty, public fight if they went through with their plans.

But Hewlett wasn't looking that far ahead. What's more, who was he to stand up to the likes of Condit, Hackborn, and Fiorina, much less HP's high-powered advisors from Goldman Sachs, McKinsey & Company, and Wilson Sonsini? With the exception of

Hackborn, he felt he knew as much or more about HP's products and technologies as anyone on the board—including Fiorina. He was chair of one of the world's largest charitable foundations, but the closest he'd come to running a business was keeping the books at the obscure lab at Stanford he'd created in 1984 to convert ancient classical music scores into digital form.

His father, as always, was never far from his thoughts—especially now, just seven months after Bill Hewlett had passed away. He felt in his bones that his father would never have let this deal get this far. One of the all-time great electrical engineers, the elder Hewlett had insisted that HP build only special, one-of-a-kind products—not the Plain-Jane PCs that brought in much of Compaq's revenues. However, when he asked his son to join the board in 1987, Bill had made it clear that Walter was not to throw his weight around. He was not to be a disruptive know-it-all. He was simply there to make sure the Hewlett perspective was represented—"to add color," as his dad had put it.

Now, entering the cylindrical lobby of Wilson Sonsini's offices, Hewlett felt like he was nearing the end of a slow-motion nightmare he was powerless to stop. During the Roaring '90s, thousands of entrepreneurs, from seasoned executives to supercilious dot-commers, had come to work out final details of the initial public offerings that would make them wildly rich. Since the bubble burst in early 2000, many now hired the firm to work out liquidation plans.

Around 2 o'clock, Hewlett joined the other board members sitting at the big U-shaped table. Among them were HP's dignified chief financial officer Bob Wayman and Dick Hackborn, the brilliant strategist who'd built the company's gold-mine printer business in the 1980s, pushed HP toward the PC business in the 1990s, and championed the choice of Fiorina as CEO in 1999. Hewlett considered both Wayman and Hackborn friends. Filling in seats around the outside of the room were some of the company's advisors, all of whom had a major interest in seeing the deal go through. Goldman Sachs, HP's investment banker on the deal, stood to bring in fees of $33 million—a much-needed haul in a miserable year on

Wall Street. Wilson Sonsini and McKinsey & Company, the elite and high-priced management-consulting firm, also had multi-million-dollar deals.

However, no one had more at stake than Carly Fiorina. When HP's board made her the company's first ever hired-from-the-outside CEO in July 1999, the news was greeted with a tidal wave of good will and high hopes. She'd earned a reputation as a "change agent" within staid AT&T during her 19-year career there, and had played a lead role in the hugely successful 1997 spin-off, Lucent Technologies. She had brilliance, charisma, and courage, yet her tenure was in deep trouble. Since she had taken over, the stock had dropped 59 percent to $23, and she was close to losing the allegiance of many of HP's employees. After failing to spot the worst downturn in tech industry history in late 2000, she'd had to make the biggest layoffs in HP history—yet was still collecting on her $70-million-plus pay package and flying in the corporate jets she ordered soon after her arrival at HP.

Fiorina must have felt the heat. Complaints about her posted to an internal HP Web site had grown so nasty that the company closed it down. Rumors of her impending demise came up so often that on one occasion she asked board members to publicly reiterate their support for their CEO. But now, it was time to power past these growing pains with a bold acquisition she felt certain would enable her to accomplish the makeover she'd been hired to achieve. Once the board signed off on the merger, she would no longer be forced to preside over a once-great company's depressing dotage. With more than $80 billion in revenues and top market share in almost every computing market, woe to anyone who dismissed HP. With those pen strokes, she would—at least temporarily—be vaulted into the highest reaches of the tech industry's power structure, right up there with Microsoft's Bill Gates, IBM's Sam Palmisano, and Dell Computer's Michael Dell. She would be positioned to achieve the biggest accomplishment of her career, and give HP a chance to return to glory.

Until she suggested the Compaq merger, Walter Hewlett says, he supported Fiorina's every move. At first, she had seemed to be just what HP needed—but his instincts about her had changed. Her soaring rhetoric, bold promises, and unflinching self-confidence now gave him pause. She was precisely the type of person who might have left his amiable father cold. The elder Hewlett loved fact-based disciplines, preferring engineers over marketers and historians over politicians. "Politics is about perception and spin, and that's the kind of thing my father was never very interested in," says Hewlett. He felt his father certainly would have been concerned with her on-the-job performance. Since she'd arrived, Fiorina had changed nearly every aspect of how HP operated—how it paid its employees, how it sold its products, and how it set its strategy. So far, these changes had not paid off. HP was moving faster and more decisively, but the company hadn't gained share in the most strategic markets or introduced many new hit products. Yet here she was, spearheading the biggest tech merger in history.

There was plenty to discuss at the meeting. The price tag for Compaq had yet to be finalized. Details of the pay packages for top executives, including Fiorina and Compaq CEO Capellas, had not been settled. There were antitrust concerns. Then, Wilson Sonsini partner Marty Korman got up to walk the board through key points of the final merger agreement. This was pretty thick boilerplate stuff, for the most part. Standing in the front of the room, he moved quickly through his 20-minute slide presentation.

Then it happened. Toward the end of the presentation, Korman showed a slide that included the following bullet point: "Unanimous Board Recommendation by Each Party." It was legalese, but the message was clear: The merger agreement would suggest that every member of both Compaq's and HP's boards, including Hewlett himself, supported the merger. Hewlett says it caught him full in the chest. Suddenly, his vague sense of doom about the whole board process crystallized. Until then, he felt he'd been behaving as a board member should, balancing his gut feeling with the need to be a team player. Now they were asking him to renounce his beliefs, and he didn't see how he could remain on the sidelines.

A deliberate, normally quiet person, Hewlett sat in silence while Korman finished his presentation. The reasons to have unanimity were obvious, Korman briefly explained. Everyone present knew the deal was bound to be controversial. No big computer industry merger had ever worked out as well as advertised, a prime example being Compaq's own purchase of Digital Equipment Corporation for $8.6 billion in 1998. And Compaq was widely considered a company with a dim future. Despite operational improvements, it had lost almost $900 million over the previous three quarters amid plummeting PC prices, falling sales, and lost market share. The stock was languishing at its lowest level in years. Having a divided board would give investors one more reason to worry. And given the intense process the board had been through to analyze the deal—13 board meetings that summer, compared to 5 or fewer for many deals—there was no reason to let that happen.

When Korman was finished, Hewlett says he broke in. "I understand what you're trying to do with this unanimity clause, but you know I can't support this." An uncomfortable hush fell over the room, he says. "You all know I'm opposed to the deal. You know my views. Do you realize what an awkward position you've put me in? I still don't know how I'm going to come out on this thing."

Hewlett waited for some kind of response.

Other attendees say they recall no histrionics. Korman insists this interchange was a figment of Hewlett's imagination. In fact, Korman says Hewlett didn't speak at all. Whether he did or not, someone suggested they take a break.

As Hewlett moved out of the boardroom into the main lobby, Sonsini appeared next to him, and the pair wandered toward the lobby, according to both men.

"Larry, I'm having a lot of trouble with this," he said.

"Yes, we know you are, Walter," Sonsini responded. According to Hewlett, Sonsini then cut to the chase. "Walter, this deal is going to go forward whether you want it to or not. And it would be best if we had unanimity," Sonsini said. If Hewlett refused to sign the agreement as written, it would be redrafted and okayed nonetheless.

At this point, Hewlett's mind went into overdrive. If he refused to give his consent, Sonsini's lawyers would have to go back to Compaq's lawyers and tell them HP's board wasn't unanimous—and by the way, the dissenter's name was Hewlett. That, he figured, could only lead to one thing: Compaq, fearful of a public imbroglio, would demand a higher purchase price from HP. His calculation went like this: He knew the final purchase price had not been negotiated. It was a stock-only deal—Compaq shareholders would receive shares of HP stock, rather than cash—but Compaq wanted to receive 0.65 of a share of HP stock for each share of Compaq stock. Hewlett claims Compaq had rejected an exchange ratio of around 0.63 just days before which HP's lawyers don't recall. If he dissented, Compaq would have more bargaining leverage. That may sound like a minor distinction, but Hewlett calculated that the difference was worth $800 million to HP shareholders. The plan was for the negotiators to hammer out the final price over the weekend. On Monday, Labor Day, the boards would meet again, respectively, to formally okay the deal.

Talk about a no-win situation. Hewlett could go along and watch HP buy a wilting company—or he could fight and cause the company to pay even more for it. It was even worse than that for Hewlett, because of the many hats he was wearing in this situation. As an HP board member, he had a fiduciary duty to do what was best for HP's shareholders. Costing them $800 million so he could make a symbolic protest did not fit the bill, and might even land him at the wrong end of a class-action lawsuit. However, he also had fiduciary responsibilities as trustee of the Hewletts' multi-billion-dollar family trust, and in his role as chair of the huge William and Flora Hewlett Foundation. How could he vote for a deal he hated to avoid spending more to buy Compaq at the outset, when that same deal could take billions out of the family and foundation coffers by driving the stock down over the long haul? Hewlett says he began looking for convenient exits. What if he simply didn't weigh in? No harm, no foul, right?

"Can I abstain?" he asked Sonsini.

"No, you cannot abstain. That does not constitute a unanimous board," the lawyer responded, according to Hewlett.

Sonsini says Hewlett never asked if he could abstain. But both sides agree that the attorney then came up with a different sort of escape hatch for Hewlett. Sonsini explained that, legally speaking, Hewlett could vote with the board to okay the deal—thereby upholding the unanimity clause—and still vote the family shares against the deal when it was put to a shareholder vote. When that day came, Sonsini was arguing, Hewlett might have good reasons to vote his shares against the deal. The issuance of 1 billion shares of HP stock to current Compaq owners would dilute the Hewlett family's interest in the company by more than a third. Still, as a board member, he had to put his own agenda second and do what was best for all shareholders. "It's okay to vote one way as a director, and another when managing your own property," Sonsini said.

Why did Sonsini do it? He says he felt legally responsible to advise Hewlett, and wanted him to feel comfortable with what he was being asked to do. "I like the guy," says Sonsini. Also, he and other insiders believed Hewlett's concerns with the deal might fade by the day of the shareholder vote. This had to be a very emotional time for him. It was the first big vote he'd been asked to consider since his father died, and it must have felt like he was being asked to give the company away. But he would come around in the end and see the wisdom of the deal.

Hewlett and his advisors would later argue that Sonsini railroaded Hewlett into supporting the merger. They said Sonsini and HP's management made a calculated bet that mild-mannered Hewlett would simply cave and go along with his boardmates, even against his personal opinions. For years, he'd dutifully supported management's wishes. Why would that change now? Even if he did vote his shares against the merger, would it really matter? After all, who cared if Walter Hewlett quietly voted his own shares against the deal? It wasn't like he was going to launch a public proxy fight, right?

Sonsini vociferously denies that anyone made such calculations. He says no one improperly pressured Hewlett. "Walter is an independent thinker and an experienced board member. He knows very well what his fiduciary duties are: to vote in the best interests of shareholders."

At some point during these discussions, a scary thought flickered through Hewlett's head: Maybe he should have had his own lawyer present? Sonsini worked for HP's board, of which Hewlett was a member—but Sonsini's primary responsibility was to the board as a whole, not to Hewlett. Because he was a neophyte when it came to corporate law, Hewlett wasn't sure if he was entitled to seek his own counsel. No matter, there was no time for such musings. Hewlett simply said "Thank you, that's very helpful," and headed back into the boardroom. "It was not heated or uncomfortable or anything like that," recalls Sonsini.

Not visibly so, anyway. But when Hewlett left with his wife for the weekend at the cabin in the mountains, he brought along copies of the pages from Korman's presentation that dealt with the unanimity clause. As the altitude rose, so did his anger. His fellow directors, some of them longtime friends, had sat by silently as he was asked to vote for a deal he hated. They were all but daring him to stand up for his convictions.

Maybe he didn't know it yet, but Walter Hewlett was at the beginning of a personal metamorphosis. Over the next eight months, he would leave his quiet, contented life to wage one of the biggest proxy battles in U.S. corporate history, and star in one of the most unlikely, high-stakes corporate soap operas ever.

1

THE SHOWDOWN

Thank God for her.
—ANONYMOUS HP INVESTOR, LEAVING THE
COURTROOM AFTER CARLY FIORINA'S TESTIMONY

The line started forming outside of the Court of Chancery in Wilmington, Delaware, at 3:00 A.M. Scruffy college students in parkas and heavy blankets set up lawn chairs to hunker down for the long wait. For $60 an hour, they held spots for the high-priced lawyers involved in the landmark case that was set to start that day. Soon after sunrise, dapper stock traders, hoping for some big courtroom news, stood sipping coffee to shake off the chill of the morning air. Law professors waited patiently to witness a chapter of corporate law history. Business reporters from around the country stood sharing war stories and speculating about who would be the day's winner. By the time a security guard opened the heavy courthouse doors, more than 200 people snaked down the side of the massive building.

They were all waiting for what was expected to be corporate theatre at its best. At the start of the working day on April 23, 2002, Judge William B. Chandler III would open the trial to consider Walter Hewlett's lawsuit against the company that bore his name.

Like most companies, HP is technically incorporated in the state of Delaware for tax purposes, so the case had ended up here. Neither civil nor criminal, the court's sole purpose is to resolve internal corporate disputes. Hewlett's suit, filed less than a month before, made one simple yet monumental request of the court: Throw out the shareholder vote taken on March 19 that had narrowly cleared the way for HP's merger with Compaq.

Like all great dramas, this one was filled with rich characters and timeless themes. Here was Walter Hewlett, the intensely private son of one of the company's cofounders, coming out of the shadows to defend his father's traditional values. Rather than pursue risky blockbuster deals, he believed HP should return to operational discipline and the hard work of inventing great products. To some, he was a courageous corporate governance hero, daring to stand up to management and its rubber-stamp board. To others, he was a meddling, spoiled scion longing for a simpler time.

His foe, Carly Fiorina, was as different from him—and from that old HP—as she could be. She was stylish, where HP was stodgy. She preferred bold moves and "transformational" management philosophies to HP's watchful, steady-as-she-goes approach. She was a marketer in a company of hard-core engineers. And she had earned her stripes at AT&T, a hierarchical world of pinstripe suits and power lunches—not the egalitarian, Western ways of HP, where the dress code was khaki and the preferred lunch spots served burgers or burritos.

Although the monetary stakes were high, this was not just another greedy corporate imbroglio. This was a fight for the soul of a company. HP had been wildly successful. It had never suffered so much as one annual loss in 63 years. But what made HP a management icon was *how* it achieved those results. For decades, the company had balanced stellar financial performance with unquestioned integrity, from how it kept the books to how it treated its employees and customers. It had plowed millions into the communities in which it did business, not only out of charity but out of a progressive self-interest in keeping them strong. Put simply, it seemed HP had figured out the magic formula for how to run a company. Everyone won—investors, customers, managers, and employees. A frequent member of *Fortune* magazine's "Most Admired" companies list, HP had been a shining example of the best that Big Business could be.

But that was a different time. During the late 1990s, HP had descended into mediocrity. Badly outpaced by rivals, the company's sales growth and morale had plummeted, and its reputation as an innovator had languished. After almost three years on the job, Fiorina certainly hadn't reversed HP's decline. In fact, some thought she had only accelerated it. Now, she would probably lose her job if the Compaq deal was voted down. This trial would determine not only the future of this powerful woman, but also how HP would try to regain that magical formula.

Well before 9 o'clock, the sweeping, spiral stairway leading up to the third-floor courtroom was jam-packed as the principals began to arrive. Hewlett's group turned up first, at 8:50. Hewlett's lawyer, Stephen Neal, led the clan, nodding gregariously as he cleared a path for his client. With his wife Esther walking calmly by his side, the slightly stooped Hewlett shuffled nervously, wearing an uncomfortable smile. An unlikely and reluctant media star, he would have preferred to be practicing his cello or working in his computer lab. He stopped to quickly shake a reporter's hand before moving into the courtroom.

It would take another 15 minutes, long after most of HP's lawyers and handlers had arrived, for Fiorina to show. Her entrance befitted one of the business world's newest superstars, one used to traveling with the accoutrements of a wealthy jet-setter. Like Hewlett, she was coming from the luxurious, $320-a-night Hotel du Pont, just three blocks from the court. Unlike Hewlett, who walked to court, she arrived in a limousine to avoid the gaggle of photographers lurking en route. She walked with a regal calm into the courtroom, flanked by her husband Frank and her lawyer Larry Sonsini. Just five weeks before, she'd presided over the shareholder meeting looking embattled and exhausted. Now, the bags under her eyes had disappeared. Despite working her typical long hours—she could go for months on four or five hours of sleep a night—she appeared well rested. A slightly clenched jaw was the only visible sign of the fierce determination that had brought her to this courtroom. It was time to give the performance of her life, and she was ready.

Neal was ready, too. It had been seven months since Hewlett had come to his office seeking counsel. From the start, Neal had been pleased with the case. Hewlett was a wealthy client from a legendary family—never a bad thing, particularly in a terrible year for business. And while Hewlett was no doubt an underdog, he was far from alone in his fears about the deal. Wall Street hated it, too. HP's shares had plunged by nearly 35 percent from the time the deal was announced to the day Hewlett visited Neal's office. Since then, the attorney had served as Hewlett's field general on the case—plotting strategy, wooing reporters, and coordinating the efforts of Hewlett's other advisors.

The case was a huge opportunity for Neal in personal terms, as well. He was the CEO of Cooley Godward, and he would like nothing better than a victory over the prestigious firm of Wilson Sonsini Goodrich & Rosati across the street from his office. The trial would pit Neal against rival Larry Sonsini, *the* "it" lawyer of Silicon Valley—advisor to stars such as Apple's Steve Jobs and Sun Microsystems' Scott McNealy. The case also appealed to Neal's love of fighting high-stakes battles, even when the deck was stacked against him. For eight years, he had defended Charles Keating, the poster child of white-collar crooks for his role in the savings and loan scandals of the 1980s. Neal had stuck by Keating, and ultimately got his 10-year sentence dismissed, after Keating had spent 4 years behind bars waiting for appeals.

Legally speaking, Hewlett's case was not much rosier than Keating's had been. Filed nine days after the March 19 shareholder vote, it hung on two allegations, neither of which would be easy to prove. The first centered on whether Fiorina had muscled Deutsche Bank, one of HP's top 20 investors with more than 17 million shares, into voting for the acquisition on the morning of the vote. The evidence was certainly intriguing. Just days before the vote, the bank had decided to vote all its shares against the deal and contemplated publicly declaring its opposition.[1] But suddenly, after a phone conversation with Fiorina and HP chief financial officer Bob Wayman at 7 o'clock that morning, the bank had thrown its shares—possibly enough of them to swing the entire vote—in support of the acquisition. But how had she done it? Was it just through the force of salesmanship? Or had HP offered big banking contracts in the future? Had she threatened to cancel existing banking work? Making matters more interesting was a phone message Fiorina had left for Wayman on March 17, which was intercepted and leaked to the *San Jose Mercury News* on April 10.[2] In it, Fiorina said that she or Wayman might have to do "something extraordinary" to win the support of Deutsche Bank and another big shareholder, Northern Trust. Just how Fiorina defined *extraordinary* was the question.

It was delicious cloak-and-dagger stuff—and very likely worthless in court. So far, there was no actual evidence of wrongdoing. Neal would need a smoking gun—a contract, a witness, or some document that confirmed that HP actually bought Deutsche Bank's votes. Many observers were convinced something fishy had occurred, but proving it was another thing. Fiorina could have delivered a promise or threat with nods and winks, without putting pen to paper. But would a judge really undo one of the biggest mergers in history on the basis of such flimsy evidence?

The second allegation had grabbed fewer headlines, but held more promise of standing up in court. It alleged a cover-up of sorts—that HP's management had withheld damning information about the merger from investors. Fiorina had persuaded many investors that this merger would be different from other failed deals, because a crackerjack integration team of top HP and Compaq staffers had spent almost 1 million hours planning every detail of how to bring the companies together.

Neal had evidence that challenged Fiorina's rosy outlook. In the weeks prior to the trial, the Hewlett camp had received a stream of information from HP insiders that told a different story, including anonymous phone calls from senior executives and unsigned letters slipped under doors in unaddressed manila envelopes. Among the 40,000 memos, e-mails, and other documents HP had been forced to hand over after the lawsuit was filed were so-called value capture updates. Prepared by members of that much-lauded integration team, these documents suggested the company was not going to hit the targets Fiorina had promised Wall Street. These reports seemed to be the smoking gun Neal needed. Fiorina had seen these documents, yet decided they were not something investors also needed to know about. Still, it wasn't enough that the documents existed. To win, Neal had to prove that Fiorina knew the reports spoke the truth. In other words, Neal wouldn't win just by proving the Compaq purchase would be a disaster for HP. He had to prove that Fiorina knew it, too. He had to prove that she was a liar.

As Neal rose to make his opening argument, he knew everyone in the courtroom was wondering the same thing: What does he have? Hewlett sat hunched at a table behind his attorney. Sonsini, the man who had advised Hewlett to vote with the board, sat just feet away from Hewlett, across the center aisle that separated the two camps. Fiorina sat against the wall at the far left of the courtroom, as if trying to get as far away as possible from Hewlett.[3]

Neal, impressive at six-foot-four with a low, resonant voice, played his best card first: the claim that HP had withheld vital information from investors that would have cast major doubts on the merger. He first needed to establish for the court what HP had promised investors, in its presentations to Wall Street, in Fiorina's speeches, and in government filings such as the S-4, the document companies use to register new merger-related shares.

Most everyone in the courtroom knew the basics. For starters, Fiorina promised huge cost savings—$2 billion in fiscal 2003, and $2.5 billion every year afterwards—but she said HP would make these cuts without sacrificing too much in the way of sales. Most analysts figured HP would take a 10 percent hit to its top line as a result of the merger, but Fiorina argued it would be no more than 4.9 percent. Then there was the question of profitability. Walter Hewlett's advisors believed the new HP would lose many high-end, lucrative computer contracts. All told, it would lose roughly $0.26 of profit per every dollar of lost sales. But Fiorina believed most of the lost sales would be in the cutthroat PC business, where margins were negligible. As such, HP figured it would lose only $0.12 per dollar of lost revenue. The bottom line: HP shareholders could expect a 12 to 13 percent increase in the value of their shares in 2003, the company had predicted. Although the math worked, Neal argued that Fiorina knew the reality was different. It all came down to how you interpreted the value capture updates. Of all the documents collected before the trial, these were the only ones that seemed to summarize how the merger was faring. A key page of each showed three columns of data.[4] One column showed the earnings per share the integration team believed HP was on track to hit for 2003 and 2004. Another showed the consensus estimates on Wall Street for those years. A third was the so-called S-4 case. HP did not include an earnings per share estimate in the actual S-4 filing sent to investors, but Neal argued that this S-4 column was what the company believed it had promised to investors in that document. And as of mid-February, HP was not on target to hit it, he argued. Even Compaq chief financial officer Jeffrey Clarke, who ran the value capture effort and was cochief of the entire integration effort, seemed to have his doubts. According to the minutes of a February 20 integration team meeting, he said "We have a mile to go on this."

Now firmly in command of the courtroom, Neal moved confidently and theatrically as he dropped his next juicy bit of evidence. It came from the personal journal of none other than Michael Capellas, Compaq's chief executive and a loud proponent of the deal. "Sobering thought," Capellas had written. "We are about to really start one of the most historic periods in U.S. business history. Case study for years. At current course and speed we will fail."

Neal then read an e-mail that Clarke had sent to Wayman on March 12, just a week before the crucial merger vote. Referring to the latest value capture update, Clarke wrote: "It is uglee [sic]. . . . Both companies are deteriorating in this slowing market and due to merger 'noise.' " Neal's case was gathering momentum. Members of the gallery exchanged glances as if to say, "This might be a lot more interesting than we thought." Investors, who had been required to drop their cell phones in a cardboard box at the door to the courtroom, began slipping out to call in trades. And Neal wasn't done. Next, he offered a study done by HP veteran Ken Wach, who had just been named financial chief of the new HP's $20-billion high-end computer business. Wach, who had just joined the integration team itself, was even more pessimistic about that part of the company than the value capture updates indicated. He sent his report to Wayman on March 10, along with a note that said: "The attached is a frightening reality check . . . I see little realistic upside and I am not alone. . . . Sure, this may be overly pessimistic, since the [salespeople are] very down right now, but I sincerely hope that we all start acknowledging the realities soon."

The reality, Neal argued, was that Fiorina knew HP's merger plan was falling off course fast. According to the February value capture update, the company was on track to deliver earnings of just $1.30 per share, versus an S-4 case of $1.65. By March 12, the internal projection had fallen to just $1.23, according to the Clarke e-mail. That was far less than the $1.37 most analysts figured HP could have posted that year *without* buying Compaq. Putting it plainly for Judge Chandler, Neal said "It hadn't gotten any better, Your Honor. . . . This was a consistent and a persistent and a declining situation throughout 2002."

Indeed, Neal continued, Fiorina hadn't even disclosed this troubling information to her own board. The directors, by then embroiled in a public fight for shareholder support with Hewlett, had not been diligent enough to ask for proof that Fiorina's plan was working. Instead, they joined Fiorina's crusade for the deal, turning a blind eye to their responsibilities as investors' watchdogs, he argued. "Your Honor, I think the board abdicated its responsibilities both to make sure it was fully informed and in turn to make sure that all complete material information was being turned over to shareholders."

Neal had masterfully played his best cards. Having done so, he quickly recounted what many had believed would be the high point of the proceedings: the Deutsche Bank allegations. There were some juicy new morsels. Deutsche Bank, for example, had a $1-million contract to help HP win its proxy fight, with a $1-million success fee if HP prevailed. But truth be told, there didn't seem to be that smoking gun to make this charge stick. Still, it was time for Fiorina's lawyers to come up with some answers.

Steve Schatz did little to defuse the sparks that Neal had set off. A member of Wilson Sonsini's top brass, he was one of the firm's top litigators. Despite his Ivy League education, Schatz stood out among the slick Silicon Valley power brokers with his thick New York accent and nervous delivery. In this case, he had slept just three hours a night for the past week as the case was being prepared, he said, and his delivery sounded more edgy than usual. He repeatedly strayed from the microphone, making himself barely audible to the gallery.

He did have plenty to work with. First, Schatz attacked the Deutsche Bank allegations, quickly stripping them of much of their remaining validity. The bank had made its own choices. There was no concrete proof that HP had crossed the line. Then he quickly moved to the allegation that HP withheld damning information from investors about the integration effort. For starters, he said, HP had never promised investors $1.65 in earnings per share in the S-4—regardless of what the heading on an obscure set of internal presentations said. No one from HP had told investors to expect such earnings. Rather, HP had told investors to focus on two key things: The new HP would cut costs by $2.5 billion a year by 2004, and it would limit revenue losses related to the merger to less than 4.9 percent. The economy might rise or fall, impacting sales and profits, but that couldn't all be attributed to the merger. As for Capellas' journal and Clarke's comments and e-mails, they were taken out of context, Schatz argued. Capellas had been jotting down notes for a motivational speech he was preparing for Compaq staffers. He knew the companies were right on course, but he didn't want employees to know it for fear that they'd ease up. As for CFO Clarke, he was frustrated that midlevel managers were unwilling to sign up for the revenue targets management had publicly promised.

Indeed, Schatz argued, the truth was that HP was far ahead of plan. Rather than $2.5 billion, management actually thought it would be able to cut expenses by as much as $3.9 billion a year by 2004. And what about the damning value capture updates? Well, the executives who wrote them didn't have the whole picture. They didn't know what staffers in other corners of the integration effort were up to. For example, a team that focused on supplier contracts had determined that volume discounts on parts and supplies would be three times greater than initially expected. Plus, Schatz argued, these managers, like managers at all companies, preferred to set nice low sales targets that could easily be achieved, ensuring big end-of-quarter bonuses. It was sandbagging, pure and simple. The full picture was that management's plan was doable, even conservative. In fact, Schatz pointed out that management had decided not to include areas in which the merger might *increase* sales—say, by selling HP printers to buyers of Compaq PC products.

Now it was Schatz's turn for moral outrage. It wasn't enough for Judge Chandler to throw out Walter Hewlett's baseless case. He had to do so in a way that would clear the good name of Fiorina and her board: "[Hewlett] has unfairly cast aspersions on HP's management, and the shareholders' will should be honored."

It all sounded conceivable, if a bit too convenient. Who really believed that Deutsche Bank had switched those votes without some kind of pressure from HP? And didn't those value capture reports speak for themselves? HP could argue that they didn't mean what they said, but where were the documents that proved HP *was* on track to hit its goals? There weren't any. In effect, HP's managers were asking the court to just trust them. Now, Fiorina was going to have to earn that trust.

When the trial schedule came over the fax machine at the Hotel du Pont on the weekend before the trial began, high fives broke out among the army of Wilson Sonsini lawyers working with HP. Steve Neal was calling Carly Fiorina as his first witness. She might be controversial as a CEO, but she was going to make a terrific witness. She was a brilliant communicator, capable of Clintonesque persuasiveness. An unbelievably quick thinker, she would understand the intent of a question before she answered. She was not going to fall into any of Neal's traps.

Fiorina was extremely well-prepped. Almost from the minute the suit had been filed, Wilson Sonsini partner Boris Feldman had been working with her to prepare for this day. Widely rumored to covet a federal judgeship, the bow-tied Feldman's erudite delivery would make him the perfect courtroom dance partner for Fiorina. And Fiorina understood the stakes. "She got it from the start," says Feldman, who spent 30 hours face-to-face with Fiorina, going over her testimony and likely questions. He describes it as a "two-week Vulcan Mind Meld." "As busy as she was, she understood that she was going to have to deliver on the stand," Feldman says.

Neal figured calling Fiorina first was his best shot. He certainly wasn't going to let Feldman call her as his witness; he would just lob softballs that Fiorina would hit out of the park. Neal had considered calling Chief Financial Officer Bob Wayman to the stand first. He had been in on the call with Deutsche Bank and was intimately aware of the financial data. But Wayman was smart and squeaky clean. After 33 years at HP without an ethical blemish, it would be hard to cast doubt on him. So Fiorina was it. Neal was convinced he could, and had to, crack Fiorina's Teflon exterior. He had the documents to prove she'd been told all was not well with the merger. If she came off as a reasonable executive who had objectively considered the documents, Judge Chandler would likely accept her explanations. But if Neal could get her to become evasive or indignant, or get her to admit she'd had concerns, Chandler might start to wonder. All Neal had to do was expose her for what her critics claimed she was: a super salesperson who would do *anything* to land the deal.

Seconds after Fiorina was sworn in, Neal went on the attack. "I have to ask you. Did you see the *Financial Times* piece over the weekend that suggested they are going to rename the Compaq Center the Carly Fee-Arena," he said, referring to the San Jose–based hockey stadium. The dig worked on many levels. It played on criticisms that Fiorina was egotistical. It might even have made Fiorina pause to think about the mostly negative press coverage, a hurtful thorn in her side considering the glowing treatment she'd enjoyed in the past. It certainly sent the message that she was not in for any walk in the park on the witness stand.

"I missed that one," she responded, with a cool, insincere smile.

To get started, Neal set out to establish what HP had promised investors in its financial filings. He held up a page from one of the value capture updates.

"You would agree, would you not, Ms. Fiorina, that the value capture team at the Hewlett-Packard/Compaq [company] . . . said that the 2003 earnings per share implied in the S-4 filing was in the range of $1.60 to $1.65 a share?" Neal asked. "I certainly would agree that that is the title of the document that the value capture team produced, yes," Fiorina said mildly, settling in.

"And the value capture document . . . stated that the earnings per share . . . for 2003 was $1.65. Correct?" Neal repeated.

Normally, witnesses are trained to give the briefest answers, to avoid offering any unexpected avenues for a smart litigator to explore. But Fiorina wasn't just any witness. Her counsel had advised her to use her own discretion.

"That is what that document says," she answered. "I don't believe you can find anywhere in the S-4 [where it says] $1.65. Nor is it what we talked to investors about for six months on the road."

Neal was not expecting a fight so soon. "But my question was more limited than that," he said, trying to get her to just answer the question. "The statement that the S-4 filing implied an EPS of $1.65 a share was a statement that came from the Hewlett-Packard/ Compaq value capture team, not from the plaintiffs in this case. Correct?" Fiorina, who had been listening with her head tilted, wearing a slightly impatient stare, blinked with disdain. "Yes, that is a document that was produced, and that is the title of the document," she said.

This cat and mouse would continue for what seemed like an eternity, as Fiorina refused to be drawn into Neal's trap. Over and over, she refused to give him the easy answers he could later use against her. Before long, it was unclear who was flustering whom. Fiorina grew more confident, even comfortable enough to make jokes. When the judge asked her to pull her microphone closer, she struggled to make room, given the computer monitor that was perched next to the mike. "We wanted to make you feel at home with computers all around," Chandler offered with a smile.

Ever the salesperson, Fiorina replied without missing a beat, "You clearly need some new ones, Your Honor."

Neal refused to back off. The questioning went on endlessly. Didn't page such and such of the December 19 presentation to shareholders say the new HP would enjoy operating margins of between 8 and 10 percent—much better than those the company achieved in 2001?

Yes, she said. But the footnote at the bottom of that page said those margins depended on overall economic activity. Good enough. But didn't that presentation say that combined revenue for the companies was $85.1 billion, before the 4.9 percent revenue loss? Didn't that imply a $4.1-billion drop in revenue? If he could get her to confirm an actual revenue figure rather than a percentage dip, HP could be held accountable if it came up short. So what if it did? she argued. There was no way of knowing what portion of the revenue loss was due to the merger or to the economy. Any dolt understood that the economy had taken a nosedive after the September 11 terrorist attacks and knew to toss aside projections made before that infamous date. More than 10 times in a row, Neal asked her to confirm that HP had projected a $4.1-billion revenue loss in its filings. Her answer: The $4.1 billion was just the result of applying a 4.9 percent drop to Wall Street's revenue estimates as of that date. Because those estimates change over time, it was no longer a relevant number. "Mr. Neal, you and I can agree there is a page that says $4.1 billion. I'm not disputing the math."

With that, Fiorina had hit on her theme for the day. For the remainder of the marathon three-hour-plus session, she would spin variations on "Your math is correct," like Mozart exploring a musical theme.

When Chandler called for a recess at 1:00 P.M., it was clear Fiorina was winning. As the packed courtroom emptied, one Wall Street investor—obviously, one with a stake in the merger passing—said simply, "Thank God for her."

Looking back, Neal said he had no regrets about his approach. But the longer he kept at it, the more gleeful the rival camp became.

"I think Steve thought he could break her," Feldman said later. "But she broke him."

2

THE EMERGENCE OF CARLETON SNEED

It's very refreshing to know that people aren't determined by their early years, that they're capable of reinventing themselves."
—JONATHAN MARSHALL,
CHILDHOOD CLASSMATE OF FIORINA

It seems that everyone who has ever worked with Carly Fiorina has a strong opinion about her. All agree that she is a remarkable speaker, an incredibly hard worker, and a top-notch salesperson with relentless drive. But agreement ends about there. Many admire her brilliance, charisma, principled toughness, and kindness. Others find her impulsive, calculating, and self-promoting—and deeply focused on pursuing goals that, even if well-intentioned, are misguided. As with many leaders of her stature, many people are also afraid of her.

She comes from a long line of proud, tough people. Her cool, polished East Coast veneer belies Texas roots. It is hard to imagine that she is just two generations removed from Texas ranchers. She was born with the name Cara Carleton Sneed—the ninth woman in her father's family to be named Carleton, a tradition that started after all of the men by that name were killed during the Civil War. Explaining her name's derivation in an interview with *BusinessWeek*, she apologized for her limited understanding of her family tree. "I can hear my Southern relatives just dying over my ruination of the genealogy," Fiorina reflected. "I still have relatives on my father's side, in Texas and Tennessee, who do this family tree thing a lot and they'd probably be horrified."[1]

If genetics count for anything, her oratorical skills and determination come as no surprise. One of her ancestors, Methodist deacon Joseph Perkins Sneed, rode his horse into the rugged prairie of East Texas, near present-day Waco, in 1839. He was a so-called circuit rider. With the Great Revival sweeping the frontier, the Methodist Church needed someone to spread the word to the settlers in the area. Before he arrived, the superintendent of the tiny mission there opened a letter sent by a Methodist bishop. "We have sent you Brother Sneed, a man who is not afraid to die or sleep in the woods," the letter told him.[2]

In the ensuing years, Sneed traveled the area delivering fiery, three-hour sermons. Years later, he settled 60 miles southeast of Waco. He started a small Methodist church in the town of Calvert, and a cotton farm nearby.

With its rich topsoil, Calvert was an ideal place to grow cotton. When the railroad came whistling through in 1869, some 30,000 hard-luck Civil War refugees poured in, along with lumber and supplies to build up the town. The boom funded construction of an opera house, blocks of opulent Victorian homes, a grand hotel downtown, and a huge cotton gin—the world's largest, at one time. There were 17 saloons to serve the more unruly fortune seekers who also migrated to the town. Calvert had a reputation for shootouts and lawlessness. One resident was Belle Starr, who ran with outlaw Jesse James. Stagecoach robberies, horse theft, and bank holdups were common.[3]

Deacon Sneed never earned much money preaching. It was ranching and natural gas that later built the family's fortune. As the twentieth century dawned, Fiorina's grandfather, Marvin Sneed, was earning a good living in the family business as a banker and cotton farmer. Fiorina's great-uncle, John Beal Sneed, a rancher, lived in

Amarillo. Beal, as he was known, was also a Princeton-trained lawyer, whose brilliance was matched only by his temper—which caused one of the more notorious family feuds in Texas's colorful history.[4]

The trouble started in 1911, when Sneed found out that his wife, Lena, was having an affair with her school-days sweetheart, Al Boyce Jr. Distraught, Sneed had her committed to a sanitarium. Fed up with the family's ongoing defense of Boyce, Sneed murdered Boyce's father, shooting the 69-year-old ranch manager dead in the lobby of Forth Worth's swanky Metropolitan Hotel. Nine months later, after taking Lena and their two daughters to stay at Fiorina's grandfather's county farm, he killed Boyce with three blasts from a shotgun in front of a Methodist church in Amarillo.[5]

John Beal Sneed never served time for either of his crimes. In the first case, with Fiorina's grandfather in the courtroom, Beal expertly survived six hours on the witness stand; the judge declared a mistrial. Sneed was later acquitted of killing Boyce Jr. Asked why, one defiant jury member responded famously, "Because this is Texas."[6] Although the Old West was on its last legs, a frontier justice remained that gave a man license to kill his wife's lover.

By the time Fiorina's father, Joseph Tyree Sneed, was born in 1920, Calvert's best days were long gone. From the start, it was clear that Tyree, as he was called, had plenty of the Sneed determination that he would later pass on to his daughter. He was born with a congenital defect that caused his head to tip to one side and limited movement in his neck and shoulder. His condition caused some around town to refer to him as a "hunchback," recalled Gracia Thibodeaux, who grew up down the block. But he didn't let his affliction slow him down. Ignoring warnings, he played on his high school football team for three years. Later, he enlisted in the military, though he would not do active duty.[7]

Sneed met Fiorina's mother, Madelon Juergens, during World War II. He was on leave from law school at the University of Texas in Austin, serving in the Army Air Force, stationed in Wichita Falls, Texas. Madelon, the daughter of an assembly-line worker in Toledo, had left an unhappy home to join the Women's Army Corps. Her mother had died when she was a child, leaving her in the care of an extended family. "My mother had a series of stepmothers who didn't think much of developing girls and a father who wouldn't pay for her college tuition," Fiorina told the *New York Times* in 1999. "So she ran away from home, in small-town Ohio, joined the Air Force, became an accomplished artist and devoted herself to being interested and interesting."[8] After the war, Sneed earned his law degree from the University of Texas at Austin, graduating in 1947. He taught at the university after graduation. Conservative and serious-minded, he declared himself a Republican when East Texas was still a Dixiecrat stronghold, and the Republican Party was still the party of Lincoln. "That was a mark of Joe's courage," said former University of Texas professor Gray Thoron, who taught there with Sneed. In Austin, Sneed also grew a private practice and started raising a family.

Cara Carleton Sneed, the couple's second child, was born on September 6, 1954, in Austin. Joe Sneed parted company with Texas when Fiorina was two. He took the family to Ithaca, New York, for a five-year stint teaching at Cornell University. When Fiorina was eight, the family headed west to Palo Alto, to up-and-coming Stanford Law School. After a brief stint as dean of Duke University's law school and as a deputy attorney general, President Richard Nixon appointed Sneed to a federal judgeship in the U.S. Court of Appeals for the Ninth Circuit in 1973. As such, the kid from Calvert moved to a comfortable home in San Francisco's tony Cow Hollow neighborhood.

In many ways, Joe Sneed would set the precedents for Carly Fiorina's approach to life. Fiercely independent, he believes deeply in the value of hard work and individual accomplishment. Unafraid of challenges, he has sought them out. "I suppose I have something of a dusty foot," he told the *Cornell Law Forum* when he decided to leave the university for Stanford.[9] "I rather like to move once in a while, to see different cultures and different people and different parts of the country. I find it stimulating and broadening." Said his former clerk Nancy Rapoport, dean of the University of Houston's law school, "As opportunities come to you, take them. He taught me that, and it's the best lesson I ever had."

Like his daughter, Sneed approaches his work with a belief in the power of his own intellect. While personally very conservative— he was a member of the three-judge panel that appointed Ken Starr as independent counsel when the Whitewater scandal was heating up in the early 1990s—he has been widely admired for leaving ideology out of his decision-making process. At times, he has taken headline-grabbing views on controversial cases. In 2001, three-time offender Leonardo Andrade faced 50 years in prison for stealing nine videotapes from a Kmart, as a result of a "three strikes" law passed by California voters in 1994. While the court ruled that the law violated the Constitution's ban on cruel and unusual punishment, Sneed dissented, arguing that the courts should not interfere with the will of the electorate.[10]

Some clerks say Sneed must have been a stern taskmaster when Fiorina was a child. Other than sick time or federal holidays, there was no time off at work. "He never missed a day of work and he didn't want anyone else to miss a day either," remembers one long-time secretary. The judge was known to flash "the look" when angered. He never raised his voice. He didn't need to. Rather than lecture clerks whose work was subpar, Sneed simply stopped giving them the most coveted work to do. On the day briefs were due, they were to be placed neatly on a particular corner of Sneed's desk.

Not all the clerks loved him. "Call me when he kicks," one former clerk snapped when asked about the judge. "I hated it," added another, when asked about the clerkship. "We tiptoed around him. It was such a cold, formal environment." Some said Sneed felt more connected to the Texas alums, though he did earn a graduate degree from Harvard. "He makes fun of people who went to Harvard and prep schools," said Ronald Mann, a University of Michigan professor who worked for Sneed in 1985. You were better off "if you were someone who grew up in oil field country, like I did." "He's a real straightforward Texan," recalls former Stanford Law School dean and Hewlett Foundation president Paul Brest, who taught with Sneed in the 1960s. "Joe is very gracious, but it's frontier graciousness. Just don't cross him."

Fiorina's mother, Madelon, was a high-spirited foil to her tough-minded, scholarly husband. She died in 1998, and Fiorina was distraught at the funeral. Friends remember Madelon as a gracious, inquisitive woman who loved to entertain. She had a passion for tennis and playing her piano, but she especially loved painting. She converted the laundry room of their San Francisco home into an art studio, and studied at the San Francisco Art Institute during the late 1980s. There, she would attack the canvas for three hours at a time, splattering paint all over her already paint-smeared smocks. In her 60s, she was leaving the 20-something students around her in the dust with her earthy, modern, semiabstract portraits. "She used paint like they did in the '60s," recalled one of her teachers, Ivan Majdrakoff. "The floor was covered with paint when she was done. It was no holds barred. She was affable and polite but really a demon in terms of putting the paint down."

At home, Madelon was a traditional wife. She kept house and entertained Joe's clerks once a year with a traditional dinner she'd cook at their home, which was crowded with hundreds of books and boasted a sweeping view of San Francisco Bay. After a formal meal, the group would sometimes retire to the living room to sing songs, with Madelon providing accompaniment on the piano.

In many ways, Fiorina seems to have been blessed with the best qualities of each of her parents. Neither she nor members of her family agreed to be interviewed for this book. But it is safe to surmise that she inherited her father's disciplined intellect, his passion for history, and his thirst for accomplishment and influence in the world. She got her mother's looks, social antenna, and zest for life. The steely resolve she inherited from both of them made her success all but a sure thing.

As the daughter of a Stanford professor, Fiorina grew up in a sheltered, yet stimulating, world of academia. It had its privileges. The Sneeds lived in a nice ranch-style house in a nice neighborhood on Stanford land called Pine Hill 1. Under an arrangement with the university, professors got low-interest mortgages on these houses. The result was a high-brow "Stanford ghetto," which even had its own elementary school system. Of the 100 or so students at Stanford Elementary, almost all were "faculty brats," including the children of environmental scientist Paul Ehrlich and renowned physicist and arms control specialist Sidney Drell.

By the time she got to Terman Junior High, named for the famous Stanford professor who helped Bill Hewlett and Dave

Packard start their company, it was the late 1960s. In some respects, her conservative home-life with her Republican lawyer father and old-fashioned mother contrasted with the upheaval caused by the counterculture surrounding her. One of Fiorina's classmates would be arrested for dealing heroin. Another would go to jail for her work with Venceremos, a radical anti-Vietnam War group that was loosely associated with the Symbionese Liberation Army, which kidnapped Patty Hearst. But mostly, she was an ordinary kid. She was more interested in the politics of her small social circle than anything else. Like so many young girls, she and her friends pretended to diet, eating only apples for lunch—but then wolfing down her mother's homemade wheat bread after school, says childhood friend Deborah Liederman.

Fiorina was studious and began playing classical piano in the seventh grade. For a time, she dreamt of making that her career.[11] She decided to study classical languages and read Aristotle in the original Greek. Fiorina would later use this as evidence of a can-do spirit from an early age. "People told me it's too hard, you can't do that, but I did it anyway," she said.[12]

That's about as rebellious as Fiorina got in her early years. Indeed, classmates remember her as the prototypical good girl—always neatly dressed in conservative clothes, bookish, and popular. She didn't play sports, wasn't a cheerleader, and didn't take part in the drama clubs, they said. Until college, her friends called her Carleton.

Her father's wanderlust may have delayed the emergence of the confident, charismatic person she would later become. Sneed took the family with him when he took a teaching assignment in London during her freshman year. Fiorina, like many other British schoolgirls, developed a crush on Prince Charles, according to Liederman, who visited the Sneeds at the time. The next year, her father took the family to Ghana. When her father took the job as dean of Duke's law school before her senior year of high school, she wasn't happy. "It was very traumatic [for Fiorina]—that's why she stayed a month of the summer with us," says Liederman. "She didn't want to leave and didn't want to leave her friends." The moving took its toll on Fiorina, some say. It may have taught her not to get too close to people or situations, to learn to welcome rather than be hobbled by change.

She did spend part of her high school years in Palo Alto, attending Gunn High School. Many students and teachers who were there don't remember her, and others were surprised to find out she was CEO of HP. She and her closer friends—Liederman, Charlotte Germane, and Rebecca Eisenberg—were members of a larger clique of smart kids, known to other students and teachers as "the intelligentsia." Brad Leva, a high school friend, recalls a typical girl who wore her brown hair long, straight, and parted in the middle, in the Jan Brady style of the day. "She was very normal," he says. But he did notice an inner fire. "I got the sense that she had a lot of energy," Leva says. "I have a recollection that when she got frustrated she would just do her work. She'd get frustrated and keep going."

Among her siblings, Carleton seemed the most likely to succeed. Classmates recall older sister Clara as the prototypical posthippie, well-known for her radical dress, wild hair, and predilection for hanging out on "Smokers' Hill." Younger brother Joe, who wasn't as studious as his middle sister, was known for his prickly personality, say classmates of hers. Intensely proud of his Texas roots, he often badmouthed California and Californians for their liberal ways—particularly his elder sister Clara. "He enjoyed goading others in the family. He enjoyed being the contrarian," says one of Fiorina's close friends from that time.

Fiorina may not have expressed her own contrarian nature so blatantly, but it was there. Although she grew up in a liberal, countercultural stronghold, she took her political cues from her conservative father. Her gripe was with the mindless adoption of leftist attitudes by many of her peers. "She loved to debate. She's a very independent thinker, and whenever the crowd moved in a direction, she would try—at first for intellectual reasons—to take the opposite view," says one friend from her college years. "She has always enjoyed challenging the conventional wisdom."

This distaste for groupthink would remain a hallmark of her career. Even as she rose to heights in corporate America at which there were scarcely any other women, she refused to accept that there was any real "glass ceiling" holding women back. After the terrorist attacks of September 11, 2001, at the risk of drawing criticism in the emotional aftermath of those events, she went out of her way to praise the historic contributions of Islamic civilization during a speech on corporate leadership.

Her refusal to accept conventional wisdom would play a major role in her tenure at HP. When she arrived, she set out to discover the true essence of the management practices that had made the company great—and to debunk the misperceptions that she felt generations of coddled workers had come up with to justify their comfortable existence. Some would say she did so brilliantly, and that the backlash she received from employees was both predictable and necessary. Others would say she was wrong in her analysis, and that she callously threw out what was best about the HP Way. And twice during her first three years, she would test a widely held truism of her adopted industry: "High-tech mergers don't work." Both her aborted $18-billion bid for the PricewaterhouseCoopers consulting business in 2000 and the Compaq merger flew in the face of decades of failed tech megamergers and HP's own miserable record with mergers.

For many of the better students among her childhood classmates, the next step on life's path was Stanford University. For children of professors, the odds of getting in were high. When Fiorina graduated high school, well more than half of Stanford professors' children were accepted. Though her father had already moved on to Duke by then, Fiorina also got in.

During her freshman year at Stanford in 1972, the antiwar activists were being replaced by the "me generation." Students replaced Bob Dylan and Joan Baez albums with Santana and Steely Dan. Many students now had their hearts set on lucrative professions such as medicine and law. Compared to more radical University of California at Berkeley across the bay, Stanford was a country club," says Beth Brust, who met Fiorina during her junior year.

At Stanford, Fiorina remained a quiet, cautious person who didn't stand out from the crowd. She wasn't a partier. She didn't do drugs. She wasn't involved in student government, sports, or the school paper. She dove into her intellectual interests rather than a more career-centric path, deciding to major in medieval history and philosophy. She would bury herself in the works of Thomas Aquinas, Bacon, and Abelard. For fun, Fiorina palled around with her roommate, Barb Miller, a Beverly Hills native with an acerbic wit and a larger-than-life Barbra Streisand–style personality, Brust recalls. If not especially popular or outgoing, she was cherished by her close friends as smart, engaging, and fun. "She made a real effort to reach out to people," says Gary Fazzino, an HP executive who went to school with her. "Different types of people tended to confide in her," from jocks to intellectuals to artsy types. Some of her peers felt she was held back by her fear that she could never live up to her father. "She had a burning desire to succeed and live up to the standards set by her father. She idolized him, and had so much respect for him and his ethical compass," says one friend from her first few years of college. "Early on, she took incremental steps in life because she wasn't sure she could measure up."

Her admiration of her father may have helped forge a personal philosophy based on the power of great individuals. A friend senses affinity for Ayn Rand, whose Objectivist philosophy championed a totally laissez-faire world in which individuals are free to achieve their greatness.[13] She said in 2001 that the German philosopher Hegel had the most influence on her management beliefs. Hegel argued that the clash of opposites can result in inspired decisions—the so-called Hegelian dialectic: Thesis plus antithesis results in synthesis. But Hegel's thinking, which has long been embraced by dictators, also supports the idea that some are born to lead and others to follow. Edwin Locke, who taught her in business school, was shocked to read of her admiration for Hegel. "Hegel doesn't believe in reality, or logic, and does believe in dictatorship. If she takes him seriously, her company and her career are doomed."

By her junior year at Stanford, she was beginning to recognize her own potential. She has said that her most important class was a graduate seminar on Christian, Islamic, and Jewish political philosophies of the Middle Ages. Says Fazzino, who was in the class, "That's when she began to blossom and feel confident about her intellectual abilities."

In her senior year, Fiorina met Todd Bartlem. The two became inseparable. Neither came from a rich family, and both had to work part-time to pay the bills. Fiorina had a variety of jobs, and worked as a secretary in HP's shipping department during the summer before her sophomore year. "We were both very serious students, and neither of us had very much cash," Bartlem says.

Part of the attraction for Fiorina seems to have been Bartlem's humble roots. He is from the farm town of Orland, California, which is little more than a truck stop on the highway that runs through California's Central Valley. His father died when he was a child, and he worked to help support the family. He made it to Stanford on scholarships. One of their mutual friends thinks Fiorina admired Bartlem because he was self-made, and because he could pursue his dreams without complications from parents with high expectations. "I think she was exploring a new side of herself," he says.

Indeed, there were still few hints of the dynamic, charismatic Carly Fiorina that was to blossom years later. She certainly didn't seem heading for a corporate stardom. "Talk about completely out of the blue," says Daniel Burd, one of Bartlem's fraternity brothers, of her corporate rise. "There was no drive toward business at all." Adds Jonathan Marshall: "It's very refreshing to know that people aren't determined by their early years—that they're capable of reinventing themselves."

One of the first steps of that reinvention might have been Fiorina's decision to be with Bartlem. Her parents, particularly her mother, opposed the relationship because of Bartlem's modest background, according to Bartlem and friends. But Fiorina had decided to rebel. "There was a great love there," says Annamaria Napolitano, a Stanford Italian professor. From the start, she worried that the pair were too different to make the relationship work. "I had a feeling they wouldn't stay together. But she was in love with him, and that's it. She wanted it, and she got it."

Fiorina hadn't completely cut the parental cord, however. Although the law didn't interest her, her father insisted that she follow his footsteps and give it a try. She tried her best to obey. After graduating from Stanford, she entered the University of California–Los Angeles (UCLA) law school—and hated every minute of it.

She found it frustrating to be bound by precedents set by others, unable to apply her passion and smarts in creative new ways. Miserable and separated from her future husband, "It was clear within a matter of weeks that it wasn't going to work out," says Burd, who also studied law at UCLA, where the two lived in the same dorm. "I had dinner with her a handful of times. She talked about how miserable she was and how she was doing it for her dad and she had absolutely no interest in the law."

She only lasted a semester. "I barely slept those first three months. I had a blinding headache every day," she said during a Stanford commencement speech in 2001.[14] On a visit home, she made the decision, as she related during the speech. "I can tell you exactly which shower tile I was staring at in my parents' bathroom when I came home for a weekend and it hit me like a bolt of lightning: It's *my* life. I can do what I want. It was an epiphany for me. In that instant, the headaches literally disappeared. I got out of the shower. And I walked downstairs and said, I quit." Fiorina later said, "It was a tough conversation. My dad was bitterly disappointed at the time."

After dropping out, she took a tiny off-campus apartment at Stanford and spent much of her time with Bartlem at Casa Italiana, where Ann Baskins, now HP's chief counsel, also lived. Fiorina learned Italian—a skill that would help her land business in that country in the years ahead. Perhaps Fiorina's first taste of business came when she worked for real estate broker Marcus & Millichap for a few months that year. She was known around the office as "the Stanford student." Hired as a receptionist, she quickly moved on from answering phones and typing to editing and financial analysis, even reworking marketing packages drafted for $100-million deals—all within three months. The incredulous office manager kept telling cofounder Bill Millichap, "Look what this person is doing," says Millichap. "She was exceptional even then."

Being the best darn office receptionist was not the life Fiorina's parents had envisioned for her. But her relationship with them always remained strong, say friends from that period. Fiorina greatly admired both of her parents, in part because they'd lifted themselves to become successful, affluent people, friends say. While she felt challenged to meet her father's high standards, she rarely doubted his wisdom. By all accounts, she had a very deep bond with her mother, who went out of her way to recognize Fiorina's accomplishments and to make her feel special.

But there was often feuding involving her two siblings that caused problems at home. Clara, who lives in Berkeley, moved toward the left. Conservative Joe went to work briefly on a ranch in Texas, and is now a lawyer there. Back then, hostilities often broke out. As the middle child, Fiorina played the mediator. "The image of an anchor comes to mind," says one close friend from that time. "Carly made a real effort to get beyond disagreements and to try to make sure everyone got along."

It didn't always work. Todd Bartlem remembers Madelon Sneed working for days to get the Christmas feast just right. But soon someone would be yelling—usually Joe baiting one of his sisters. "Within an hour there was yelling and someone was leaving the table," Bartlem says. "Madelon would end up crying in the kitchen. The father would go upstairs or try to make peace." After a while, Fiorina and Bartlem avoided her home when they knew her brother was going to be there, he says.

Family tension was also present when Fiorina and Bartlem got married in 1977. The reception was at the Sneeds' San Francisco home. The food, prepared by the chef at Stanford's Casa Italiana, was great. The mood was not. "The wedding was a very tense affair," recalls one of the couple's friends. Bartlem's mother, feeling she was in enemy territory, hung around her son like a tent, and the new in-laws hardly spoke to each other. "It was obvious that the [Sneed] family thought she was marrying beneath her," says another friend, "[Her parents] were not very keen about her marrying Todd."

Soon after the wedding, Fiorina and her new husband headed to Italy, where Bartlem was starting the first year of a two-year international studies program through Johns Hopkins University. Bartlem describes these days as golden. "It was wonderful. It was a great adventure." Fiorina was traveling without her family for the first time, he says. The couple shared a one-bedroom apartment in downtown Bologna with a "godawful" bright orange floor and a view of a dismal courtyard. She got a job teaching English, while he studied. They went to art museums. They'd spend hours at a local *osteria,* sitting at the family-style tables and drinking $2 bottles of wine.

When the year was over, they returned to Washington, D.C., where Bartlem was to complete the second year of his degree. Fiorina had been toying with the idea of getting her MBA. Her part-time jobs at Marcus & Millichap and at HP had piqued her interest. And Bartlem says they agreed that going into management might be smart for her. She could make good money for a few years. If they had kids, she would have the option of leaving the workforce for a while to raise them. So she applied to Washington-area schools, including the Robert H. Smith School of Business at the University of Maryland in College Park, Maryland.

She almost didn't get in. Thanks to the slow Italian mail system, she wasn't sure whether her application had made it to the school in time. Soon after the Bartlems arrived in Washington, she drove straight to the office of Smith School Dean Rudy Lamone. When his secretary told her that her application was in fact late, Fiorina asked to speak to the dean. "Tell her to go over to the MBA office," he told his secretary.

"No, she says she wants to talk to the dean."

When he came out of his office, he ran into a pretty, 23-year-old MBA candidate with a brown Dorothy Hamill haircut who wasn't going to take no for an answer. "So, can a liberal arts student from Stanford compete with the analytical jocks you have around here?" Lamone recalls her asking.

Lamone was impressed. They proceeded to talk for two hours, about her medieval history degree and her other experiences. Fiorina thought she might like business, but wanted to hear a dean's perspective, to find out if an MBA was the way to go. "She was testing her own intuition about what her next move should be in life. I don't think it was a done deal in her mind," recalls Lamone. He agreed to recommend her to the admissions committee, which quickly admitted her when they saw her impressive Stanford grades.

Almost from the start, it was a remarkable awakening for Fiorina. Although Robert H. Smith is now ranked by *Business Week* as one of the nation's top-30 business schools, back then it was mainly a commuter school—a way for Washington bureaucrats and middle managers to pick up an MBA working nights and weekends. This was not a school for ambitious young Ivy Leaguers looking to set the world on fire.

But Fiorina was determined to learn as much as she could, and she quickly became one of the school's shining stars. "She was the most poised and confident person in the program. She was the pre-ordained superstar," says Gene Podsiadlo, a fellow student. Her professors agree. "She's the smartest MBA I've ever taught," says Edwin A. Locke. "A lot of people have high IQs but can't deal with the real world. But she has Jack Welch's kind of business intelligence. She can really see the big picture."

Carly Fiorina was not a wallflower. When he first met her, marketing professor William Nickels thought that Fiorina was more interested in becoming a consumer advocate than in becoming a businessperson. But she was such a standout in one of his first-year courses that he asked her to be teaching assistant for his 500-student principles of marketing class. When he began giving her advice on how to teach her section, she cut him short. "Is this my section?" she asked him. "Then let me teach it the way I think it should be taught."

"She was extremely self-confident, even then," says Nickels. He thinks her experience as a teaching assistant helped Fiorina recognize some of her skills as a communicator and manager. "When you stand up in front of 45 students three times a week, taking all kinds of questions and getting grief about grades and such, you learn to handle yourself in front of people. You don't have any fear in front of people anymore."

Years later, when the school considered putting together an MBA program designed specifically for women, she was unenthusiastic. "She wasn't against it, but she felt it's not about being a man or a woman," says Lamone. "It's not that she was negative in any way about women wanting to come together to break the glass ceiling. But in her heart, it's all about performance. She doesn't play any of the gender games. If you perform well, you can't be denied."

That toughness was also evident in a term paper she wrote for a doctorate-level seminar on worker motivation, taught by Locke. At the time, the latest buzzword was *participatory management*—the idea that letting workers participate in making decisions that affected their jobs was a powerful tool to increase morale and raise productivity. When Locke asked the class to analyze one of the key academic studies on the subject, Fiorina dug in.

Her paper, "The Coch and French Study: A Critique and Reinterpretation," was so good that Locke worked with her to have it published in the scholarly journal *Human Relations*.[15] In the paper, Fiorina questioned the central thesis of the earlier management study. The original study posited that worker productivity at a pajama factory rose significantly after workers were allowed to help with job scheduling, production targets, and the like. But Fiorina came up with a different explanation. Productivity rose not because workers were given more of a say, but because they got more job training and a pay scale that rewarded them for their performance. In other words, she argued, the employees were more motivated by the fair pay.

Throughout her career, Fiorina—like most high-tech executives—would rely heavily on rich bonuses and other financial incentives to motivate her employees. However, HP's culture was always the exception to the high-tech rule. Many of its employees knew they could make more money elsewhere, but chose HP for the feeling of collegiality and the authority they were granted to do their jobs as they saw fit. Fiorina's term paper gives one the sense that she thought such motivations couldn't compete with hard, cold cash.

By the time graduation day approached, Fiorina "knew what she was going to do with her life," Lamone says. "I think she really felt good about the world of business—because she saw that she could make an impact." Once, Locke suggested she stay on and become a college professor. "No," she said easily. "I want to be where the action is."

But where to go? The Robert H. Smith School of Business was no hotbed for MBA recruiting. But there was one coveted opportunity. Each year, AT&T held spots for promising grads to work in its nearby Washington office and to enter its management development program. It wasn't an obvious fit for Fiorina. AT&T's federal division was an old-boy network of hardened veterans who had grown up in the Ma Bell monopoly. Lamone advised her to apply anyway. AT&T was changing, already embroiled in the antitrust suit that would lead to the breakup of the monopoly in 1984. It was clear that Ma Bell was going to have to get off her duff and compete, and that she'd need some sharp marketing by fresh young thinkers to do so. "That's saying a lot to a freshly minted MBA," recalls Lamone, "but I felt she could really go places."

Needless to say, 25-year-old Fiorina got the job. She began as a midlevel sales manager within AT&T's old Long Lines Department. She oversaw an account team that attended to the needs of some smaller federal agencies, such as the Department of Health and Human Services. Long Lines was the source of most of AT&T's profits, and its staffers were just as complacent—and just as male—as Lamone had warned. "Everybody was a 42 long. Carly just didn't look like the typical Long Liner," says Frank Lombardi, an AT&T veteran whom Fiorina later worked for.

Fiorina quickly made her mark, even among the young hotshots in the management development program. "Carly always stood out. She was smart and confident and outspoken, all at once," says ADC Telecommunications CEO Richard Roscitt, who came up through the AT&T system with Fiorina. "It didn't matter who you were, once she made up her mind about something. You could have been the chairman, but you were going to hear about it." She was very popular with her staffers, who were dubbed "Carly's Angels," and she was a sensitive people manager. Tony Bardo, one of her account managers, remembers coming in one day, depressed about a personal problem. In a flash, without his saying a word, she recognized his sadness and approached him. "Come on, let's go down the street and get a cup of coffee. Let's talk." At the same time, she was clearly keeping an eye on how to get ahead. The first time she flew on one of AT&T's corporate jets, she carefully noted the seating protocol, so as not to make the mistake of sitting in one of the top executives' seats the next time she took the plane, says Maureen Rosen, a friend at the time.

As a woman in the mostly male AT&T system, there would be times when she might have used a shoulder to lean on. AT&T had gone out of its way to promote the careers of talented women and minorities to higher-level careers. But Fiorina never asked for any

special treatment for being a woman. Instead, she bravely stared
down sexism. Once, an unhappy customer called to arrange a lunch
meeting with Fiorina and some colleagues. Driving to the address
alone, she realized only when she arrived that it was a strip club.
Unwilling to be intimidated, she walked in. The others, all men,
were already seated and snickered as she approached. Stone-faced,
she calmly sat down. When one of the men called a stripper over to
perform at their table, Fiorina didn't flinch. The stripper, sensing
Fiorina's rage and not wanting to embarrass her, declined the invi-
tation. When the lunch ended, Fiorina got up and coolly left. "It was
her way of saying, 'Nice try, guys, but go screw yourselves,' " says former colleague Harry Carr, who heard the story from Fiorina.

Within a few years, Fiorina had drawn the notice of AT&T's top
executives. Bob Allen, who became CEO in 1988, traveled to the
University of Maryland to turn on the switch of a new multi-million-
dollar phone network the company had installed on campus. During a lunch, a cheeky Lamone told the CEO, "You owe me a lot, Mr.
Allen."

Allen gave him a surprised glance. "What do you mean?" he
asked.

"I gave you Carly Bartlem."

"That was the best gift you could ever give anyone," Allen
responded.

On the home front, Fiorina's life was changing. For the first
few years after the couple's return from Italy in 1978, her
marriage to Todd Bartlem was easy and comfortable, according to
Bartlem and mutual friends of the couple. After renting for a while,
they scraped together enough money to buy a brick Cape Cod–style
house in Silver Spring, Maryland. When she wasn't studying, Fiorina
played the baby grand piano her parents had shipped out. Often,
they'd throw casual dinner parties, where they'd share bottles of
Italian wine, play with their beagle, Suzie Q, and have long games of
Scrabble and other word games. Every June, they hosted a big soft-
ball game and barbeque for 50 of their friends.

Rosen remembers one night, when she and Gene Podsiadlo
went to dinner with the Bartlems to a popular D.C. restaurant called

44

G.D. Graffiti. To pass the time, they decided to make up nicknames for each other. Fiorina dubbed Rosen "Captain Confection," because of her baking ability. Podsiadlo was "Nick Danger." Bartlem was "Dr. Excitement." And Fiorina? After a few moments, Rosen came up with it: "the Silk." "She was so incredibly smooth," remembered Rosen. "There was not a situation that rattled her. She dressed beautifully. She always knew how to handle herself, knew the right thing to say. It wasn't like she was phony. She was just always charming. And she had a great giggle." Fiorina was also a good friend. Rosen says Fiorina lent her a few thousand dollars when Rosen got into financial trouble during these years. "She really saved my butt, and she did so without a moment's hesitation, and with no questions asked," Rosen recalls.

The marriage began to sour in the early 1980s, says Bartlem, who remains very bitter and has been estranged from Fiorina since 1984. Part of the reason, say friends, was that he was often gone for weeks at a time on business. "She really put a lot into that marriage, and sacrificed a great deal for him," says one mutual friend. Another source says Fiorina told him that Bartlem had been unfaithful, a charge Bartlem denies.

According to Bartlem, Fiorina was becoming enthralled with the world of business—the intellectual challenge, the thrill of success, and the monetary rewards. She began devouring management books such as John T. Molloy's bestseller *Dress for Success* (New York: Peter H. Wyden, 1975), a guide to dressing smart while climbing the corporate ladder. "It became a bible for her," Bartlem claims.

Fiorina began working long hours, Bartlem says. By the time the weekend rolled around, all she wanted to do was curl up with a Robert Ludlum book or sleep, he says. It was hard to get her to go to a movie. "She would be inside moping. She just put her heart and soul into the work. She became a unidimensional person. Anything that didn't enhance her business life, she didn't want to know about."

The couple divorced in 1984. One day soon thereafter, Fiorina came to his house to pick up the last of her things. After quickly packing, she met him on the front lawn as she was preparing to leave. "I will never see you again in my life," Bartlem says she told him. He protested, saying there was no reason for that, given how close they'd been for their 10 years together. According to Bartlem, she said, "After my business training, I've come to the conclusion that there are certain things I need. You have to make up your mind and act on what you believe is right. You just have to do it. That's why I'm doing this."

"Wait a minute," he claims to have responded, "this is not a Harvard University case study. This is a marriage. It's not black and white." But she left, without leaving a phone number or forwarding address. True to her word, she has never seen him since.

Bartlem doesn't deny he's got an ax to grind. "I wish I could wish her the best, but I don't. I want to see her fail," he says. Clearly, this is the bitter bile of lost love—emotions that might be discounted and not considered in an examination of a business figure.

However, the circumstances of her first marriage say a lot about the evolution of Carly Fiorina. As in many first marriages that fail, she found herself traveling down a path that no longer worked for her. When she walked away, she cut all ties. In the process, quiet Carleton Sneed seemed to take a big step toward becoming iron-willed Carly Fiorina. Her divorce is not a total explanation, to be sure. But it may not be coincidence that, from this point on, she would be known by colleagues and observers for her willingness to battle ferociously to achieve her goals, whether in closing a sale, winning a job, or pushing through a merger. At times, her resolve would lead her into treacherous ethical territory. One small example involved the divorce hearing. Maureen Rosen claims Fiorina told her on numerous occasions that she was her best friend, and asked Rosen to testify on her behalf at the hearing. "Does Todd know about this?" Rosen asked. Fiorina said she had told Bartlem, and that he was comfortable with Rosen testifying.

That wasn't true, as became painfully obvious from the look on Bartlem's face when Rosen entered the courtroom. Bartlem soon forgave her, and they remain friends. As for Fiorina, Rosen hasn't heard from her in years. Rosen has no ill feelings, and figures Fiorina was simply going through a difficult time. Still, "I was laboring under the impression that we were better friends than we were." When Fiorina remarried the following year, Rosen wasn't invited to the wedding.

In the grand scheme, this was no great crime—probably the kind of thing that ambitious, hard-driving people do from time to time. However, the sense of betrayal Rosen felt is a common theme among many people who have done business with Fiorina. Many tell a similar tale. They were charmed and inspired by her at first, and gladly returned the devotion and loyalty that she professed to have for them. But at some point, when this was no longer expedient, she was able to turn her back. "People want to believe she's this really warm human being, but that's not what she's about," says one HP executive. "The things she says are very warm and disarming. The things she does can be very different." This may be a testament to the power of her charisma and sales ability. Many successful business leaders leave long lines of hurt people behind them. Not all had so successfully won them over in the first place.

Fiorina's controversial character stands in marked contrast to that of Bill Hewlett and Dave Packard. From the start, friends say, they never strayed from a simple, now seemingly old-fashioned set of values. Somehow, that simple code helped them build one of the most successful companies in history.

3

INSIDE THE HP WAY

People think it's all schmaltz, but it really happened.
—JOE SCHOENDORF, FORMER HP
MARKETING EXECUTIVE

One of the most influential, admired partnerships in business history began with a camping trip. The year was 1934, and Bill Hewlett and Dave Packard had just graduated from Stanford University. They decided to take a two-week backpacking trip in the remote San Juan mountains of southwestern Colorado—far from the verdant Sierra Nevada where Hewlett had vacationed as a kid, and closer to Packard's hometown of Pueblo, Colorado. Setting off with a horse they rented for a dollar a day to carry their gear, they must have made an unlikely looking pair. Packard, with a heavily muscled six-foot-five frame, would have dwarfed the compact, fine-featured Hewlett.[1]

At that point, they were acquaintances who shared a mutual love of engineering and the outdoors. By the end of the trip, they sensed that they had much more in common. Both wanted to build a company that would use technology to benefit society. Neither was particularly concerned with following anyone else's footsteps. Both seemed to strike a balance between adventure and pragmatism.

When the two weeks ended, they knew they would make a good team. "We trusted each other not to get lost," Hewlett said many years later.[2]

They didn't get lost. Over the next 50 years, HP would provide a blueprint for generations of entrepreneurs. Their approach boiled down to basic ideas: By giving workers respect and autonomy, they would build innovative products that would both contribute to society and generate big profits. For the time, it was a revolutionary way of doing business. While many companies were structured as "Yessir!" military-style hierarchies, "Bill and Dave" insisted on being called by their first names and going for beers with their workers. The ubiquitous cubicles dotting offices around the world today? They were originally an HP innovation, meant to encourage employees to work together. Managers were asked to keep their doors open and to walk around, so they would stay connected to their people and their projects. Because success depended on everyone's hard work, the company was among the first to offer benefits such as catastrophic health insurance, profit sharing, and tuition assistance. "If I want them to be loyal to me, I've got to be loyal to them," Hewlett once told author Michael Maccoby.

All told, HP was remarkable in a thousand unremarkable ways, and those who worked there felt privileged. The perks helped, as did the pride in working for such a successful company, but it was more than that. HP was like a capitalist utopia, built on a set of sound, admirable values. Everyone, from the lowest line worker to suppliers to customers, was to be treated with respect. Humility, thrift, hard work, teamwork, and integrity were expected—and rewarded. While other companies cut corners or exploited workers, HP prospered thanks to its higher code. "I had the conception that you could either make money, or be good people—but you couldn't do both," says retired HP executive Austin Marx. "HP completely reversed that. Being good to people was the reason they made money." Adds former HP marketing executive Joe Schoendorf: "People think it's all schmaltz, but it really happened. It was hardheaded, soft-hearted management—and it worked."

Like all great leaders, Hewlett and Packard knew how to get others to rise to their level. The barrel-chested Packard, credited as the business genius of the pair, had a larger-than-life presence and a finger that grew longer as he wagged it at you, as former HP archivist Karen Lewis recalls. Hewlett was an engineer's engineer, with a mischievous sense of humor and an insatiable curiosity. They led by example, not through motivational talks or big bonuses and were concerned with employees' "work/life balance" long before it became a catchphrase. Most people who worked for them believed they were better for the experience. "Companies are societies, and people live in them—and HP had a very positive effect on my character as a human being," says Paul Ely, a retired HP manager. "Silicon Valley is infected with the HP Way—not perfectly infected, but infected."

The founding of HP is the original Silicon Valley creation myth, an important milestone in the history of business. After their summer camping trip, Packard headed east to take a job at General Electric in New York, a position he was lucky to land during the Depression. Hewlett went to complete a graduate engineering degree at the Massachusetts Institute of Technology (MIT). However, in 1937, Stanford electrical engineering professor Fred Terman lured them back to Palo Alto, hoping both men could help him realize a dream of creating a West Coast technology hub around Stanford. Terman got Packard a Stanford fellowship that paid him $500 a year, so he left New York, bringing his new wife, Lucile, or "Lu." Hewlett returned from MIT to design lab equipment for a local doctor.[3]

In 1938, the pair, with $538 between them, set up shop in the now-famous garage at 329 Addison Avenue. The Packards rented the first-floor apartment of the two-family house. Hewlett slept in a cottage behind the house until he married his childhood friend, Flora Lamson. The new company got off to a humble start. The partners often worked through the night, amid the dim light and dirt floor of the garage, taking whatever work they could get. They designed optical toilet flushers, electrical muscle stimulators, air-conditioner parts, and bowling-lane foul indicators.[4] Advertisements for some of their first products advised customers to write to Department B. "There wasn't any Department A, but they didn't want to sound small," recalled longtime HP manager Al Bagley.

They didn't have a particular business plan, a fact made clear by the generic name they'd planned to use for the business, the Engineering Service Company. Only at the last minute did Hewlett and Packard decide to use their last names. Hewlett won the coin toss to decide whose name would go first.

They might have been living on the edge of solvency, but it was thrilling. Back then, the area that would later be called Silicon Valley was a sleepy agricultural region covered with fruit orchards, dubbed the Valley of Hearts' Delight. Although the term *electronics* wouldn't come into vogue until the invention of the transistor at Bell Labs in 1947, a crop of "radio engineering" companies had sprung up in the area. In nearby Redwood City, Charles Litton was laboring over vacuum tubes. Philo Farnsworth had invented television in San Francisco. Far from being cutthroat competitors, advancing the technology was the common cause. Litton lent his factory to HP to build parts, and Hewlett and Packard were quite happy to return such favors. The spirit of collaboration, and the belief that working together can lift all boats, would be a key hallmark of the HP Way.[5] If Microsoft is the signature technology company of the past 20 years with its ruthless, monopolistic ways, Hewlett-Packard set the tone for high tech's first half-century. The basic rule, as Hewlett once put it, is: "You show competitors what you are doing—they will learn soon enough. Just don't tell them what you are thinking."[6]

The company's first big break came when it landed an order for a device called an audio oscillator, which was used to generate and measure sounds. The model was based on one of Hewlett's designs from his Stanford days. It caught the fancy of an engineer from Walt Disney & Company. Disney needed an oscillator to fine-tune the soundtrack for the new movie *Fantasia,* which would play in theaters on a special surround-sound multispeaker system. Disney liked HP's asking price—it even paid more per unit—and bought eight of the devices.

The Disney sale helped put HP on the map. At the end of 1939, the company posted sales of $5,369 and profits of $1,563—the first in an unblemished string of profitable years that continues to this day. Eager to get out of the garage, they rented new space from John "Tinker" Bell, about two miles down the road. It was nothing special, but they made do with what they had. Packard even converted a refrigerator into a stove that they kept out back for firing glaze on the instruments. They used sandbags to block the front door from leaks during rainstorms.[7] But they were off and running.

In many ways, Hewlett and Packard were like generations of ambitious Stanford grads who have started their own businesses over the years. Yet from the start, they had goals that would set their company apart, says Jerry Porras, who profiled HP as a coauthor of *Built to Last* (New York: HarperBusiness, 1994). Most entrepreneurs get started to get rich, or to develop a particular product or market opportunity. Hewlett and Packard had a different checklist. They wanted to create a company for the joy of working with each other, to provide a place where like-minded engineers would enjoy working, and to put technology to work for the greater good. "Profit is not the proper end and aim of management. It is what makes all of the proper ends and aims possible," Packard later told Porras.[8]

Packard got a taste of just how radical his view of the world was in a conversation in 1942 with Stanford professor Paul Holden, a top management guru of the time. A group had gathered to talk about the challenges of running a business during wartime. After posing the question "What is the responsibility of management?" Holden argued "Management's responsibility is to the shareholders—that's the end of it." Packard objected. "I think you're absolutely wrong," he said. "Management has a responsibility to its employees, it has a responsibility to its customers, it has a responsibility to the community at large. And they almost laughed me out of the room."[9]

In 1943, HP moved into its first company-owned building, a no-frills 10,000-square-foot building at 395 Page Mill Road. Designed to double as a supermarket in case the electronics business didn't work out, it hardly looked like the home of a future corporate juggernaut. Even then, however, the company was introducing practices that would make it an icon in business circles. There were no internal walls in the new building, just a big open space to facilitate teamwork. The founders focused on creating products that would be the most reliable on the market—a decision that would enable HP to command premium pricing for decades to come. Ray

Rooney, who was HP's thirty-first employee, remembers Packard tearing into him for not cutting cardboard cartons for HP's products neatly enough. "Take that thing over there and do it right!" Packard yelled. "He had a short temper," remembers Rooney. "If someone didn't do his job right he'd say 'If you can't do this job I will get somebody who can.' Afterward he would be sorry and he'd apologize."

Packard's tirades would remain a fixture at HP until his death in 1996, but he was quite the opposite of the overbearing, uncaring boss. With Hewlett away serving in World War II, he began to develop the egalitarian corporate culture the company became famous for. Every morning, the employees collected change to buy coffee and donuts, which everyone shared during twice-daily breaks. Lu Packard gave a baby blanket to every baby born of an HP employee. On Friday nights, employees would hit local dive bars such as the Old Pro or the Heidelberg Beer Garden. Often, Packard, who had a celebrated ability to hold his liquor, would lead the group in singing old songs such as "The Eddystone Light" and "Heard a Crash on the Highway." "Someone always had a guitar," says former HP executive Carl Cottrell. "Dave loved to sing."

HP offered groundbreaking perks almost from the start. As of 1941, the company paid an incentive bonus to every employee. Originally tied to hitting production targets, it later became a profit-sharing plan. HP wasn't the first to offer such a system. Procter & Gamble did it, and General Radio, HP's top competitor, offered bonuses to engineers. However, HP extended the program to cover every employee—and this was just a start. When an employee contracted tuberculosis, the company decided to pay the costs—and then instituted a catastrophic medical insurance program, one of the first in the nation. To minimize the chance of layoffs, the company decided not to be a defense contractor, so that it would not have to resort to fire-and-hire tactics at the start and finish of big engagements. In 1954, it instituted a program that helped pay for top engineers to get advanced Stanford degrees. When the company issued 300,000 shares in an initial public offering three years later, part of the reason was to share the wealth—60,000 shares, to be exact—with employees.

Critical to the HP Way was the idea that everyone's opinion mattered. All employees were expected to speak their minds if they saw a better way of doing things. Says former HP CEO Lew Platt, "I heard them say it many times—if you hire good people and give them the right environment to work in, you'll get great things from them." Employees were to be trusted, until they abused that trust. All supply closets remained unlocked, for example, so employees could take whatever supplies or electronic components they needed. The founders wanted employees to have access to tools to come up with new inventions, whatever the time of day or night, and there was no use tempting a thief by locking a door. Once, when Hewlett found a storeroom locked, he broke it open and left a note insisting it not be locked again. "HP trusts its employees," the note said, according to former executives.

As word spread, many talented engineers flocked to the new company. After graduating from the California Institute of Technology in 1948, Al Bagley interviewed with HP because it had a reputation as a company "that would try anything." When Bagley told Hewlett and Packard during an interview that he didn't have any new product ideas, they directed him to spend three months in the library and come up with a market need for a product. Then, he was given another three months to come up with a product design. Ultimately, he invented a product called a frequency counter that brought in millions of dollars by the mid-1950s.

As Bagley discovered, HP was no laid-back country club; you had to prove yourself and get the job done. Managers were expected to hit their financial targets and maintain morale. If they failed, they could find themselves quickly transferred. One time, Packard flew to HP's Colorado Springs campus to visit an executive named Cort Van Rensselaer. "What brings you here?" Van Rensselaer asked, as Packard walked into his office. "I'm here to take you back to California and replace you." Within hours, the two men were on the plane. Van Rensselaer went on to a long career at HP, but in jobs that better matched his skills.

Of course, the HP Way wasn't for everyone. Extremely entrepreneurial people often were frustrated by the constant need to consider other opinions. Some people didn't like all the camaraderie. Top performers sometimes found the pay packages too egalitarian. But most people, if they stayed long enough, found it was a great place to spend a career.

Most successful businesses benefit from luck and good timing, and HP was no exception. Although it wasn't a defense contractor, World War II and the Korean War generated a huge demand for HP's products. With the dawn of the Electronic Age in the 1950s and 1960s, HP's catalog of products grew thick as the company invented new kinds of instruments to help electrical engineers do their work. In some ways, it was almost too easy. Because HP was an engineering company selling to engineers, there was no need to develop a slick brand or worry much about marketing. An HP engineer had only to ask the engineer sitting next to him to know if engineers at other companies would like a creation. This "next-bench syndrome" would remain deep within HP's genetic code. It would create a distrust of slick marketing types that would remain until Fiorina's arrival in 1999.

If HP benefited from good timing, it thrived by emphasizing practicality. Its engineers were trained to think more like Thomas Edison than Einstein—to always exploit ideas that would bring in the most profits the soonest. So long as HP stayed disciplined, the system worked. By plowing its profits back into research and development (R&D), the company moved amoebalike into an endless series of new markets for products with geeky names, such as voltmeters, harmonic wave analyzers, and oscilloscopes. Each time an engineer came up with such a gizmo, a team of managers was set loose to build the business—with predictable results. These instrumentation markets often grew to $200 million in just a few years. Because customers were willing to pay more for such reliable gear, HP's profits were obscene. Often, the company would earn nearly all the profits to be had in a particular business, leaving its rivals to fight for scraps. Profits provided fuel for the company to attack the next opportunity that came around. "It was just a magical formula," recalls former HP CEO John Young, who joined the company in 1957.

Hewlett and Packard had the good sense to leave well enough

alone, and the management skill to organize the company so it wouldn't get knocked off course. By 1957, HP had 1,500 employees, more than 300 products, almost $30 million in annual sales, and a huge new headquarters in the Stanford Industrial Park.[10]

Concerned that HP might drown in bureaucracy as it grew, the cofounders had made some decisions that paved the way for another 40 years of success. For starters, they decided to slice the company into divisions, each with an executive team responsible for running it like an independent business. This institutionalized HP's small-company feel and afforded up-and-coming managers plenty of opportunities to run their own show. So long as the company continued to grow, "You didn't need to do a lot to manage your career," recalls former HP executive John Russell. "If you waited a while, they'd come tap you on the shoulder." As a result, HP was able to cherry pick graduates of top-rated engineering schools, and it became famous for its deep ranks of top-notch general managers.

Hewlett and Packard also wanted to codify their core management beliefs, to make sure every employee would see them in writing. In 1957, the company's top managers holed up at the Sonoma Mission Inn, in the wine country northeast of San Francisco, for a two-day meeting. There, Packard shared a list of six "Corporate Objectives."[11] Most important was profit—not to pad executives' or investors' pockets, but because it was vital if the company was to pay for the R&D and perks that were essential to HP's business formula. Second, HP would stick solely to its chosen field of expertise— instrumentation—and would produce only products that made a technical contribution, technology that rivals couldn't easily match and that customers would pay a higher price to get. The company would offer secure, satisfying work to its employees, and would contribute to the communities in which it did business.

Last on the list was revenue growth, an area in which Fiorina and Walter Hewlett would later clash during the war over the Compaq merger. Fiorina would argue that the merger was necessary because it would double HP's revenues and give the company a huge market share. Hewlett, like the cofounders, believes that chasing market share at the expense of profit was shortsighted. Under

Packard, HP would buy a company only to break into a promising market. Knowing Packard's disdain for the idea of growth for growth's sake, it is likely that he would have hated the Compaq merger. "Bill and Dave would be turning—no, twisting—in their graves over this deal," says Paul Ely.

Fiorina's obsession with growth wasn't the only area in which she parted ways with HP's founders. Whereas she aimed high and took big gambles, Hewlett and Packard had been pragmatic, even cautious. In 2000, Fiorina was criticized for setting earnings goals that HP couldn't hit. Packard had once demanded that the cover of an annual report be reprinted because it included a graphic in which a line traveled up and to the right. Packard feared the drawing would give the impression that HP's stock was going to rise over time. He had been known to bellow "The price of the stock is too damn high!" during analysts meetings. Of course, he'd had the luxury of handling Wall Street however he pleased. He and Hewlett then owned most of the stock.

Fiorina's view of the role of the CEO differed from Hewlett and Packard's, too. Like many of her high-tech brethren, Fiorina's team rarely turned down an opportunity for a well-placed article that could boost the CEO's image. Though not reclusive, Hewlett and Packard didn't court the press. It wasn't their way. James Collins, the other coauthor of *Built to Last,* says Hewlett and Packard never liked to talk about themselves. In 1972, when writing a letter on their behalf for an IEEE Founders Award, Barney Oliver noted that Hewlett, when describing his success, attributed it to being "on the nose of the rocket when the market took off." Packard added: "Well, at least we didn't louse it up completely."

A famous example of Hewlett's humble side occurred in 1964. With HP's twenty-fifth anniversary approaching, Hewlett pitched an idea to public relations head Dave Kirby: to have engineers create a tiny gold-plated model of the original oscillator to present to Walt Disney. After HP machinists built the trinket, Kirby made the arrangements to visit Disney. When they arrived, they were led to the studio chief's offices. He was wearing a sport shirt and moccasins, and "in 30 seconds we realized that he didn't know HP from a sack of cement," recalls Kirby. When they presented the miniature oscillator to Disney, he responded, "Oh, this is very nice. I'll give it to my grandkids."

Rather than add to the humiliation, Hewlett and Kirby sheepishly backed out of the office. Then, Kirby squirmed through what seemed like an eternity of silence as they got back in the car and drove off. Moments later, with a twinkle in his eye, Hewlett finally said, "Well, that didn't go over very well, now did it?"

When Kirby retired years later, Hewlett praised him for his work. "The only screwup I can remember was the Disney affair. But it all turned out okay, because they thought it was Packard."

The HP Way was a direct reflection of the company's founders. Many of Hewlett's ancestors traveled from Arkansas to California in a covered wagon. Hewlett's father, Dr. Walter Albion Hewlett, was a brilliant surgeon who became dean of Stanford's medical school in 1916. Dr. Hewlett was an innovator, as his son would become. While most doctors were studying corpses to gather medical information, Dr. Hewlett and colleagues pioneered a new movement to study patients' clinical data such as blood tests and electrocardiograms. That way, the focus could shift to keeping people alive, rather than inspecting the dead.

Bill Hewlett's brilliance was not apparent as a child, probably due to his dyslexia, which was diagnosed years later. He'd only been admitted to Stanford when his high school principal found out who his father was and agreed to recommend him. By then, however, Hewlett's father had passed away from a brain tumor. At Stanford, he had to wake up at 4:00 A.M. to do his homework because he was such a slow reader. However, he found his stride in Terman's engineering labs, earning a reputation as a top-flight engineer by the time he graduated.

Hewlett was the driving force behind HP's record of technical innovation. He loved nothing more than hanging around engineering labs or talking with technologists at other companies. His curiosity extended to other subjects, as well. An expert in California wildflowers, he became a noted photographer. "He was one of the most inquisitive people I ever met in my life," says former CEO Platt. "When I look out the window, I'd see a tree. But he'd want to know what kind of tree it was, how it worked, what was its genesis—and he was that way whether it was art or music or botany or electronics. That was the seed that was planted inside HP. He was the guy who gave the invention DNA to HP."

If Packard became famous as the management innovator of the pair, he was also a technologist first. He spent his youth scouring the *World Book Encyclopedia*'s entries about natural science, conducting his own experiments and building vacuum-tube radios. The son of a lawyer father and a schoolteacher mother, Packard even ran an amateur radio station, erecting a tower in his yard.[12] At Stanford, he was the first undergraduate to be asked into Professor Terman's elite graduate radio engineering class.

Of the two, Packard was by far the more volatile. Managers lived in fear of crossing him. Once, when he didn't get a straight answer to one of his questions during a board meeting, he got up, walked slowly all around the boardroom table, and sat back in his chair, fuming all the way. "That would cause you to gulp," says retired executive Bill Terry. Indeed, Packard had two nicknames, recalls Al Bagley: "Pappy" (for his benevolent side) and "the Mean One" (self-explanatory). Though he was the architect of the company's egalitarian ways, Packard allowed no doubt as to who made the final decisions. Executives laugh about how he hated the term "corporate controller." "If there's any controller around here, it's me," he once snapped. Another time, hearing complaints about how the corporate culture was changing, he roared at a staffer: "The HP Way is what I damn well say it is."

His powerful personality extended to his personal life. He could be a remote, demanding father, say longtime friends. "This was not a warm and cuddly person," says Jay Keyworth, who considers Packard a father figure. "People used to say that if he was dropped out of a plane over the North Pole, he'd swim out in Seattle six months later." Nonetheless, he had a magic touch for helping his wife and children fulfill their own dreams. He helped Lucile found the Stanford Children's Hospital just before her death in 1987. Some people would say Dave made his wife work too hard in her final days, recalls Keyworth. "Others would say he gave his dying wife her ultimate wish." Later, Packard helped daughter Julie start the world-famous Monterey Aquarium, and helped fund son David Woodley Packard's renovation of an old 1930s movie palace in downtown Palo Alto.

Perhaps the most remarkable thing about Hewlett and Packard was their partnership. They were a tandem unique in business history. They were best friends who were able to finish each other's sentences. Their united front made it very difficult for internal fracases to go very far, because managers could never play them against each other. "It got to be a joke," Hewlett said in a 1984 interview with the Institute of Electrical and Electronics Engineers (IEEE).[13] "People are like children: When they don't get the answer they want from one person, they move on to the next person, and they very quickly found that independent of each other we came up with the same answer. Dave and I worked together for so long we really felt very much alike."

Both men shared a common view of how to use their vast fortunes. Basically, the money was to be given away. In 1964, Packard set up the David and Lucile Packard Foundation. Hewlett followed in 1966 with the William and Flora Hewlett Foundation. Both men put more than 95 percent of their wealth into charity. They gave more than $300 million to Stanford University. "[Our parents] went to a lot of trouble to explain [their wealth] to us," says Walter Hewlett. "The money had come to us a quirk. It had to be given away." The same spirit infused the company. HP employees have long been a fixture in education and civic groups. Says marketing consultant and author Regis McKenna, "We'd really be lost without HP's leadership in the community."

Both men were avid anglers and hunters, and loved nothing more than working with their hands. When they purchased the 30,000-acre San Felipe ranch south of San Jose in 1952, Packard bought tractors and personally paved 20 miles of road. They were more than fake weekend ranchers. One year, guests were shocked to see Packard deal with a cow whose innards had somehow become exposed while giving birth. Packard took a look, calmly rolled up his sleeve, and shoved his arm into the cow to its full length. "He was undaunted by anything," says Al Bagley.

The founders' feeling of friendship extended to HP's management team. Many of Fiorina's critics point out that she arrived at HP without any longtime allies, and that she never established particularly close ties with many of her managers. Not so with Hewlett and Packard. They loved inviting managers to an annual deer hunt at their ranch. Hewlett would happily wake up the hunters at 4:00 A.M. with a serenade on his accordion, and Packard would bark orders at the guests, assigning them to one of many jeeps.

If it was clear that they were the bosses, they were also just two of the guys. In 1952, Ray Demere was driving to an elk hunt in Idaho, with Packard in the front seat. Demere flipped the truck going around a bend. Packard was thrown from the truck, blacked out, and suffered vision problems. Demere, who broke his back in the crash, feared his boss's ire when he awoke in an adjacent hospital bed. It never came. "He couldn't have been better about it," says Demere.

Even as the company grew, the bond between management and the employees remained strong. In 1967, John L. Cooper, now an attorney in San Francisco, was a summer intern, as low on the totem pole as was possible. Like Packard, he had grown up in Pueblo. After Packard discovered this during a morning coffee break, he took notice of Cooper. When Cooper began having trouble with his eyes in September 1967, he went to see a doctor at Stanford Medical Center. To his shock, the doctor told him he had detached retinas in both eyes and was in danger of going blind. Although he had no medical insurance, a renowned doctor performed the surgery. When Cooper awoke and asked how this would all be paid for, he was told not to worry. HP had paid for the whole thing. "I don't know for sure that David Packard did that, but I was one happy guy," Cooper says.

Both partners found endless energy for public service. Hewlett tended to work behind the scenes. He would buy land in the Sierras that was threatened by developers. Packard, on the other hand, sought out ways to have higher-level impact, says Karen Lewis, who helped him write his book, *The HP Way* (Boston: HarperBusiness, 1995). Packard founded the American Electronics Association, a large trade organization. From 1968 to 1971, he served as deputy secretary of defense for the Nixon administration. While in the job, he pushed through procurement reforms that took millions out of the pockets of corporate contractors—and injected himself into the center of the raging debates over Vietnam. He once called Jane Fonda a traitor.

Although the partners were demanding taskmasters, they created an environment in which managers were free to speak their minds. Steve Gomo was a young midlevel manager when he was asked to present the capital budget to the board of directors in 1978, because the executive that normally did the job was not available. Terrified, Gomo slaved to create a 12-slide presentation, and remembers practicing in front of a mirror for hours. Finally, he was called in to the meeting. Gomo's presentation went well until he showed a slide filled with financial data. Suddenly, Hewlett piped up. "What is this gross asset and accumulated depreciation stuff? We only show one thing: net assets."

There was total silence. Gomo swallowed hard, and said, "Actually, that's wrong, Bill. We don't just look at net assets."

"Yes, we do," said Hewlett firmly. Then, turning to CFO Ed van Bronkhorst, he said, "We never look at anything but net assets, right, Ed?"

"No, Bill. He's right," said van Bronkhorst.

Suddenly, the whole board room burst out laughing at the thought of this rookie showing up Hewlett—except for Gomo, who just wanted to get the heck out of there. Fumbling with his papers, he moved toward the door, when suddenly Packard stood up, dominating the room with his huge physical presence. "Oh shit, this can't be good," Gomo thought.

Gomo's fears quickly vanished. "I just want it recorded in the minutes of this meeting that this was the best presentation on the capital budget that this board has ever received," said Packard, shaking Gomo's hand.

Gomo, glowing inside, made his exit. "There was no reason for Packard to do that—except to make a young kid feel good. I will never forget that as long as I live."

In the 1960s, after more than 20 years of quietly going about its business, HP began to be recognized around the world as a great company. It provided the security of working for a corporate giant and a generous one, at that. The company continued to pioneer new perks, including flextime and job sharing for working mothers. The company also bought up a series of properties that employees could use for recreation. It bought a redwood grove in the Santa Cruz Mountains, a lake in Scotland, and a Colorado ski resort. The founders' generosity impressed employees.

"I have the impression that Bill and Dave are working for me, rather than the other way around," an employee once told Barney Oliver, the longtime manager of HP Labs.[14]

All told, by the end of the 1960s, HP was an organization on top of its game—high tech's answer to Harvard, the Yankees, or the Green Berets.

Camaraderie was clear in the skits that were performed at annual management reviews. Sometimes, executives poked harmless fun at each other—such as forcing one guy who pronounced the word *satellite* as "statellite" to repeat the word countless times. More often, the skits were designed to not so subtly point out a person's character flaws or excesses. One year, Paul Ely, whose booming voice could be heard two conference rooms away, it was said, was called on stage to participate—and was given no lines.

Perhaps the most telling skit of all involved just Hewlett and Packard. The set consisted of two chairs, arm to arm. Packard sat in one, and then Hewlett walked on stage: "Hey, this seat is vacant. Can I sit here?" After he sat down, the two began boasting, each claiming to run the world's best company. Despite HP's success, it was funny because neither man would ever talk that way. "They couldn't even read their lines, they were laughing so hard," recalls Dave Kirby, who helped write the skit.

Hewlett and Packard didn't have the only formula for building a company. Fairchild Semiconductor had a ruthless, "stab-your-neighbor culture," as management consultant Geoffrey Moore puts it, which led the best managers to leave and found their own companies. One of those companies, Intel Corporation, was built on the Darwinian idea that competition and confrontation would lead to brilliant execution and inspired strategies. But HP, arguably, had the greatest influence of all—as important to the technology business as Louis Armstrong was to music or Babe Ruth was to baseball.

Just ask Steve Jobs. As a 12-year-old, in 1967, he was trying to build a frequency counter. He called HP, and Bill Hewlett happened to come on the line. "Hi, I'm Steve Jobs. I'm twelve years old and I'm trying to build a frequency counter," Jobs said. Hewlett spoke with Jobs for 20 minutes, promised to get him the parts he wanted, and even offered him a summer job. Jobs has been a fan ever since, and has used many of HP's philosophies in creating Apple Computer. "They believed that humans were noble," he said during a 1998 interview. "HP was definitely the fundamental DNA of Silicon Valley."[15]

For years now, the Hewlett name has been synonymous with vast wealth, but that was not the case when Walter Hewlett was growing up in the 1940s and 1950s. Vacations were spent up at the Cedars, a rustic collection of cabins deep in the Sierras that had been owned by the same middle-class families since 1900. After his father and Packard bought the ranch at San Felipe, Walter would spend many weekends there as they built roads or irrigation dams. There was no sense that his father would one day be a business magnate. Told by her father that HP made "measuring equipment," eldest child Eleanor reported to her third-grade class that her father made rulers.

After HP went public in 1957, the fortune started to build—slowly, at first, and then in great leaps. In the 25 years following its establishment, the William and Flora Hewlett Foundation would balloon into one of the nation's largest charitable organizations. When Flora passed away in the late 1970s, the family created a separate minifoundation dedicated to teaching young family members the proper practice of philanthropy—a foundation on training wheels. Through it all, Walter and his four siblings, who own roughly $125 million in HP stock between them, have chosen to live modestly, given their wealth. "It's not like we were born Fords or Rockefellers," says Eleanor. "We are not a bunch of spoiled rich kids."

4

TROUBLE IN PARADISE

Dave and Bill never really liked the computer business.
— FORMER HP EXECUTIVE DOUG CHANCE

nyone reading the headlines about Carly Fiorina and the
HP soap opera in recent years might think the company's
problems started in the late 1990s, when it entered the
most prolonged slump in its history. However, the roots of the problem began far earlier, in the late 1960s. That was when the company
began to move out of the safe electronic instruments business into
the stormy computer industry.

The migration was ultimately successful. By the time HP bought
Compaq, it was the second largest maker of computing products in
the world, and had outlasted a throng of one-time powers such as
Burroughs, Wang, and Digital Equipment Corporation (DEC). But
the journey was long and painful. Many factors contributed to the
trouble. Bill Hewlett and Dave Packard backed away from day-to-day
operations in the 1980s, leaving the HP Way open to the interpreta-
tion of others. To continue growing in a far more competitive and
complex world, the company had to invent new approaches to business. Without the founders on hand to steer the way, HP's executives struggled to map a clear course. That set the stage for Carly

Fiorina—and the violent reaction that occurred when she tried to impose her will on the company.

HP's computer age began innocently enough. In early 1964, an engineer in HP's oscilloscope division named Kay Magleby had just completed his PhD at Stanford, with HP paying half the tuition. Having discovered a love of computer science, he found himself a job in HP's new central R&D lab and told his boss, Paul Stoft, that he was done making oscilloscopes. A square-faced bull of a man, Magleby wanted to build a computer. It was seven years after the invention of the integrated circuit, and companies from mighty IBM to red-hot start-ups such as DEC were using these bits of silicon to build powerful new machines—and an exciting new industry that seemed to have limitless opportunity. Because HP's customers were already using computers, it was clear that HP was going to be affected. Stoft gave Magleby the go-ahead. "It was new, and I wanted to learn about it as well," Stoft says.

When Dave Packard got wind of what they were working on, he wasn't happy. Computers weren't an area of expertise for HP. Packard stormed into Stoft's office. "What have you got Kay Magleby doing?"

"He's designing a computer," Stoft replied.

"What? Is that the best thing you can have him do?" Packard said. Then he stomped out.

Magleby and Stoft, wanting to keep on with their research, came up with a way to sell it to the boss. Magleby's computer would be used to improve HP's core business, instruments. HP's customers had to fuss with lots of dials and buttons, then write down the measurements collected from their HP voltmeters, electronic thermometers, and other products. By attaching all their HP gear to a computer, customers would be able to see, store, and make calculations on a single monitor.

Their argument almost didn't pass muster. After Magleby gave a three-hour pitch, Packard did what he always did at the end of important meetings: asked for Bill Hewlett's opinion. Hewlett hemmed and hawed. "We don't know about computers," he said, according to Magleby. "I'm not sure we should mess around with them." Packard chewed on his partner's comments, and asked Stoft again: "Do we really think Kay's time is best spent on this project?" When Stoft replied in the affirmative, Packard said "I think Kay's got something here" and told him to continue with his efforts.

If he'd had his doubts, within a few weeks Packard was knee-deep into figuring out HP's entrée into the computer business. He flew east and talked with DEC founder Ken Olsen about possibly purchasing his fast-growing company.[1] That looked like too difficult a merger, so Packard decided instead to purchase technology from a struggling computing subsidiary of Union Carbide. When HP came out with the HP 2116A in 1966, it was a hit, with all the reliability and innovation HP customers had come to expect. While other computers were crash-prone and had to be monitored constantly in air-conditioned rooms, Magleby's computer was rugged enough to be used right out on the factory floor.

HP's venture into computing might have stopped there. Hewlett and Packard were so concerned that HP would draw the ire of IBM that they almost refused to let the 2116A be called a computer. "Dave always insisted that we're not going to compete with IBM, ever," recalls Magleby. IBM was too big and powerful in that business. HP was asking for trouble if it tried racing up that heavily defended hill, Packard said. But thanks to HP's decentralized culture, HP's more gung-ho employees would not be denied. A version of the 2116 was created for high school and university use, to offer computer training and to maintain records. So-called time-sharing companies bought banks of the machines and rented out their use to companies that couldn't afford their own. By the early 1970s, it was clear there was no turning back. Computers were going to be a vast market, and HP was going to be a part of it.

HP's first effort to attack the computer business head-on did not go well. Tom Perkins, who would later play a key role in the HP–Compaq merger as a member of Compaq's board, was in charge of an effort to build a machine, code-named Omega, that would have been a revolutionary step forward in computer design. It was too revolutionary a step, it turned out—both technically and culturally. The many long-haired computer scientists brought into the company did not understand the HP Way, and the project flopped. "We were a hardware company and suddenly there's these strange people who ride bicycles around and don't wear shoes and mumble to themselves," Stoft says, describing the oddball programmers who were suddenly making their way around campus. Though HP was great at designing hardware, it struggled to develop the massive software programs Omega required. When the cofounders cancelled the project, Perkins, who went on to cofound the powerful venture capital firm Kleiner Perkins Caufield & Byers, was given a placeholder position as an assistant to Bill Hewlett, say some former executives.

After the Omega disaster, HP got to work on a less ambitious design, known as Alpha. This project didn't go well, either. Introduced as the HP 3000 in November 1972, customers quickly found the product was not up to snuff. It hadn't been properly tested, was plagued by software bugs, and couldn't do many of the things HP claimed it could. It was a huge embarrassment for a company that was famous for the reliability of its products. Packard, who had just returned from his stint at the Defense Department, was furious. He ordered the company to take back the 50 or so units that had been sold, and tapped HP veteran Paul Ely to re-launch the product.

Working behind the scenes with Ely was Dick Hackborn, then an up-and-coming young engineering manager. Already, he boasted a unique combination of management skills. He was considered a "scientist engineer" among HP's more down-to-earth inventors, says Stoft. Like an Einstein among Edisons, he was more interested in sweeping theories of how technology could influence the world than in inventing the next widget. Yet he was also a great day-to-day manager. Though he was quiet, private, and unassuming, he somehow was able to fire up his staffers to pull off great achievements. "He was a great teacher," says former HP executive Bob Frankenberg. "He was a big part of why HP became an icon." However, he was as enigmatic as he was capable, say many former HP managers. Hackborn hated confrontation—to the point that it became common knowledge that if you wanted to know what he thought about a conversation you'd had with him, it was best not to rely on what he said. The trick was to talk to the next person he spoke with, with whom he would invariably share his real opinions.

For someone who hated confrontation, Hackborn would inject himself into major strategic debates throughout his career—even those not involving his businesses. As a result, many of his peers were not quite sure what to make of him. Some saw him as honest and straightforward; others sensed a political savvy and simmering ambition they distrusted.

He didn't seem to fit the HP mold. He wasn't big on hunting, skiing, or golf, like so many of his peers, but rather preferred wine, books, and art. Later in life, he developed a deep interest in yoga. Most HP employees planned to spend their entire careers with the company, but Hackborn was forever talking about ditching the whole thing to become a dentist, lawyer, or politician.

Hackborn's impact on HP started with the HP 3000. After the machine was pulled from the market, he helped rein in the troubled engineering effort to get the product reintroduced six months later. "He was the guy who came in on the white horse," says Dick Watts, a former HP executive. The product would become one of the most reliable machines in the history of the computer business, with huge sales to companies that could not afford IBM mainframes.

Still, the computer business required an entirely different approach for HP. In the instruments business, a small group of people spent a few hundred thousand dollars to develop a new product. Building a major new computer, on the other hand, cost millions and required a host of parallel efforts—one team to build the basic hardware, one to come up with the semiconductor brains, one to design the software, another to build the disk drives. In the instruments business, the new product could be simply added to HP's catalog, to be sold to rank-and-file engineers right along with HP's other products. In the computer business, HP would need a legion of high-priced salespeople and sophisticated marketers to convince big corporations to commit to HP over IBM or some other rival. "The customers were suddenly people who didn't know how to use a screwdriver, and, God forbid, didn't want to," recalls former HP executive John Russell.

Even Hewlett and Packard had their doubts. They wanted to hold onto the proven formulas that had worked so well: Only enter businesses that can be grown profitably from the start, and hand them over to managers to run like independent companies. Computers took years of up-front investment, and didn't fit into HP's nice, neat organizational structure. "Dave and Bill never really liked the computer business," says former executive Doug Chance. Says former CEO John Young: "In the computer business, the pieces are less important than the system as a whole. That is something we would wrestle with for a long time." Young would have to oversee that struggle, and it would not be pretty.

Not all of HP's moves into the computer age went badly. The company's HP-35 handheld scientific calculator was the company's first consumer hit.

The calculator started off as many HP products had: as one of Bill Hewlett's inspirations. In 1971, Hewlett walked into R&D manager Stoft's office holding a small Japanese calculator roughly the size of a paperback book. "You know, this is kind of a nice deal," he said, and began musing with Stoft about the new low-power chips and other components that were then being developed. Before he left 10 minutes later, he told Stoft to get to work on a calculator that would have as many functions as bigger desktop models, but which he could fit in his shirt pocket. "I want something I can carry around," he said.

It was a radical idea to think small in the age of Big Iron. The market research firm Hewlett hired said HP could never sell enough to make a profit. But Hewlett was sure it would be a hit, and he okayed some radical departures from how HP did business. The HP-35 wouldn't cost thousands; it was priced at $395. To keep costs low, the company procured chips and other parts from outside suppliers rather than develop them in-house. Rather than simply add a page to the HP product catalog, the company established a distribution network that included electronics shops, department stores, and other retail locations. This new territory was about as familiar as the moon to the HP executives in charge. Computer division chief Bill Terry remembers going to Macy's in San Francisco and being shocked when the store's buyer told him that HP would have to stock the shelves before they knew exactly what demand would be. "You guys don't understand," the buyer told him. "I can't sell it if I don't have it in the store."

It all worked, brilliantly. The product was developed in record time—7 months versus the more typical 18. Sales went through the roof, as students and others waited for hours outside stores around the country. To many inside the company, this was proof that the HP Way could be applied to completely new markets, in completely new ways. By 1980, HP had been almost completely metamorphosed from the narrowly focused instruments company of old. That year, for the first time, more than half of HP's sales and profits came from computers rather than instruments.[2] There were 40 divisions.

John Young, who replaced Bill Hewlett as CEO in 1977, struggled to maintain HP's small-company feel. "Management by walking around" was no longer possible in such a vast international corporation. Informal coffee breaks gave way to mandatory "coffee talks" to maintain communication between management and the troops. Young and his successors would fight a constant battle to convince employees that the HP Way wasn't dead—it was only changing.

Dick Hackborn was about to make sure of that. After his work on the HP 3000, he'd been utterly exhausted. Frustrated with the endless meetings and strategic debates at HP's headquarters, he decided to take the summer off. Heading north from Silicon Valley with his family in a rented mobile home, his first stop was to visit fellow HP executive Chance, who ran an HP division in the bucolic community of Santa Rosa, California. During his visit, he decided to take "the next general manager's job he could get that was not in Palo Alto or Cupertino," remembers Chance.

Before long, Hackborn was running a division in Boise, Idaho. He soon began building HP's most successful business ever: printers. It started in 1979, when he got wind of new printer technology developed in Palo Alto. An HP engineer had noticed that droplets trapped underneath a chip he was researching would vaporize when the chip was powered on. Over the next few years, using tiny nozzles and sophisticated software to control the flow, HP developed inkjet cartridges that could squirt vaporized inks onto paper with much greater resolution than the clunky dot-matrix printers of the day, and at a much lower cost than the high-priced models HP had been selling with the HP 3000.

The inkjet technology would take years to perfect. In the meantime, Hackborn spearheaded the company's first huge printer hit: the laser printer. He broke many of HP's old rules to do it. At the time, HP was selling an expensive $60,000 model made by Japan's Canon, Inc. When Canon executives proposed building a smaller, cheaper model using their laser technology and HP's distributors and salespeople, HP agreed. PCs—including those from a Houston-based start-up called Compaq—were selling like hotcakes, and Hackborn figured most of them would have an attached printer over time.

To ensure a meaningful profit, Hackborn flipped HP's approach on its head. Rather than spending gobs on R&D and charging high prices, HP let Canon provide the technology while it focused on selling as many units as possible at as low a cost as possible. The approach worked very well. The first LaserJet, unveiled in 1984, sold more than twice as many as forecast. As the PC market boomed, HP quickly cornered the printer market, combining strategic brilliance, operational excellence, and even great marketing; for example, HP was first to figure out that documents should be printed so they came out in proper order. Time and again, HP introduced models that offered greater capabilities at a fraction of the price of the rival offerings.

By the late 1980s, the inkjet printer market began to take off. Again, Hackborn and his troops found new ways to make the business successful. While headquarters pumped billions into R&D to build the inkjet technology and lock up crucial patents, the boys in Boise cut costs to the bone in other areas. And just as Gillette always made its money on razor blades rather than the razors, HP began racking up huge profits by selling ink cartridges. Even after prices and profits for PCs and printers collapsed in the late 1990s, this inky river of profits would continue to rise. Before Carly Fiorina made her bid for Compaq in late 2001, the $9-billion printer supplies business was bringing in all of HP's profits, covering losses from the rest of the $45-billion company.

Despite its success, Hackborn's printer empire was extremely controversial inside HP. The engineers and salespeople who had built HP felt Hackborn's lean-and-mean approach ignored Hewlett and Packard's devotion to invention. Hackborn disagreed, arguing that the printer business was just a new way to innovate and run a business. Wasn't that what HP was all about? "I used to ask Hewlett and Packard regularly if I was violating the HP Way," he said. "Every time, they assured me I was very much within the HP Way, if you look at it as principles rather than practices."[3] He gave maximum responsibility and respect to his employees, and he certainly delivered huge profits and revenue growth.

Still, the once tight-knit company was becoming one with three different heads. There was the old instruments business. While still growing, it was fast being marginalized in terms of its overall importance to the company. There was the computer business, which still followed the old R&D-intensive guidelines. Young, intent on making HP a serious rival to IBM, poured huge up-front investments into the so-called Spectrum Project. Though ultimately successful, it would throw the computer business into the red for much of the 1980s. Finally, there was Hackborn and his supporters, who fumed at having to help pay for all of Palo Alto's perks, when they were bringing in most of the profits.

By then, a state of almost perpetual war had engulfed the company.

Hackborn was at the center of the debate. For a time, he ran his printer empire from a tiny office in a strip mall in Boise; he didn't like even the hustle and bustle at HP's main Boise facility. Yet he had a habit of weighing in on how other parts of the business should be run. At times, he would fire off long missives, commenting on how someone else was running their division.

This rubbed many colleagues the wrong way, especially since he refused to actually get involved in many aspects of running the company. HP's top brass found it almost impossible to get him to come to Palo Alto for meetings. He'd complain of an inner-ear problem that made flying uncomfortable, or use his wife as an excuse. "Dick was a funny sort—quick to criticize and slow to help," says Lew Platt, who would become HP's CEO. "Dick had a very nice deal. He could sit in Boise and focus on running his business. He knows a lot about running a business. He doesn't know much about running a company." He almost never got involved with visiting customers, entertaining dignitaries, or dealing with public policy issues.

HP's computer troubles continued in the late 1980s. To align all parts of the company toward battling IBM, Young had created a system of interlocking committees to replace the tried-and-true divisional structure. Some of HP's most talented executives jumped ship, frustrated with the bureaucracy that seemed to be taking the place of the old HP Way. "It was like pushing on the end of a 300-foot rope to get anything done," says Paul Ely, Hackborn's old boss. Worse, the egalitarian toughness of the old days had been somewhat replaced by a sense of entitlement—the idea that one deserved nifty perks and job security, and the right to heard. "I got very tired of the collegiality," says Dan Warmenhoven, who went on to run Network Appliance, Inc. "It was like the U.N. National Security Council. Everyone had veto power."

Dave Packard had seen enough, as well. Although the Spectrum Project was finally nearing its end, it had fallen years behind schedule. At board meetings, Packard would listen to Hackborn's printer group report another blowout quarter. Then computer division chief financial officer Robert Wayman would deliver more bad news. "Dave Packard would sit there tearing his hair out," says board member Jay Keyworth. Young's support of Bill Clinton for president in 1992—an unforgivable sin in Packard's mind—didn't help his cause, either. Platt also suspected that Hackborn was quietly lobbying the cofounders to oust Young.

In 1992, the founders decided to make Hackborn the new CEO and chair of the company—but they were in for a surprise. Hackborn didn't want the job. He had refused an offer from Bill Gates to become Microsoft's chief operating officer, says former HP manager Steve Gomo, who worked closely with Hackborn for years. Even when Gates doubled the multi-million-dollar pay package, Hackborn resisted. "I guess I can't be bought," he told Gomo.

Packard tried repeatedly to get Hackborn to take the top job. He even once mistakenly told the board that Hackborn had accepted, according to Young. When Hackborn held his ground, the job went to Platt, an affable engineer and operations expert. Once voted the "class plugger" at his high school in upstate New York for his work ethic, Platt had started out managing facilities for HP in the Boston area in 1966 and worked his way up.

Hackborn didn't last long working for Platt. He later told Walter Hewlett, "I've spent my whole life fixing things. I'm tired of fixing other people's problems." After he quit, Hackborn accepted Packard's offer to join HP's board. At Gates's request, Hackborn also joined Microsoft's board—a decision that later caused flags to go up for Hewlett.

"I couldn't understand it," says Hewlett. "Microsoft is such a different company from HP. There's a ruthlessness there that I think Dick was fascinated by. He says his heroes are Bill and Dave. I sometimes wonder if his real hero isn't Bill Gates."

Lew Platt took over HP at a very opportune time. The printer business was booming. The Spectrum Project was finally paying off, causing HP's computer business to roar to life. Revenues zoomed from $12.5 billion in 1992 to $31.5 billion in 1995. With all cylinders firing, Platt concentrated on HP's culture. Widowed as a young executive with four children, his devotion to the HP Way had been cemented when his managers had given him all the flexibility and time off he required to be an attentive father.

As the 1990s progressed, however, HP's prosperity came to rely on an un-HP-like foundation: PCs based on software from Microsoft and chips from Intel.

In the past, HP had doubted the PC business. While HP's printers used homegrown technology and expertise, PCs could be made by almost anyone. That was one reason that HP had passed when a low-level engineer named Steve Wozniak had showed them a prototype of his user-friendly computer in 1975.[4] (When he failed to garner interest even from his immediate boss, the Woz and his partner, Steve Jobs, used the idea to create Apple Computer.)

By the early 1990s, HP had a small, struggling PC business that existed to serve those customers that wanted to use PCs to access HP's more powerful computers. Some executives wanted to tap into the soaring PC market more aggressively, but Dave Packard warned against letting it get too big in its own right. HP veterans tell of a business review session at which Packard was looking over a prototype of one of HP's newer PCs. "You know the only thing worse than a shitty business?" he muttered. "A big shitty business."

The story may be apocryphal, but there's no doubt about Packard's view. Doug Chance, who ran the business for a time, says "It was not particularly helpful to have him going around saying 'Why the hell are we in this business?' "

Soon after Platt took over, HP's board nearly made the decision to kill the PC business entirely. Only when Hackborn pleaded for its life and offered to run it did the board reconsider, says Bob Frankenberg, whom Hackborn tapped to whip the money-losing business into shape. Frankenberg succeeded in that effort, and HP moved from twenty-seventh in market share in the early 1990s to become a leader by middecade. Slowly, the company began to refocus its strategy around the PC standard. In 1993, Platt decided HP couldn't sustain the billions of dollars required to maintain the PA-RISC chips that powered its higher-end computers. Instead, he made a deal with market leader Intel Corporation. By combining HP's PA-RISC technology with Intel's famous manufacturing and marketing might, he hoped to have a leg up in setting the future direction of the entire computer industry, with powerful machines at PC prices. (So far, that decision hasn't worked out as planned. Originally due out in 1996, the Itanium family of chips that resulted from the partnership was only beginning to make a dent in the market in 2002.)

Still, the PC boom did lead to some years of rollicking growth for HP. One big reason: Rick Belluzzo, Hackborn's longtime protégé, drove down costs while expanding HP's presence in retail stores and distributors, as millions of consumers and businesses loaded up on PCs and printers. In 1995, the company posted a remarkable 26 percent sales growth, with profits growth of 52 percent. Platt, an unlikely media star, began to appear in cover stories, but he knew the good times were not sustainable. Even as HP racked up great numbers, Platt repeatedly warned Wall Street that this could not continue.

By the time Platt's warnings came true, HP would be a far different company. It spent the 1990s chasing market share in PC-related markets that were rapidly commoditizing, and in which rival Dell Computer was able to sell products far more profitably, given its approach of selling via the Internet. These were just the kind of markets that Packard would have gotten *out* of in the old days, say many longtime HP executives. The deeper HP waded in, the more difficult it would be to wade back out.

The situation brought the debate between HP's two major camps to a head. Belluzzo, Hackborn, and their supporters were convinced that the PC would dominate the future of the computer business, and that the market for HP's higher-end computers based on PA-RISC chips and Unix software would slip. Willem Roelandts, head of the Unix computer business, warned that HP would end up losing its ability to innovate—and command decent profits—if it relied too heavily on Microsoft and Intel. Hackborn was right about the general trend, but his view was too simplistic, Roelandts felt. Even if Intel computers were a better bargain, they simply couldn't handle many of the jobs that HP's Unix machines could tackle— and PCs weren't profitable enough to enable HP to provide the top-notch support HP gave its Unix customers.

The two sides clashed at a tense series of meetings in early 1995. Belluzzo, with Hackborn's backing in the boardroom, won the war. On August 28, 1995, Platt put Belluzzo in charge of the entire computer operation. Roelandts, who resigned, was shocked. His division had gone from a $200-million loss in 1992, with negligible growth, to 25 percent annual growth and hefty operating profits, above 10 percent. Roelandts felt the invisible hand of Hackborn. "I've always respected Dick Hackborn, but his ideal role is as éminence grise—the power behind the throne. He doesn't want to be public, but he craves power."

Belluzzo insists he never intended to trample HP's Unix busi-ness, but that business quickly lost momentum—just as the Internet boom was about to send demand for such systems through the roof. Belluzzo would also be criticized internally for a sweeping deal with Microsoft. HP sources say the company had discovered that Microsoft was infringing on a host of HP patents—potentially worth hundreds of millions of dollars, according to some sources—but Belluzzo licensed them to Microsoft for roughly $100 million plus a price break on Microsoft's Windows software.

The fight wasn't only about future strategy, but about the com-pany's culture. By this time, the HP Way had become like a religion. It was revered by some and ridiculed by others. For certain, it could be used to justify a wide range of positions. Some looked up to Platt as a keeper of the HP Way; others began to feel he was overly focused on the trappings of the founders' philosophy—the perks, the diversity, the community service—and not focused enough on the business end of the founders' thinking. "With Lew, it's like every grade on the report card counted the same," says one former executive. "Your business could be going to hell, but it was like—well, you did very well on worker safety." Says Belluzzo, "Bill and Dave were pretty tough guys. Somehow, we lost that. You had to be careful not to hurt people's feelings."

By the mid-1990s, Dave Packard was keeping busy in his old age. His hearing had failed, and he missed his wife, who had died in 1987, but he took joy in bringing friends from the old days, from dignitaries such as former CIA chief Dick Helms to the ranch hands at the San Felipe ranch, up to his fishing camp in British Columbia. He spent hours sitting with his friend Bill Hewlett, who had suffered a stroke. He tinkered in the woodworking shop he built at his house, and built a waterwheel to generate electricity at his property on the Big Sur coast. However, Packard was growing disillusioned with what he saw as a decline in business ethics, with politics, and even with HP. "Dave got pretty irascible in the 1990s," says Karen Lewis, who coauthored *The HP Way* (Boston: HarperBusiness) with Packard in 1995. "He was not happy with the direction of the company."

Indeed, when Packard attended his last general managers meeting, in 1996, he had Platt accompany him to the podium so he could address the company's top executives. Few could understand him; in fact, most felt horrible that the great man could hardly be understood through his garbled speech. But what he read from the podium was a poignant metaphor for HP—an Oliver Wendell Holmes poem titled "The Deacon's Masterpiece," about a carriage that was designed never to wear out.[5]

> *She was a wonder, and nothing less!*
> *Colts grew horses, beards turned gray,*
> *Deacon and Deaconess dropped away,*
> *Children and grandchildren, where were they?*

As the "one-hoss shay" approached its hundredth anniversary, it showed "a general flavor of mild decay," but there was nothing much to worry about. Then, on its hundredth anniversary, the shay suddenly fell apart in a heap.

> *Little of all we value here*
> *Wakes on the morn of its hundredth year*
> *Without both looking and feeling queer.*
> *In fact, there's nothing that keeps its youth,*
> *So far as I know, but a tree and truth.*

Then the poem ends as follows:

> *You see, of course, if you're not a dunce,*
> *How it went to pieces all at once,*
> *All at once, and nothing first,*
> *Just as bubbles do when they burst.*
> *End of the wonderful one-hoss shay.*
> *Logic is logic. That's all I say.*

Packard died on March 26, 1996, eliciting an outpouring of testimonials. More than one HP employee sent a good-bye note to Packard's e-mail account. The *San Jose Mercury News* ran a special section about his life. At a private memorial service, his son David Woodley Packard hung a photo of him sitting on one of his beloved tractors. The caption: "David Packard: 1912–1996, Rancher, etc."

The company also held a memorial service for Packard, by a stand of trees at the company's headquarters. Bill Hewlett was there in his wheelchair, and he listened as employees expressed condolences and their longing for the good old days. Some time later, Hewlett turned to his secretary, Judy Arluck, to ask her an important question. Some who had written to Hewlett after Packard's death argued the HP Way was dead.

"Judy, is the HP Way dead?" he asked.

"No," she told him, after considering the question for a minute, "but it's on life support."

After Rick Belluzzo won control of HP's computer business, he tried to make the kind of draconian cuts that would be necessary for the company to prosper in the hypercompetitive industry he and Hackborn felt was coming. If HP was to compete against the likes of Dell, it could not afford the vast fleet of Ford Tauruses it maintained for its workers, or its extravagant overseas headquarters. He wanted to nix profit-sharing, and somehow get HP to rediscover its competitive fire. During the Christmas break of 1996, after HP's Atlanta office lost a big deal with no evident signs of disappointment, Belluzzo penned a memo exhorting the troops to get tougher. He even declared a "no-lose" policy under which any salesperson could call on him to help close a deal.

Belluzzo didn't get all he wanted, but he did put through massive changes in 1997. He formalized HP's ties with Microsoft with a multipronged partnership. In April, he pushed through a $1.2-billion purchase of Verifone. In the three weeks that followed, he worked late hours and weekends to come up with a total overhaul of HP's organizational chart. Among the changes: a sweeping reorganization to merge all of HP's sales efforts into one—a precursor to the "one face to the customer" concept Fiorina would later demand.

Belluzzo didn't think it was enough. As the heir apparent of the company, he decided that if he were going to be CEO in three years, he may as well push his agenda now or end up with a sick, uncompetitive company. "I decided I was going to get these issues on the table," he says. "If people are uncomfortable with it, then so be it." Platt wasn't ready to impose all of Belluzzo's shock treatments on the company, but neither did he make any strong calls about HP's future direction. As a result, HP remained in a treacherous limbo—stuck with a declining PC business, an underperforming computer business, and a printer business that the company increasingly relied on for its profits. The company was also an embarrassing no-show when it came to the Internet. Platt "seemed like a chess guy in a video-game world," says one consultant.

By 1997, the company began to miss its financial targets. Some quarters it would fall short of its sales projections, the next quarter miss on profits. Clearly, the icon was losing its edge quickly.

In all, the company would disappoint Wall Street for nine straight quarters. The overall trend was most disturbing: In its continuing efforts to adapt to tougher competition, the company seemed to have lost its ability to create new markets. Sun Microsystems' Scott McNealy happily dissed HP as "the printer company." Though HP executives fumed, there was little argument but that he was right.

Platt knew the problem wasn't likely to correct itself. In 1995, he had commissioned a study to look at the growth records of $40-billion companies. At the time, it was a prescient effort to avoid an inevitable problem. After all, if HP had kept growing at its historical clip, it would have hit $80 billion in sales by 2000 and $250 billion in 2006. In 20 years its revenues would be bigger than the current gross domestic product of the United States.

It was a fascinating project. Over the next few years, a core group of HP executives looked at financial data of many companies that had grown larger than $20 billion since the 1890s.

The results, in many ways, were flattering. HP had grown faster, for longer, than any company in history. Even putting aside the company's first 20 years, HP had grown an average of 20.2 percent per year between 1958 and 1998, says James Mackey, the project research director.

However, the findings were also terrifying. The study showed that HP was in fact poised to become the *only* company, other than Wal-Mart, to reach $50 billion without hitting a major, permanent stall in revenue growth. Almost each and every time, that stall caused a huge drop in profits. In almost every case, the CEO was replaced, employment fell by more than 25 percent, and the market capitalization fell, on average, more than 50 percent—never to return to its previous heights. Usually, the hit to profits caused the company to skimp on R&D, which caused many of the best people to leave. "The stall was the end of the company as it was known before. It might as well be given a new name," says George Bodway, the executive in charge of the project. The scary conclusion: Unless HP pulled off some kind of management miracle, it was likely to hit the wall—and soon.

When Bodway and Mackey made their final report to Platt and his staff, and later to Hackborn, the conclusions were clear. HP had better quickly spot some new growth opportunities or make some hard decisions about what businesses to abandon. Clearly, Platt was going to have to take a much more active role in setting HP's course. When Bodway presented these findings to HP's board, "they all got quiet, and said 'Let's study this further.' What they didn't say was 'This isn't going to happen to us,' " says Bodway.

Making matters worse was the Internet boom that was breaking out all around HP. Even gargantuan IBM, under Louis Gerstner, had mobilized for this new frontier. "We've got the wrong Lew," some wags inside the company sniped, comparing Platt to Gerstner. Dell and others were selling reams of equipment via the Net, but Hackborn railed that HP didn't even have a decent Web site. By late-1997, Platt was beginning to wonder if he was the guy for the job. Annual sales growth had dropped from 26 percent in 1995 to 22 percent in 1996 and 12 percent in 1997. With the annual general managers meeting set for that January, he decided to do something about it. He commissioned a study from consultant Richard Hagberg to define what was wrong with HP's culture and to critique himself and his top staffers.

The meeting did not go as planned. A few days before it began, Belluzzo suddenly announced he was leaving to become CEO of rival computer maker Silicon Graphics, Inc. Belluzzo had become increasingly critical of Platt. Platt, in turn, had been expressing his concerns about Belluzzo's aggressive tactics to the board, so Belluzzo must have known that his status as heir apparent was in danger. "Belluzzo wanted big change, and Lew didn't. And Lew drove him out, and it was more transparent to the board than I suspect Lew thinks," says board member Jay Keyworth.

The timing of Belluzzo's departure was not good. Here, the leading lightning rod for change was walking out the door, just as Platt was going to deliver his own call to arms. Not surprisingly, the day did not go well. First, Platt unveiled the results of Hagberg's study on HP's culture. CFO Bob Wayman presented the disturbing results of the growth project. Then Platt issued a challenge. "Look, folks, we've been doing an analysis of where we stand, and we have to change our ways," Platt said, before demanding to know how each of the attendees would change the way they did their jobs. Instead of acquiescence, he was barraged with thinly veiled hostility during a difficult 90-minute question-and-answer session. Visibly crestfallen, he mumbled "I'm going to have to quit," as he left the stage. "This organization needs big changes, and I may be part of the problem. I'm not the person to lead this company anymore," he said.

By the summer of 1998, Platt sought help to figure out a plan for the future. A special committee of the board was named. At that point, Hackborn had decided to quit the board. Insiders say he was angry at how Belluzzo had been treated, and wanted to focus on philanthropic activities. He was a trustee of the Hewlett Foundation, had his own family foundation, and was building a new house. But Platt convinced him he meant to take drastic action. Platt and the board even hired McKinsey & Company to look at various strategic options. Hackborn agreed to stay on.

The company looked at a variety of options. It considered organizing itself as a holding company, akin to General Electric. In the end, McKinsey suggested that HP be broken up. Clearly, the original instruments business would be better off on its own. It got no benefit from being part of the printer and computing colossus. With instruments division chief Ned Barnholdt as its CEO, the stand-alone company would be able to get back to an approach much more akin to Hewlett and Packard's old formula—lots of innovation, lots of profits, and lots of attention to employees.

What to do with the rest of the company was a dicier subject. According to many former HP executives, including board members, McKinsey felt the remaining HP should also be sliced into two, as well—one company to make computers, another to make printers. That way, the printer company would have an easier time doing deals with HP's computer rivals, such as Dell and Compaq. Also, the computer business would no longer be able to rely on the printer division's profits. Once and for all, the computer business would have to make some tough decisions and get its house in order. Furthermore, the three companies that would result from this three-way split would be much better focused—and therefore much more manageable for whoever had to run them. Even with the instruments company out of the picture, recalls one former HP executive,

"There was a fear we wouldn't be able to find a CEO who could manage all of what remained."

However, this second split had major downsides. Who would get the HP name? The instruments business probably deserved to get it. After all, it was the direct descendant of the company founded in the garage, and it would most likely hew closest to the HP Way. But the printer and computing companies would then have to establish a new brand name—a task that could cost $1 billion. At that price, the instruments company would have to give up its claim to the name. Looking back, this might have been a mistake. In the ensuing years, the instrument company, renamed Agilent Technologies, would earn kudos for sticking to the HP Way even as HP seemed to head in the other direction. This raises the question of whether Fiorina would have had an easier time trying to shake the company up if it had been the one to get the new name. "If Agilent were called HP, everyone would be happy," says former executive Doug Chase.

Ironically, there were signs of a reawakening inside HP's computer business while these major decisions were being finalized. A group within Ann Livermore's enterprise computing business started making waves with an Internet strategy called e-services. Nick Earle, a smooth-talking Brit who was tired of watching HP sit in neutral, led the charge, along with consultants who had helped craft IBM's successful Net branding campaign. Before long, HP employees were inundated by glossy posters and booklets proclaiming a grand, if hard to grasp, plan to become a Net standout. Earle began talking up the new strategy to analysts and at investor conferences—even pledging $100 million on an ad campaign before Platt gave his okay.

It was almost completely hype—but for a company that had always prided itself on not showboating, it had the desired effect. As shareholders became convinced HP was finally "getting" the Net, the company's shares rose from $60 in February to $116 in early July.

By the end of that month, there would be far bigger news than that to catch investors' attention—for better or worse.

5

THE MAKING OF A STAR

Carly Fiorina is truly focused on the success of Carly Fiorina, and of the organization she is leading. Which comes first, I'm not sure.
—FORMER LUCENT EXECUTIVE

By 1985, Fiorina had closed the door on a seven-year marriage to her college sweetheart, and she would not look back. She had a golden future ahead of her as a fast-rising young executive. Rushing to catch a flight to AT&T's New Jersey headquarters or driving to her local office in Washington, D.C. Fiorina appeared the picture of a Reagan-era yuppie, right down to the power suits and pumps.

She had a new husband, as well. That year, she married Frank Fiorina, a longtime AT&T salesperson and marketing executive who worked in the D.C. area. From the moment they returned from their honeymoon, say coworkers, it was clear the pair were a perfect match. Friendly and gregarious, with thick hair and a stocky build, Frank was well liked and respected at AT&T. The couple lived in a handsome two-story colonial in a stately neighborhood in Arlington, Virginia, riding stationary bikes most mornings. While friends say she's no sailor, they spent many weekends on Frank's 19-foot boat with his two daughters, who were then 8 and 12 years old.

Forced to sleep crammed together under a blanket in the open-bowed boat, Fiorina found a warmth that had gone out of her first marriage.

Clearly, she had found a soul mate. She and her new husband were similar in many ways. They were both top-notch, aggressive salespeople. They dressed well, had a talent for giving presentations and for courting the press, and had a lust for landing the big deal. But there was something more: She'd found a husband who saw her potential and was willing to take a back seat to help her achieve it. Already, it was clear within AT&T that she was the superstar in the family—in AT&T-speak, the high-potential candidate. And whereas her first husband thought her love affair with business was an afflic-tion, Frank totally supported it. He had risen from a job as a techni-cian to become a vice president, but he knew he wasn't going much farther. In 1998, he would retire early, to commit himself to his two daughters and his wife's career.

To climb that corporate ladder and feed her need for accom-plishment, Fiorina sought out tough assignments. There were plenty of such opportunities at AT&T in 1984. That was the year of the landmark settlement that broke up the Ma Bell system, in which AT&T agreed to spin off seven regional local phone companies and focus on long-distance service. Fiorina took a job that put her on the front lines of this new competitive world. She took a job with AT&T's troubled Access Management division, which connected customers' long-distance calls to local phone companies. "Access Management was in the worst shape," she wrote in a column in the *New York Times* in September 1999. "I decided that's where I wanted to work."[1]

In her new role, Fiorina pored over floor-to-ceiling boxes of bills, uncovering overcharges. After reviewing her findings, AT&T designed a bill verification system that saved the company hundreds of millions of dollars, she wrote. "This is not something most people would think of as fun," Fiorina recalled. "We had great fun accom-plishing something nobody thought we could."[2]

Then she got her first big opportunity: She was put in charge of the 30-plus-person team that served the General Services Adminis-tration (GSA), the behemoth agency that buys everything from pencils to cars for the federal government. GSA was one of AT&T's biggest, but most troubled, accounts. Spoiled by decades as a monopoly, AT&T's staffers didn't jump to return phone calls or upgrade equipment. The result: By the time Fiorina took over, AT&T's business with GSA had fallen from $500 million to $225 million a year.[3] "Carly was brought in to stop the bleeding," says Tony Bardo, a salesperson who worked for Fiorina at the time.

She wouldn't have much time. GSA began working on a set of specifications for a massive new telecommunications contract called FTS2000. GSA wanted to give the whole contract, up to $25 billion over 10 years, to a single supplier—the biggest nonmilitary government contract ever awarded.

It was a must-win contract for AT&T. Losing would cost the company hundreds of millions in revenue a year and give upstart rivals Sprint and MCI a chance to prove they could handle the biggest deals. AT&T needed to show it could compete in the post-divestiture world. "It would probably have been a big embarrassment to us if we lost," says former AT&T CEO and chair Robert Allen. "AT&T could not afford to let MCI win that contract, at any price," says Paul Goulding, a former GSA administrator whom Fiorina hired as a consultant. When GSA released its request for proposals on December 31, 1986, Fiorina found herself at the center of a historic deal—and surrounded by problems. The GSA was almost openly hostile toward AT&T and was doing what it could to encourage other bidders. "AT&T had an enormous problem over at GSA. They were universally hated," Goulding says. Texas Republican Jack Brooks, head of the Government Oversight Committee, was an anti-monopolist who didn't want AT&T to win the entire FTS2000 contract. And Fiorina's biggest difficulty might be convincing AT&T's own top brass that they might well lose GSA's business if they didn't deal with these realities.

As she would do repeatedly during her career, Fiorina grasped the big picture and quickly mobilized on many fronts. She hired Goulding to provide a real-world perspective on what AT&T was up against. Ambitious as she was, she was pragmatic enough to call in for high-powered backup. She appealed to her boss Mike Brunner that the company needed to appoint a full-time corporate officer from AT&T headquarters to manage the contract, rather than leave it in her hands. She wasn't lacking confidence, to be sure—but she was just a midlevel regional sales manager. Brunner agreed, and soon a high-ranking executive named Louis Golm was assigned to the case. "Carly saw that if we took our traditional approach, we would not be successful," says Golm.

Golm quickly pulled together a six-person core team that worked nearly around the clock to win FTS2000. Fiorina was the marketer among the group, but she was in many ways Golm's second-in-command. From the time he arrived, she attacked the task at hand with a passion that amazed him. She'd be in his office within 10 minutes of his arrival each morning, strategizing and giving orders. "She had to talk about everything she was thinking about," recalls Golm. "She was just ready for war." Often, days would end with a working dinner at an upscale restaurant near headquarters.

Fiorina did much of the heavy lifting as Golm's team put together AT&T's bid. She hired and organized the efforts of consultants and lobbyists such as Goulding, and she lobbied the staffs of key Washington decision makers. She was the driving force in making sure that AT&T understood exactly what GSA wanted to see in the bid.

She was also learning to be tough—a quality she would become famous for later in her career. When GSA awarded two-thirds of a $55-million electronic tandem network (ETN) contract for computerized phone switches to AT&T's rivals, Fiorina decided to play hardball. AT&T had always won such contracts in the past, and this time she had personally negotiated an attractive volume discount that had not even been factored into the agency's final decision.[4]

After receiving the news in a phone call on October 16, 1987, she charged into a room where some staffers were meeting. "This is unacceptable. We have to fix this," she snapped, according to Harry Carr, who was the lawyer on the team.

"When Carly gets really mad, she doesn't let go a load of expletives," says Goulding, who was also there. "She gets more determined that she's not going to let someone get away with it. She decided to just slug it out with the GSA."

AT&T quickly filed a protest against the GSA, alleging that some of the awards were illegal. To help prove that GSA had discriminated against AT&T, Fiorina hired former congressional investigator Frank Silbey. Silbey had made a career ferreting out crooked contracts, and he knew what rocks to look under. He was expert at dealing with the press and ruthless in pursuing his targets. "If you met him on the street, you wouldn't think he's a dangerous character," says Carr, who considers Silbey a friend. "But I wouldn't want to be on the other side of Frank. He'd professionally slit your throat, and you wouldn't know it had happened until it was too late."

Golm jokingly called Silbey "Deep Throat," and admits that he worried that Silbey might employ unseemly hardball tactics that were not in concert with AT&T's aboveboard ways. "I sometimes worried that we had a loose cannon on deck," says Golm. "But he had amazing insights."

Soon, Silbey and Fiorina were quietly leaking tips to the press. Reporters began getting calls that suggested that GSA contracting officials might be on the take—what kind of cars they drove, what kind of neighborhoods they lived in, and the like, say AT&T employees and advisors and a reporter who covered the story. AT&T's lawyers soon discovered that the company's fears were justified. A GSA official named Sureshar Lal Soni had shared details of AT&T's bid with other phone companies, so they could slip in with a better price to win the ETN contract. Lawyers even found a receipt for a lunch a BellSouth executive bought for Lal Soni and his daughter, where the three discussed the ETN contract and Ms. Lal Soni's future in the telecom business. A few months later, the company had hired Lal Soni's daughter.[5]

Fiorina was a natural at dealing with the press, says Calvin Sims, who was covering the story for the *New York Times*. She always seemed to be available, he recalls. He could call her at home anytime; he recalls hearing birds chirping in the background as she gave him the latest news. Other times, she'd meet him at the Jefferson Hotel when he arrived from New York to cover the story. She was a hard source to resist. "She'd stand there and look you straight in the eye" without a hint of nervousness, he says. At times, she seemed too good a source, making Sims check himself to make sure he wasn't being used. Once, after GSA officials chewed him out for writing stories questioning the agency's ethics, word got

back to Fiorina—who used the information to cement her relationship with the reporter. "I feel really bad about what they did to
you," he recalls her saying. "Even back then, she had a sense of how
to use the media."

By the time Fiorina arrived at HP, she was confident in her abilities to steer the press. The assumption among her handlers was
that one meeting with Fiorina would be enough to charm a new
beat reporter into her way of thinking. Reporters who didn't toe
the line were blackballed. She could play defense, as well. Once,
the *Wall Street Journal* ran a story that suggested that AT&T may
have considered bribery. Fiorina was furious. The morning the
story ran, almost before press relations staffer Herb Linnen could
suggest it, she demanded that they hold a press conference, which
she would run. "I remember vividly her walking into the room with
this aura about her. People just warmed up to her," Linnen recalls.
After shaking hands with all 15 reporters in the room, she took to
the podium with the same ease she'd later display during the proxy
fight. "Hi, I'm Carly Fiorina," she said, before calmly shooting
down the allegations. Somehow, she managed to be firm and outraged, without seeming emotional or defensive. As the press conference came to an end, Linnen leaned over to a peer and said:
"That woman is going to go a long way. She's going to move right
up the ladder." She also won her case. All the ETN contracts that
were given to AT&T's rivals were unwound and awarded to AT&T,
except for one.

In late 1988, AT&T won 60 percent of the FTS2000 contract.
The company left a huge amount of money on the table—it under-
bid the nearest competitor by $500 million over the 10-year life of
the contract, say executives and GSA staffers involved in the deal.
Still, it was a huge victory, worth billions to AT&T over the next 15
years.

By the time the AT&T team got the good news, Fiorina had
already moved on. Her performance had established her as one of
AT&T's top up-and-comers. She'd had the opportunity to present
directly to AT&T's top brass—a rarity for a midlevel sales manager—
and had made a lasting impression. Bob Allen, for one, recalls being
very impressed on first meeting her. Fiorina had also won a huge fan

in Lew Golm, who recommended her for the Sloan Fellowship program at the Massachusetts Institute of Technology (MIT) in Cambridge, Massachusetts. For decades, AT&T had sent promising young executives each year to the prestigious program, whose alumni include Boeing CEO and HP board member Phil Condit, Ford Motors CEO Bill Ford, and U.N. Secretary-General Kofi Annan. Only 55 executives are invited to the program each year.

Normally, ambitious young AT&T managers maneuvered for years to win the "Sloan beauty contest." "It's the ultimate kiss on the forehead," says Dan Hesse, who worked with Fiorina at AT&T and was one of three Sloan fellows chosen from the company that year. In AT&T's militaristic culture, "you are clearly being identified as someone that can become a general," Hesse says. To win one of the coveted spots, candidates would spend years collecting the right mix of jobs on their resumes—overseas duty and stints in everything from R&D to sales. But Fiorina, who'd worked only in the Washington sales office, came out of nowhere to get the nod. Her name had never come up in the rumor mill before, "but [FTS2000] made her a star overnight," says Hesse.

For once-shy Carleton Sneed, who'd been to a second-tier business school, it was a chance to see if she really stacked up with the best and the brightest. At MIT, for the first time in years, Fiorina was not the obvious star. "I did not see her as particularly aggressive. She was soaking it in," recalls Alan White, senior associate dean of the Sloan School.

She was also enjoying the break from the corporate grind. Among the mostly male Sloan fellows—there were only 9 women in the 55-person class—Fiorina was very much one of the guys. Many of the married class members commuted to Cambridge from big homes in tony suburbs west of Boston, but with Frank home in Washington, Fiorina was among the single "townies" living in Boston's Back Bay neighborhood, just over the bridge from MIT. On many nights, she'd leave her brownstone to meet Hesse and other classmates at the Plough & Stars or the bar at the Eliot Hotel to discuss the day's events over a pint.

During her year at MIT, she seemed to put business on hold to let her intellectual side take priority. In one of her favorite classes, called Choice Points, she read books that posed moral dilemmas that could be applied to business—Greek tragedies, Shakespeare, Flannery O'Connor, Kafka, and Ibsen. Fiorina could talk for hours about these works, often resuming the discussions over late-night drinks. She was particularly interested in Sophocles's *Antigone,* the story of a woman who fights to bury her dead brother, defies her king, and ends up killing herself. As a woman who hoped to take on responsibilities traditionally reserved for men, "she really identified with this person," says Hesse.

Fiorina's thesis topic, though important to the community at large, was curiously academic. Most of her classmates set out to solve hard-core business problems that could be applied when they returned back to the job—say, how to adopt a particular management technique or deal with a certain country's trade policies. Hesse's paper was about Japanese phone giant NTT's relationship with its main equipment providers. But Fiorina chose a far broader topic that was then being debated in the press: secondary school reform in the United States.[6] It was a choice that might have made more sense had she been attending Harvard's John F. Kennedy School of Government, just down Memorial Drive. "For me, as a sociologist, it was really refreshing," says her thesis advisor, John Van Maanen, a professor of organizational studies. "But it didn't seem to be written with AT&T's issues in mind. It wasn't a utilitarian career-building move."

After graduating from Sloan, Fiorina was a hot commodity within AT&T. Executives, including Joe Nacchio, head of AT&T's consumer and small business unit, vied for her services. In the end, she opted to work for Network Systems division executive Bill Marx. It was another challenge she couldn't resist. Before divestiture, Network Systems was a sleepy manufacturer that built equipment used solely by AT&T. But in the deregulated world, Network Systems would have to start going after other corporate accounts. Rather than just wait for orders to flow in, Marx wanted Fiorina to get out there with customers—figure out what they wanted, then spur the division to make it for them.

It was certainly a change of scene from the polite halls of the Sloan School. Network Systems traced its roots to Elisha Gray, who dropped off his patent application for the telephone just hours after Alexander Graham Bell on February 14, 1876. Then, in 1880, he cofounded Western Electric, which became the country's dominant electrical manufacturing company. A century later, Network Systems was easily the least hospitable place within the Bell system for a female hotshot with a marketing degree. It was almost entirely male, and engineering and manufacturing were the disciplines that mattered. Heavily unionized, its blue-collar workers quickly made their feelings known to female managers. Nina Aversano, who met Fiorina at the time and would be a close ally for years, remembers one factory worker staring her in the eye at one of her first meetings and saying "What the hell can you do for us?" "These guys didn't know how to *spell* marketing," Aversano says.

Fiorina helped to show them. By 1991, she was setting strategy for the company's international operations, and gained a reputation for driving to hit high growth targets. This brought her into some conflict with her old friend Dan Hesse from MIT. He was running the division's international operations, and contended that there was no way AT&T could take market share in the middle of a recession from French and German rivals that enjoyed government support. Fiorina disagreed, and pressured him to hit the high growth goals that had been handed down by higher ups. "We agreed on a lot of things, but we did butt heads a number of times," says Hesse. This can-do optimism, which some believe can be a willingness to ignore reality, would be a hallmark of her career. In the trial that followed the HP-Compaq merger, for example, she testified that the managers whose reports claimed the company's business plan was way off target were simply being pessimistic.

Fiorina's rise through Network Systems' ranks accelerated in 1994. In just over a year, she welcomed three big promotions. On October 24, she was named sales head for the Eastern United States and Canada, a territory that included huge customers such as Bell Atlantic, Ameritech, and NYNEX. Before she could even settle into that job, she was named president for all North American sales about a month later.

She quickly established herself as one of the great salespeople of her industry. No one worked harder to understand the customer,

the market, or the politics inherent in every big deal. She understood how all of the company's products and services could be
pulled together. She knew what price or financing package would
be required to win the deal. She was the one person with the charisma, the contacts, and the determination to corral all of Network
Systems' capabilities to meet a customer's needs. "She was the glue,"
said Harry Bosco, a longtime colleague.

She was extremely focused on customers. In 1996, for example,
the division was in danger of getting the boot from US West, whose
phone service failed so often that the company was ridiculed as "US
Worst." HP board member Bob Knowling, then head of operations
for the Denver-based carrier, asked Fiorina to fly out to Denver to
discuss the problems. At the meeting, held in early December,
Knowling read Fiorina the riot act, in front of her boss. "I'm sure
that's not the meeting she signed up for," says Knowling. By January
1, she had replaced the entire support team serving US West, and
turned adversity into more opportunity. "I became a real big Lucent
fan," Knowling says.

Not everyone was so enamored. In the mid-1990s, Network Systems struck a multi-billion-dollar deal to help Pacific Bell, now part
of SBC Communications, Inc., build a $16-billion broadband net-
work throughout California that would be capable of delivering
voice, data, and video to millions of homes. The Network Systems
division bid aggressively to land the deal, which required Lucent to
develop a variety of types of new equipment and to do the installation work—a labor-intensive job that required digging a trench in
the front yard of every new subscriber. Fiorina didn't negotiate the
deal, but by late 1996, when it was clear that the companies had
vastly underestimated the cost and complexity of the job, she was
called in to clean up the mess.

According to one Pacific Bell executive, Lucent claimed Pacific
Bell owed it roughly $500 million for the work it had done on the
contract. Pacific Bell refused to pay, because Lucent was far behind
schedule in delivering the necessary products. "We all bit off more
than we could chew," recalled Nina Aversano, who says Fiorina was
trying to make the best of a bad situation. But Pacific Bell executives
remember the situation differently. "She made a couple of overtures

to gracefully withdraw from the deal, and then she got very nasty. She was very abusive. There was yelling," says one Pacific Bell executive. "We felt she was manufacturing excuses as to why her company was not accountable."

In the end, the companies settled, and the project was officially scrapped in June 1997, but Fiorina didn't win fans. According to one high-ranking Lucent insider, "Carly was not allowed in the door at PacBell."

Inside AT&T, attitudes about Fiorina were also becoming polarized—a phenomenon that would become more intense as her authority grew. Many appreciated that she was always willing to invest time in people she believed were as committed as she. She rarely got emotional or raised her voice when disappointed. She was appreciative of hard work, and could be extremely thoughtful. When Herb Linnen, her PR staffer during the FTS2000 days, retired from AT&T in the late 1990s, Fiorina surprised him by showing up at his going-away party. "Well, I just wanted to come and wish you well," she told him with a smile. "I heard that you told people at AT&T that I'd make a good executive some day."

Others had a very different view. They saw an executive who was ruthless in pursuing her goals—both for the business and for herself. "She can read people as well as anyone I've ever met," says one former colleague. "She'd be great at running a spy ring." Others, either admiringly or disparagingly, marveled at her ability to "manage up"—MBA-speak for the ability to ingratiate herself with higher-ups and always make herself look good. "Carly can market the tar out of herself. That's what she was known for," says one former Lucent manager.

Fiorina's next assignment would put her at center stage of one of the biggest, most significant deals in AT&T's 120-year history: CEO Bob Allen's decision to spin off the Network Systems division as a separate company. Although Network Systems was a money-maker that helped prop up AT&T's battered stock, it was clear it would one day need to be off on its own. Many of the Baby Bells, given the choice, would rather buy from companies such as Nortel or Alcatel. AT&T seemed likely to be a future phone service rival, given all the talk of deregulating the phone business, as later occurred with the Telecommunications Act of 1996. "The whole industry was going through the roof and the telephone companies weren't buying from us," says one former Lucent executive.

Fiorina wasn't in on the talks in early 1995 that led to the spin-off decision. She was brought into the loop around July, says a person who was involved at the time. But she really got busy after Allen announced a three-way reorganization of the company on September 20, 1995. The AT&T name would stay with the company's core long-distance division, which would still sell phone service. The troubled computing businesses, in disarray due to a botched 1991 acquisition of NCR Corporation, would be spun off. All of AT&T's hardware businesses, from huge multi-million-dollar phone switches to old-fashioned rotary phones, would be combined with world-famous Bell Laboratories and AT&T's Microelectronics chip-making unit to create a $20-billion-a-year telecom equipment powerhouse.

Allen had asked AT&T board member Henry Schacht to be the new equipment business' CEO and chair. McGinn would be president. However, as top management struggled to figure out the details of the massive transaction, Bob Allen turned to Fiorina often. "I had a lot of respect for all of my senior managers, but I always felt like she was closer to the customers and to people inside the company. She had the good judgment to know how they were going to react to things, more than the rest of us at the top," says Allen.

When it came to executing the spin-off, McGinn turned to Fiorina to manage the project. On November 20, 1995, she was promoted to executive vice president for corporate operations. This put her in charge of overall strategy, mergers and acquisitions, and investor and press relations.

There wasn't much time, and there was a lot to do. Allen wanted the spin-off to be complete by early April 1996. Fiorina was charged with creating a new identity for the company—its name, its logo, its branding strategy. She led an effort to figure ways to revamp AT&T's slow-moving corporate culture, so the company could post double-digit growth rather than trudge along at its midsingle-digits rate.

One of the first stops was HP, one of the fastest-growing big companies in the world. Ironically, HP had already started a study of its own, to see if it could keep up its pace of growth at its huge size. The answer, which came a few years later: probably not.

Most of all, her job was a marketing assignment—not of the company's products, per se, but of the idea of the new company. It was her job to get the world's investors champing at the bit to buy its shares. Although she had little financial background, she worked closely with investment bankers to tune that message to fit what Wall Street wanted to hear. The theme that emerged: Lucent had more technology than investors knew about, thanks to the fact that it had inherited world-famous Bell Labs. This meant that the company wasn't just going to start life as a market leader in many existing markets, but could also dominate in emerging opportunities such as wireless communications and optical networking, a much faster means of transmitting data than AT&T's traditional switching gear. "She put the gloss on the whole thing," says Jeff Williams, who was an investment banker with Morgan Stanley, which would take the company public. "She figured out what the right story was, and then she told that story."

Fiorina brought all her attributes to the task—her capacity for hard work, her gut instincts, and her ability to build and motivate a team. An example was the effort to define a new identity for the new company. A 10-person team ran through a detailed process that included interviews with 33 AT&T executives, almost 500 customers, and more than 1,000 randomly selected Americans. In the end, she approved the name Lucent Technologies, which means "marked by clarity" or "glowing with light."[7]

Fiorina also gave the thumbs up to Lucent's new logo—a red swirl meant to symbolize the "innovation ring," combined with the words *Bell Labs Innovations* to maintain that tie with the glorious past. Fiorina later told reporters she liked the swirl because it reminded her of one of her mother's paintings.

Many of the skills Fiorina developed while launching Lucent would help her win the proxy fight with Walter Hewlett, but none more than her role in the road show to woo investors. For most executives, it's a miserable forced march of repetitive presentations and hotel stays. Fiorina thought otherwise. Rather than leave logistical planning to underlings, she made sure the right executives got in front of the right investors at just the right point in the process. "A large part of our success was due to her attention to detail," says Williams.

When it came to actually pitching the deal to investors, Fiorina was masterful. She, corporate controller Jim Lusk, and Schacht made up one of the teams to sell the deal. They often did seven or eight meetings a day. Schacht would kick off the meeting, and Fiorina would lead investors through a deeper analysis of the new company. Lusk claims that Fiorina convinced many investors that the company's executive team could pull off what would be the biggest spin-off in history, and that they weren't just a bunch of stodgy Bellheads. "She [got] so psyched in these meetings," Lusk says. "It's like the Super Bowl, the Emmys or something." Lusk says he'd never met anyone with Fiorina's energy level. "She's not cranked up on coffee or chocolate or anything, but she's cranked up on energy. No one does [presentations] like Carly. These presentations get boring after awhile. When Carly's talking it was like it was the first time she was doing it. You'd think it was the only set of investors in the world who mattered."

Fiorina could work the same magic on employees. Lusk is an example. When the road show began, he was visibly nervous—both at the prospect of having to pitch to Wall Street investors for the first time in his life, and at having to travel with the company's chair, Schacht, day after day. Fiorina repeatedly bucked him up, calmly making suggestions as to how he could improve his performance. "She treated him like a little brother. In the end, she gave him the ability to have a very powerful voice, with no expectation of getting anything in return," says a banker who sometimes traveled with the team.

Her sense of humor also offset the toll of hard work, Lusk says. One time, they flew in to do a meeting in a Midwestern town, and their car wasn't waiting. Panicked they'd be late, Fiorina chatted up a pilot, asking if she could borrow a car. The pilot lent them a friend's car, an old wreck with ripped seats. Instead of getting upset, Fiorina wrote out a sign that said "This is what cost cutting is all about" and hung it on the car door. The pair took a photo to bring back to show executives who were beefing about the need to control costs. "Even though she's intense, she enjoys the moment," Lusk says.

She certainly enjoyed the moment of Lucent's birth. On April 4, 1996, the first day shares were offered, Lucent staged a highly choreographed event at the New York Stock Exchange. Nellie Perkins, a line worker at a Lucent plant in Oklahoma City, flew to New York to buy the first 500 shares. By the end of the first day, Lucent had raised $3 billion—by far the biggest initial public offering (IPO) in history. At the end of the day, Lusk and Fiorina rang the bell to close the market. An exuberant Fiorina told the *New York Times,* "I feel like I've given birth here, literally."[8]

Six months later, Fiorina's contributions were rewarded with a new assignment: president of Lucent's consumer products division. It was a reward from Fiorina's standpoint, anyway. The post marked the first time she was given total operating responsibility for a business, from R&D to sales and customer service. This experience would give her the management breadth she needed to move up the ranks at Lucent. If she ever wanted to be a CEO, this was a must for her resume.

However, the division was a mess, and it was at the bottom of McGinn's list of strategic priorities. It made phones, cell phones, and answering machines—markets that had long been stripped of any decent profit margins by foreign competitors. It was a low-growth, break-even-at-best business with nothing in common with Lucent's preferred business: selling multi-million-dollar switches and related products and services to big phone companies.

When she arrived, most of the heavy lifting was done. Bill Marx, who had first brought Fiorina to Network Systems, decided to shutter 338 AT&T retail stores as a way to cut costs. Fiorina continued to work at repositioning the division, but she couldn't figure out a strategy to make it a winner, say former colleagues. As months passed, she became convinced that it would simply cost too much to improve Lucent's brand versus the likes of Sony—especially relative to the paltry profits in the offing.

Fortunately, a new path emerged in early 1997, when executives from the Dutch company Philips Electronics visited to discuss combining the two companies' consumer products efforts. At first, Fiorina was a taken aback by the idea, say former managers close to the negotiations. If she agreed to create a joint venture, she'd no longer be running her own show. It was clear she'd have to find another job. But the more the Philips executives talked, the more she liked the idea. Philips needed a phone for the U.S. market, and Lucent's engineers were working on the necessary chips. Lucent had little market share overseas, where Philips was strong. In many ways, the thinking was similar to the argument for HP's purchase of Compaq. As with PCs, the phone business was a rapidly maturing business that was expected to consolidate to just two or three global players. By joining forces, Lucent and Philips—much like HP and Compaq—would have huge market share and plenty of redundant workers and other assets that could be trimmed to pump up profits. Also like the HP-Compaq merger, neither Lucent nor Philips was considered a top performer in these markets. Combining them, it seemed, was the best way to try to turn two laggards into a winner.

Some of Fiorina's direct reports did not like the idea. Almost everyone knew the division was a sinking ship. Joining forces might look good on paper, but integrating two large companies located across an ocean would be an operational nightmare. Mike Bond, a director of Lucent's corporate mergers and acquisitions office, saw a better way: Simply sell the division before it got sicker. He'd spoken with executives at Matsushita, Sharp, and others, and knew interest was high, in large part because Lucent had rights to use the AT&T logo until 2000—a logo that consumers were willing to pay 10 percent extra for. "I thought the better course would have been to sell it off," he says.

Once Fiorina decided the joint venture was the way to go, she was not going to back down. At one point, she called her top team together to discuss the joint venture, ostensibly to make a group decision. However, as she shot down any opposition, it quickly became clear what would happen. "It wasn't about should we do this. It was about how do we do this," recalls Bond. "Carly's a great consensus builder, so long as the consensus goes her way." She was simply too well prepared, too determined, too quick on her feet, and too well thought of by the higher-ups to pick a fight with. She'd win the fight in the end, so what was the use of sticking one's neck out? "Ultimately, some people just stepped aside and said 'It's your problem,' " recalls Bond.

After just a few meetings, the deal was announced in June 1997. The new venture, which would have roughly $2.5 billion in annual sales, would be called Philips Consumer Communications (PCC). It would be 60 percent owned by Philips and 40 percent by Lucent. Fiorina would be chair, and Philips executive Mike McTighe would be CEO. "This company will be able to hit the ground running," Fiorina stated in the press release.[9] All involved were hugely impressed with Fiorina. "I trusted her," said Cor Boonstra, Philips' CEO. At a party in Brussels to celebrate the signing of the joint venture, Boonstra and others say Fiorina seemed strangely ambivalent, as if she were slightly ashamed that she had to resort to the joint venture. "She felt she had no chance on her own, and she was convinced this was a good deal to do," says Boonstra. "Her wisdom was bigger than her emotions."

Initially, hopes for the joint venture were sky-high. Besides some start-up-related losses, they expected the venture to grow to $3.5 billion in sales within a year and to start churning profits within a quarter or two. Fiorina and McTighe hosted opulent trade show events to kick off the venture.

However, divorce would follow quickly after the honeymoon. By early 1998, Philips executives realized that Lucent was more like the old AT&T than it was like the nimble, fleet-footed New Economy star that it was widely portrayed to be. Despite the need to cut costs, Lucent refused to close some R&D centers and factories. Unwanted old phones were piling up in Lucent warehouses, and there were too few new products to take up the slack. As a result, the joint venture racked up tens of millions of dollars of losses in the first quarter of 1998, its first full quarter of operation, say former Philips and Lucent executives. From there, things went downhill fast. The real killer was Lucent's sluggish product development. Lucent had promised Boonstra that it would finish development of powerful chips for new mobile phones within five or six months, but the Philips CEO determined that it would take two or more years for the

103

chips to be completed. "It was denial of business reality. We had our heads in the clouds," says another top executive involved in the joint venture.

Where was Fiorina? Officially, she was chair of the venture.

The June 17, 1997, press release announcing the merger said she would "assume another senior management role at Lucent Technologies when the transition was complete."[10] However, soon after the joint venture was announced, she and some loyal supporters moved to headquarters in Murray Hill. "She just packed her bags and walked away," says one of the managers who left with her. A few months later, Fiorina called Lucent's consumer products team together to formally notify them that she was moving on to another assignment. "I'm leaving for a new assignment, and I'm not going to be able to be there for you anymore," she said, according to two attendees.

Some members of the team cried, touched that Fiorina was thinking of them with all that she had to do. Others figured she was only being realistic. The joint venture had been a good idea, but hadn't worked out—and she was just the chair, not the day-to-day chief. It was understandable that she would focus on her new assignment. Some saw it differently, though. Mike Bond and a high-ranking executive tried to stifle laughter during her impassioned speech. To them, it was a shameless effort to put a good face on the truth: that Fiorina was washing her hands of the impending disaster and skipping out of town before the blame landed on her. "We thought it was hysterical, like a bad Western," says Bond. "She was basically saying, 'Don't call me, I'll call you—and I'm not going to call. Thank God I'm out the door.' "

By summer, Boonstra had pulled the plug on one of the most disastrous joint ventures in telecom industry history. Philips had swallowed a loss of around $1.5 billion in less than a year. Lucent would close down its mobile phone operation and would later sell what remained of Ma Bell's phone business for far less than it would have been worth before the joint venture. At a press conference that October to announce the divorce, Boonstra said: "I'm not proud to get first prize for this, but this is the fastest dismantling of a joint venture that I ever did."

Boonstra professes no ill will toward Fiorina. "There was never a bad word between Carly and me," he says. "I believe she was as disappointed as we were. It was a very bad experience." However, some top Philips executives left the experience unimpressed with Fiorina. Says one, "I believe she makes too many speeches, without knowing enough details about her organization. She has no clue how resistant an organization can be to change. Lucent was never really changed; it was still the old AT&T. I think her intentions are good, and her ideas are okay or not completely right. But she has no idea what really goes on inside a company." Four years later, in the midst of her fight to save HP's merger with Compaq, Fiorina publicly denied any role in the Philips Consumer Communications mess. She said she had moved on to other things before problems became apparent. "What happened after that I had nothing to do with," she told financial analysts at a meeting in New York in February 2002. Maybe so, but critics of the Compaq deal worry about similarities to the Lucent-Philips debacle. Both deals looked good on paper. Both were built on the assumption that combining two poor performers could create one strong one. In the case of PCC, many agreed that the lack of day-to-day execution—getting products out the door and quickly integrating two distinct organizations—was a critical problem. Certainly, HP's success with integration planning in doing the Compaq merger suggests that Fiorina learned a great deal from the PCC debacle. Whether the Compaq merger is a long-term success remains to be seen.

Having washed her hands of PCC, Fiorina was on to bigger and better things. The first stop was an assignment to help Rich McGinn, who had replaced Henry Schacht as Lucent's CEO, define a new strategy for the company. By this time, the Net boom was in full swing, and the heroes of the business world were the fast-moving, fast-growing firms of Silicon Valley. Fiorina and Lucent Vice President Dick Sadai began traveling to the West Coast three or four times a year to meet with executives from Microsoft, Intel, HP, and Sun about forging closer links.

At Lucent, many eyes were on Cisco Systems and its charismatic CEO, John Chambers. While Lucent made the big switches that phone companies used to connect callers, Cisco specialized in so-called data networking gear used by corporations to move Internet traffic, e-mail, and the like. Because Internet traffic was expected to grow far faster than voice traffic, Lucent would have beat Cisco at its own game. At one internal meeting in 1998, Lucent even put up "Wanted" posters featuring Chambers, Nortel CEO John A. Roth, and other executives.[11]

McGinn hired Delta Consulting, which specialized in helping CEOs fundamentally transform their companies, to figure out a new approach for Lucent. He then assigned Fiorina to be the point person to work with the consultant to manage the effort. By the end of the year, the plan had taken form. Since its inception, Lucent had been organized into a few large divisions, organized to address all the needs of its main customer segments, from an entire network for a phone company to a voice-mail system for a small business. The new strategy called for McGinn to split the company into eleven smaller, more entrepreneurial units. The idea was to free each business from Lucent's sprawling bureaucracy, and give each unit's top executive the freedom to move faster. The plan would have appealed to Dave Packard, a devoted believer in decentralization.

Part of Fiorina's role was to sell the strategy to AT&T's board of directors. At one board meeting in Boca Raton, Florida, she was the primary presenter. "Carly was very smooth. It was a consummate performance. None of us could have done it better, not even Rich," says one of the dozen or so executives that had worked with Fiorina and Delta to define the plan. When the plan was formally unveiled in October 1997, it was greeted with much excitement within the company. "People felt reenergized. We were going to make Lucent run like Cisco. We were going to make it work," says the executive.

The plan certainly wasn't all Fiorina's doing, but like many of her major initiatives, it was bold, sweeping, and had a sky-high degree of difficulty. Getting AT&T to operate as a coterie of fast-moving little companies was about as simple as getting Mark McGwire to give up home runs to become a base stealer. Later, she'd try the opposite at HP, where she centralized aspects of what had been a devoutly decentralized company. In both cases, the result would be organizational and operational chaos. The new structure at Lucent ignored the fact that its big customers liked the fact that all of its products worked together. But freed to do their own thing, each of the new unit chiefs set out to follow his or her own strategy.

These problems became obvious later, when Fiorina was put in charge of one of the 11 units, called the Global Service Provider business. The title was something of a misnomer. She wasn't running a business, exactly. She wasn't responsible for designing or making Lucent's products. She didn't have so-called profit and loss responsibility. Her group was a sales and marketing arm.

Still, she was McGinn's right-hand person, say many former Lucent managers. She and McGinn had a lot in common. Both were college history majors from middle-class backgrounds; his father was a photographer and his mother a secretary with AT&T. Both were bold; when AT&T had decided to purchase struggling NCR in 1991, he had tried to convince the company to think bigger and buy HP instead.[12] Both were charismatic. She was polished, prepared, and could outwork anyone. McGinn was less of a detail guy, but could come on like your best pal. He was quick to loosen his tie, share a laugh, and get down to the brass tacks of getting a deal done.

McGinn and Fiorina were also kindred spirits when it came to business philosophy. Both believed in setting sky-high sales targets. They viewed stock price as an ultimate measure of business success. Many executives—including Dave Packard and Bill Hewlett—believed stock price was a flawed reflection of what really counted: the health of a company, in terms of profits, products, and corporate culture. Fiorina and McGinn bought into the philosophies of a new wave of Internet executives, who were creating vast wealth by doing everything possible to lift their stock prices—right now, as opposed to tomorrow. According to this approach to business, revenue growth was king. A vast new Internet economy was under construction, and the ultimate winners would be those who grabbed market share now. If mistakes were made amid the rush, so be it. Mistakes could be fixed later, but lost opportunities were lost forever.

Fiorina made the most of the company's opportunities. It was the perfect time to be selling communications gear. The 1996 Telecommunications Act, designed to bring competition to the regulated phone market, had spawned hundreds of new carriers, including such long-distance providers as Qwest and Global Crossing. When the Net took off in the late 1990s, spending went into the stratosphere. To a great extent, it was all a sham, sustained by hype. There was not nearly enough demand for Net traffic to make use of all the gear that was sold. But Lucent was in the right place at the right time, with everything a would-be Internet powerhouse could want—from plain old phone switches to speedy optical gear to zip traffic around the world.

Lucent had already been cruising along even before Fiorina became its sales czar, but its best days came after she got that job. Lucent quickly landed a string of huge soup-to-nuts deals. In the summer of 1998, for example, Lucent announced a $700-million, three-year deal with Sprint and a $2.4-billion, five-year deal with SBC. Thanks in large part to her efforts, the company gained market share overseas. If a Lucent salesperson was close to landing a big deal, the company "would send Carly in like a cruise missile and she'd charm the hell out of them," remembers Marc Schweig, a former Lucent sales executive. With her Italian name and her fluency in the language, executives at Rome-based Italtel "thought she was a goddess. She absolutely mystified them," says Schweig.

Schweig also credits a new compensation system Fiorina put in place for the company's increased vigor. Rather than just salespeople, almost every employee was eligible to earn a bonus. The system had three tiers: a meager bonus if the company just hit its publicly stated quarterly goals, a higher bonus if the company hit a higher internal target, and a big payday if the company hit a sky-high "aspirational goal," says Schweig.

In 1999, Lucent would post a stunning 20.4 percent sales jump—a remarkable achievement for a $30-billion company. The performance made Lucent a high-tech star, right up there with Microsoft, Sun Microsystems, and, yes, Cisco. For a time in 1999, it would be the second most widely held stock in the world.

Quarter after quarter, Fiorina demonstrated an ability to hit the financial targets McGinn had given to Wall Street, in part due to her close ties with a handful of big phone companies that brought in the bulk of Lucent's sales. Says one consultant who worked at

Lucent at the time, "Carly was the informal CEO of Lucent. The whole organization turned to her to deliver the quarter. She was the one who would figure out the gaps, figure out how to make the quarter."

She was also developing her larger-than-life persona inside the company. Known to some as "Carly Armani," former Lucent managers say a core group of devoted employees surrounded her. "It was as if they'd all drunk Carly juice," says one former Lucent manager. "Everything was 'We have to check with Carly.'"

Her celebrity would rub some executives the wrong way, but Lucent's salespeople adored her. And why not? Her ability to close big deals helped them meet their rich quotas. Even B-class salespeople could bring home $250,000 or more a year. She was equally comfortable selling Southern-style in Arkansas, with a brassy edge in New York, or talking tech in Silicon Valley. "She's very good at being a chameleon," says one former employee. She once described her seven basic rules this way:[13]

1. Seek tough challenges. They're more fun.
2. Have an unflinching, clear-eyed vision of the goal.
3. Understand that the only limits that really matter are the ones you place on yourself. Most people in businesses are capable of far more than they realize.
4. Recognize the power of the team. No one succeeds alone.
5. Never, never, never, never give in. To quote Winston Churchill, "Most great wins happen on the last play."
6. Strike a balance between confidence and humility—enough confidence to know that you can make a real difference, enough humility to know that you can ask for help.
7. Love what you do. Success requires passion.

Fiorina's most famous bit of showmanship came a few weeks after Lucent purchased Ascend Communications in early 1999. With a price tag of $19 billion, by far Lucent's biggest acquisition ever, it was her job to figure out how to integrate Ascend's sales force with Lucent's. Ascend was known for its highly paid, fiercely independent salespeople. They liked to be able to do their own deals and not have to answer to anyone back in the corporate office. No one personified the company more than sales executive Mike Hendren. A native of rural Kentucky, he had a badass reputation as a hard drinker who loved the ladies. A "rags-to-riches hillbilly," Hendren had once been caught by police urinating on a city street, say former Ascend managers. Not fond of computers, he used pen and paper to track his schedule, and sometimes wore flip-flops, a T-shirt, and sweatpants to company meetings.

Tensions were running high when the sales teams for the two companies met at a hotel outside of Pheonix. Hendren and Fiorina took the stage together at the meeting. He spoke first, sharing his thoughts about how the two sales teams could make the merger of such disparate parties a success. For one thing, Lucent's salespeople needed to get a lot more aggressive—or as he put it that day, "Nobody at Lucent has any balls." With that, Fiorina quietly walked behind a lectern on the stage, and, with her back to the audience, began shimmying and shuffling around. Only partially concealed, attendees couldn't imagine what she was doing. Was she changing her clothes? Scratching an itch? "What the hell is she doing up there?" thought Nina Aversano, who was in the audience.

Suddenly, Fiorina turned around, to expose a huge bulge in her crotch, where she'd stuffed socks down her pantsuit. "Mike, I just want to let you know, that despite what you might think, some of us at Lucent do have balls!" she proclaimed, as the room full of hundreds of salespeople let out a collective roar. "That's when Hendren decided he liked Carly," says Aversano. "It definitely put her on the map with the Ascend people."

Companies rarely stay as hot as Lucent was during the late 1990s. Lucent's refusal to recognize that fact would lead to a sickeningly fast fall from grace for the company. Many observers trace the trouble to September 1998, when CEO McGinn all but promised a roomful of Wall Street analysts that the company would grow at a 20 percent per year clip. It was an audacious goal for a company of Lucent's size—a growth clip that only HP and a handful of other companies had even come close to approaching. Once he'd publicly made this promise, there was no backing off. With many smaller companies posting that kind of growth thanks to the Internet boom, investors would quickly ditch Lucent's stock if it came up short. In fairly short order, it became clear that the company would have to pull out all the stops to make good on McGinn's promise. It started in predictable fashion. By early 1999, the company's outstanding bills began to climb as Lucent began easing up on its credit terms, say analysts and former managers. Rather than insisting that customers pay their bills in 30 days, Fiorina's salespeople would let customers slide for 90 days or longer if they'd place an order, say former Lucent managers. Salespeople were pressured to get customers to buy immediately rather than put it off—a tactic that essentially borrowed from future quarters to make the current one. "You were asked to come up with the wildest ideas to move product," says Bob Hewitt, a former sales vice president.

Some of the wildest involved a tactic called vendor financing, in which an equipment supplier such as Lucent floats a customer a loan to help cover the cost of high-ticket gear. It is by no means new or limited to the telecommunications market. Boeing does it for planes, and Maytag does it for washing machines. But while these companies typically put up only a small portion of the price of their products, Lucent and some of its telecommunications rivals took the practice to new extremes. Although they typically lacked the expertise and controls that banks put in place to mitigate the risk of nonpayment, these companies began loaning the entire purchase price to customers—and even threw in more funds to help cover installation and maintenance of the gear. The practice had a crazy logic during the heady days of the Net boom.

A host of companies, many of them start-ups, were clamoring to build huge, multi-billion-dollar networks. Because they had yet to earn any money themselves, the only way they could get the job done was with someone else's money. By forwarding the loan, a supplier like Lucent would be able to land a big sale—and would be locked in for more business when the start-up hit it big and needed to expand its operations further. Trouble was, no one gave much thought to the fact that these cashless companies might simply flame out, with their debts unpaid. One Ascend salesperson even remembers fronting $20 million to a young entrepreneur in Sweden who somehow thought he could wire all of Scandinavia and then Europe for Net access. "It was literally a guy, his girlfriend and his dog," says the salesperson. "He didn't have a business plan, or a budget.

Interviews with more than 15 former Lucent executives and customers confirm that Fiorina was a key player in Lucent's vendor-financing activity. In March 1998, she championed Lucent's first big transaction of this sort, a $200-million loan to Advanced Radio Technology, says Leslie Rogers, who ran the company's North American customer finance operation at the time. In October, Lucent agreed to front as much as $2 billion to Winstar Communications, a tiny start-up with an audacious plan for making the phone network wireless.[14] Fiorina "certainly was supportive," says former Lucent sales executive Nina Aversano, who negotiated the deal. "That deal left a lot of heads shaking," says Rich Nespola, president of TMNG, a telecom consulting company: "In our view, Lucent read too many press clippings and was lulled into or cajoled into euphoria rather than reality." Lehman Brothers analyst Steven Levy was shocked to learn that Winstar was free to use Lucent's money to buy equipment from other equipment providers. "That was a unique deal at the time," says Levy, who says that Lucent ultimately took losses of $825 million after Winstar went bankrupt in April 2001.

By the time Fiorina left for HP in July 1999, Lucent had a reputation for its willingness to float the biggest loans in the industry, and to float them to some of the iffiest credit risks. In the first half of 1999, the company inked deals to lend hundreds of millions to companies such as Global Crossing, KMC Telecom Holdings, Jato Communications, and One.tel. Former Jato CEO Brian Gast says, "I know we had her blessing on [our] deal." Before too long, Global Crossing, One.tel, and Jato had all declared bankruptcy. All told, Lucent's loan commitments jumped from $2.6 billion in 1998 to $7.2 billion in 1999—more than twice the exposure of archrival Nortel, says Lehman Brothers' Levy. Lucent hasn't itemized how much each of its financing deals cost, but Levy says the company had to write off $3 billion in vendor financing loans between late 2000 and late 2002.

To be sure, Fiorina's responsibility for these losses is a controversial subject. Many of the most egregious deals were struck after Fiorina left for HP. Rogers and Aversano insist that Lucent was repaid in full on almost all of the loans made while Fiorina was at the company. Many sources also say that as pressure to maintain sales grew in 1999, Lucent CFO Don Peterson and Lucent's board started okaying deals that would have been laughed out of the room in preboom days—even over the objections of the treasury personnel whose job it was to analyze such deals.

Fiorina's aggressive salesmanship was one reason Lucent became the vendor financing king. "There is no doubt that she bears some of the responsibility," says analyst Levy. Normally, corporate financiers are expected to provide a check on salespeople who want to offer cushy terms to a customer in order to land a big deal. With Fiorina running sales, that relationship often seemed to be flipped on its head. "If Carly wanted a deal to get done, our job was to get it done," says one former manager involved in Lucent's vendor financing program. Most sources believe Fiorina truly believed the loans were good bets, but that leads some to question her business judgment. "The only reason you would loan hundreds of millions of dollars to a company with lousy credit is so someone else wouldn't do it first," says the manager. "It was begging for trouble."

For all her attributes and accomplishments, many HP insiders would come to question Fiorina's wisdom, as well.

By late 1998, Fiorina was an executive at the top of her game. She knew what she wanted, and didn't want to be denied. At one point, for example, she decided that Lucent should spend $70 million to buy a sleepy Australian equipment maker called JNA Telecommunications. JNA's products were mediocre at best, but it had close relationships with some of Australia's largest phone companies. Fiorina felt Lucent could just disregard the products, and use JNA to sell Lucent's competing products to those carriers. Lucent executive Bill O'Shea, whose unit made those Lucent products, was against the idea. However, he missed the executive meeting to discuss the merger, say two managers who were there. Executive Vice President Patricia Russo, who was in charge of mergers and acquisitions, suggested they wait to get O'Shea's opinion, but Fiorina held her ground: "Look, Bill has done umpteen acquisitions without calling me to find out how they would be integrated into my [sales organization]. Now, I want to do a deal, and he's not here. Well, I'm not walking out of this room until I have a decision."

Russo, taken aback, asked for an extra day to get O'Shea's buy-in, confirm the managers.

"I'm not waiting a minute," said Fiorina. "I want a decision now." Russo had the authority to put off the decision, but she was evidently not ready to do battle with Fiorina that day. Says one of the attendees, "It was a great example of Carly's resolve."

However, many former Lucent staffers say that Fiorina was realizing she was not going to get the authority she felt she deserved at Lucent. She was not among the company's top-five best-paid executives. She wasn't on the board of directors, as was Russo. According to the organizational chart, she didn't even report to the CEO, former managers say. When people talked about McGinn's heir, Russo's name came up far more often than hers. "I think she and Rich were somehow at odds," says former AT&T CEO Bob Allen. "I don't know the details, and I don't want to. But I think it was clear that she wasn't going to have the freedom to operate that she thought she deserved, and that she had probably earned."

Some believe that Fiorina may have also been growing more and more uncomfortable with McGinn's sky-high sales targets. If she had concerns, she never stopped pushing her troops. On February 11 and 12, 1999, she held a pep rally of sorts for the top staffers within her division. Afterward, the group traveled to corporate headquarters for some final thoughts from McGinn. According to one attendee, he killed the mood, warning that he didn't see how Lucent could possibly hit all of its financial targets. That night, as the group dined at the Hunt Club Grill Restaurant at the ritzy Grand Summit Hotel in nearby Summit, New Jersey, Fiorina got up on a chair to repair the damage. She appealed to her staffers not to despair, but to know that it's only in difficult times that real heroes are made. When they looked back on their lives, they'd remember the times when they beat the odds. "She gave the speech of a lifetime," says the attendee.

Still, by early 1999, many inside Lucent were coming to terms with the fact that Lucent was not quite the business miracle it had seemed. Much of its success had come from its cash cow, phone switches. It was being badly beaten in some of the key markets of the future. Its efforts to crack data networking had failed to make much of a dent against Cisco, and Nortel was running away with the crucial optical networking market. Many of the new Internet companies Lucent had loaned money to were running out of gas. "I saw the writing on the wall. It was obvious the clients were running out of money, and it was getting ugly," says Doug Sabella, a former executive who left in 2000.

Try as she had, Lucent's Bell-heads were not moving much faster. They still took years to roll out new products, while competitors updated theirs every 8 to 12 months, says Frank Dzubeck, president of Communications Network Architects, a networking industry consultancy. "Fiorina was thought of as being an exceptional person because she advocated change. But the change she advocated only went down so deep."

If she was tiring of Lucent, some in Lucent were tiring of her, too. Some company veterans wondered if she really deserved her superstar status. While she had prospered during the boom, she had never remained in a job long enough to prove she could build a business for the long haul. Even Fiorina's refusal to use e-mail—she preferred the phone or even sending letters—rubbed some the wrong way. Her lack of technical sophistication might have contributed to her willingness to support high growth goals. "She really didn't have a broad, deep understanding of the technologies," says a former top executive. "That left her vulnerable to the hype and the smoke."

Many also thought Fiorina was a bit too good at advancing her own career. Like other Lucent executives, Fiorina had her own public relations staffers, but hers seemed to be much more successful in landing laudatory personal profiles. The best example: the October 1998 cover of *Fortune* that named her America's most powerful female executive—an article that was noticed by the board members over at Hewlett-Packard, among others.[15] Some Lucent executives felt Fiorina had oversold her role in Lucent's success. "She let herself be represented as saying she was COO without the title. The reality was that she ran sales," says one former manager. Says another: "Early on, you couldn't find anyone who didn't adore her. Towards the end, people weren't sure if it wasn't all about Carly."

In her final months at Lucent, she became increasingly inaccessible, says Dick Sadai. Once a close confidante, he says it suddenly took three months to get on her calendar. Sadai remains a fan, but others became disillusioned.

"You don't want Carly against you. It's not a pretty thing," says one former manager. "She can be unbelievably sweet, and an unbelievable viper." Adds Sadai, "She is able to move on with the company's agenda, and to easily dismiss the people whose loyalty to her was deep and long-term. Loyalty was not among her high priorities."

Of course, Fiorina is not the first corporate executive to be accused of being too ambitious or ruthless. Why, then, was she so controversial? Maybe it was because she didn't meet the stereotype of the woman executive. That stereotype suggests a manager with a deep empathy for workers, a consensus-building management style, and a commitment to the company rather than ego. Fiorina, on the other hand, was pragmatic, decisive, ambitious, and ruthless when necessary.

"Women are in this double bind," says Joyce K. Fletcher, a professor at Simmons School of Management and a researcher with the school's Center for Gender and Organization. "They have to display enough masculine characteristics to be taken seriously, but if they go too far they get labeled the B word. Men could do those same things and be perceived very differently."

Fiorina would remain controversial at Lucent even after she left to take the HP job in July 1999. Within months of her departure, it would be all too clear where the company was heading. With few hot new products and demand for older models drying up, Lucent came up almost $1 billion short of its revenue targets in the quarter that ended December 31, 1999.

Lucent stands out even among the dismal tales from the tech slowdown. With McGinn's 20 percent growth goal a distant memory, he lowered Lucent's earnings estimates four times in the year after Fiorina left. In the final quarter of 2000, with the Securities and Exchange Commission (SEC) investigating the company's books, Lucent reduced revenues by $679 million, to erase bogus sales from earlier quarters.

By mid-2001, things were so bad that Lucent managers took to removing lightbulbs from unnecessary light fixtures to reduce the electric bill.[16] As of late 2002, 100,000 employees had lost their jobs, and the stock of the descendant of once-proud Western Electric was trading around $1 and was in danger of being delisted. The *Wall Street Journal* reported that the SEC was looking into possible accounting violations dating back to the mid-1990s.[17]

What to make of Fiorina's role in this sad tale? Her supporters point out that before she left, Lucent never missed on its earnings estimates to Wall Street. They say that when she left, Lucent lost the one executive who could make things come out all right—who could somehow land the necessary deals to make McGinn look smart at the end of each quarter. They point out that Lucent was hardly alone. Nortel's stock also fell below $1 in 2002.

Others don't buy it. They say Fiorina had a lead role in pumping air into the Lucent bubble, and that she escaped just before the situation exploded. This much is sure, however: Even Fiorina would not have been able to hold off financial disaster at Lucent for long, so imagine if HP had happened to wait another year to find its new CEO. Says Harvard professor Rakesh Khurana, the author of *Searching for a Corporate Savior* (Princeton, NJ: Princeton University Press, 2002), "It's unlikely she would have been considered for the HP job, once it became clear that Lucent's success had more to do with loose credit terms and creative accounting than any reinvention of the company as the Second Coming of Cisco." In fact, Fiorina might have even been fired, if for no other reason than that she was head of sales. She would have been a likely scapegoat. That happened to the woman who replaced her in that position, Pat Russo. Had HP not come calling when it did, the Carly Fiorina story might have been entirely different.

6

SEARCHING FOR A CEO

The first thing we have to do is get rid of the HP Way.
—HP BOARD MEMBER SAM GINN TO A CEO
CANDIDATE, ACCORDING TO WALTER HEWLETT

Early on the morning of January 16, 1999, HP's board of directors began arriving at the elegant Garden Court hotel in Palo Alto. The hotel has long been one of the digerati's favorite spots for making history. On the ground floor is Il Fornaio, one of Silicon Valley's most famous deal-making restaurants, where entrepreneurs and venture capitalists congregate to do deals and be seen. Each of the conference rooms overlooks a sumptuous Mediterranean-style flower garden. On this day, the board was there to discuss what could be done to jolt HP out of its stupor.

For many of the board members, the time had come for drastic action. Like the proverbial frog in a pot, HP had been lulled into complacency by years of prosperity. The company, once so admired, seemed like an embarrassing relic at a time when the Internet appeared to have rewritten all the old rules for how to compete. "We thought this company needed a revolution," says Jay Keyworth. "You don't miss two big technology shifts, the PC and the Internet, without thinking that something's wrong. We knew there was a big, big problem—with a capital B." Dick Hackborn, whose opinion mattered most of all, also wanted to see some bold moves. He had two reasons, say close friends. He cared deeply about the company, and wanted to see it do well. Also, he wanted nothing more than for HP to get back on track so he could be left alone to retire in peace in Boise.

The day's events started at 8:00 A.M. Consultant Rich Hagberg walked the board through the cultural assessment that CEO Lew Platt had commissioned a few months before. The results came as no surprise: HP rated off the charts in terms of corporate integrity and employee loyalty, but it had lost its aggressiveness and much of its confidence. HP's fierce competitiveness had given way to a culture of entitlement, and a nasty case of passive-aggressiveness had taken hold. Employees paid lip service to the old notion of respecting other HPers. But when confrontations occurred, many staffers would dutifully talk the HP talk—and then go off and pursue their own agendas. Managing the place was the corporate equivalent of herding cats—and it wasn't working.

The board decided that HP needed a change in leadership. For months, Lew Platt had been openly questioning whether he had the vision to solve the company's problems. Finally, the board—particularly Hackborn—had come to share his view. According to Platt, Hackborn had been interviewing many of Platt's lieutenants: "Dick was running around talking to people, finding all the criticisms he could about me." Platt didn't resent Hackborn checking up on him—that was a board member's right—but he did resent that Hackborn never confronted him about his findings. "I'm a big boy, and I can stand almost anything," says Platt. "The only thing I don't like is all these hush-hush meetings, and people who won't be straight with you."

What kind of person should take the helm? There was a long list of requirements. A more charismatic leader was a must—someone who could raise HP's profile. He or she needed to be strong in marketing and sales, where HP was weak. It had to be someone who could challenge HP's hallowed traditions. HP needed a leader who could change the culture without breaking it, someone with a gentle touch and a spine of steel.

Job one was to consider executives already at the company. Hagberg handed out hefty 50-page reports on a handful of candidates.

None jumped out as having the right combination of skills and ambition. Carolyn Ticknor, who ran HP's laser printer business, was a stellar nuts-and-bolts executive, but was not interested in leaving Boise. PC chief Duane Zitzner's divisions had performed inconsistently over the years, and he lacked the cool polish required of a big-time CEO.

That left only two more serious internal candidates: Antonio Perez and Ann Livermore. Perez was a wild card. He had the best track record. He had masterfully built up HP's last remaining goldmine business, inkjet printers. In many ways, he was proof that the HP Way could in fact still work. He knew how to take smart risks and was respected by his staffers. As a kid in the seaport town of Vijo, Spain, he had spent summers rising at the crack of dawn to buy tons of fish at auction for his father's business. Paying a dime more per pound of fish could spell disaster, so Perez learned subtle ways to read the competition. "If that guy puts his hand in his pocket, he's going to bid," recalled Perez. His hunches had continued paying dividends throughout his career for HP. Among his accomplishments, he'd led development of HP's Photosmart digital photography gear. Hagberg told the board, "If you want to take a risk, choose Antonio. He'll break glass, but he's what you say you need."

There were problems, though. Perez and Ticknor had been competing for years. If Perez became CEO, Ticknor and much of her laser printer team would probably quit, some argued. Others wondered if he had the expertise to fix HP's stubborn computer business problems. Hackborn, say insiders, worried that the opinionated Spaniard might rock too many boats.

At that point, discussion turned to Ann Livermore, head of HP's corporate computing business, which sold high-end gear and services to big corporate customers. She also had a spotty record for delivering results, but the popular Livermore wanted the job. Badly in need of an image makeover, she'd hired a PR specialist named Atchison Frazer to help raise her profile. The result was a stream of press releases, speaking engagements, and glowing news articles. Still, Livermore didn't seem quite the ticket. Try as she might to play the rebel, she couldn't avoid her basic nature. She was HP through and through—too nice, too stodgy, and too vanilla. The board wouldn't rule her out, but wouldn't rule her in, either. "Ann was lacking sizzle," says former board member Jean-Paul Gimon. The board decided Livermore was the only viable internal candidate—but *how* viable was the question.

That meant only one thing: HP would have to consider the unthinkable. It would have to hire an outside CEO. The company that had prided itself on empowering workers and on people-oriented management had failed to groom someone to lead the company forward. But if it was time to break the system, then so be it. No one present objected, not even Platt. At 58, just two years away from HP's traditional retirement age, Platt agreed to step down after overseeing the spin-off of HP's instruments business. That way, the new CEO could get a fresh start with a new, more manageable HP. "It had become clear that the board would be happy if I left sooner than later," Platt says. "So this was a nice way to end things, all the way around." In a world in which too many CEOs put their own desires first, it was a stirring last act to some—well in keeping with HP's old-fashioned brand of integrity. "He's one of the most courageous CEOs I've ever run into. He puts his ego second," says Hagberg.

Platt resolved to stay involved in the search for his replacement, a controversial move for an outgoing CEO, but the real power would reside with the board's search committee, to be appointed by Platt. One member he chose was Dick Hackborn, the man he was convinced was lobbying against him. The others were Sam Ginn and John Fery, the former CEO of paper products giant Boise Cascade and a longtime friend of the company's cofounders. As for Walter Hewlett, he had planned to join the board of the new instruments company and drop off the HP board. Still, he recalls being puzzled that there were no family members on the search committee. "In retrospect, I certainly should have been part of that search committee," says Hewlett. "It was an error on my part. I wasn't watching things as closely as I should have been."

Little did Hewlett know that within two years, he would be the only family member on HP's board. David Packard would resign in 1999 in protest of the Agilent spin-off. Susan Packard Orr would resign in 2001, citing her lack of corporate credentials and her confidence in Fiorina. Then there was Gimon, Walter Hewlett's brother-in-law. An opinionated retired banker who'd been put on the board by Bill Hewlett in 1993, some board members thought he was too disruptive. Gimon protested bitterly when told he would not be renominated in 2000. Then he complained to Walter Hewlett, and the pair demanded that there be at least one board representative from the Hewlett family. As a compromise, the board agreed to have Hewlett stay on. Platt admits the board would not have minded having no family representation, but Hewlett wasn't likely to make any waves for the new boss. "I was probably a lot more trouble than Walter," said Gimon in an interview in 2002. "At that point, Walter did not seem likely to fight for anything."

The world got a double dose of big news from HP on March 2. For starters, its $7.6-billion instruments division, later renamed Agilent Technologies, would be spun off as an independent company. That was shocking enough, particularly for employees in that business. In Japan, HP was so highly regarded that some employees of the instruments business worried that their marital prospects might be dimmed if they couldn't say they worked for the company any longer. The second blockbuster announcement was that Platt would step down—and HP would begin a search for an outside CEO.

There were more questions than answers about who HP might bring in. The board said it wanted someone with tech industry experience, but there were literally only a handful of people who had ever run a technology company of HP's size. And who would want the job? Thanks to ridiculously inflated stock prices, many of the likely candidates had massive options-laden pay packages. They were already getting all the glory they could want in the press and from investors.

Then again, the chance to run HP was nothing to sniff at. It was a world-renowned company with huge deposits of untapped potential. With a little marketing and an organizational kick in the pants, it could be as sexy as stars such as Sun, Oracle, and Cisco. HP had unique advantages and assets—those loyal employees, a blue-chip customer list, and a printer business that would crank out enough profits to hide problems elsewhere. "It wasn't a turnaround situation," says former Sun Microsystems president Ed Zander, who was a leading candidate for the job. "HP was a profitable company with a lot of good things to work with. It needed leadership." Adds Gary Daichendt, a high-ranking Cisco executive who was also approached: "This would have been my dream job. It was on the West Coast, it was a great company, and it would have been a chance to show the world that integrity can win."

Running HP certainly looked like a better career move than the other big CEO job that became available on April 18. On that day, Compaq gave CEO Eckhard Pfeiffer his walking papers and announced that it, too, was in the market for a new boss. Compaq was stuck in the humidity of Houston, a far cry from temperate Palo Alto in the heart of booming Silicon Valley. While HP was showing signs of a rebound, Compaq looked to be heading south, and fast. Its PC business was getting clobbered by Dell, and its merger with DEC was a mess. "We're infinitely better off" than Compaq, Platt said in an interview in early May. "We know where the hell we're going. We're not confused. I would argue that Compaq is confused."

If HP wasn't confused, the search process seemed to be. To start with, candidates say the company did not seem to have a clear idea of what it was looking for. Platt agreed that the HP Way needed a tune-up, but he did not think it needed a drastic makeover. Though it seemed passé at the height of the Net boom, HP's culture would once again prove to be a competitive advantage once the market returned to normal. At least two of the three search committee members did not share this assessment. Hackborn wanted a strong new leader who could inject new thinking: "There's some aspects of the HP Way that have evolved that weren't a part of the original HP Way, and I'd just as soon see them go away," he said in an interview at the time. "There are other parts of it that we need to reinforce."

Sam Ginn, who chaired the search committee, felt even more strongly. His views were made crystal clear in his first interview with Antonio Perez. Perez had traveled up to Ginn's San Francisco office at cell-phone giant AirTouch Communications, expecting to spend the day talking about his qualifications. After a few minutes of small talk, Ginn got to the heart of the matter. According to Walter Hewlett and another person familiar with the conversation, Ginn told Perez: "The first thing we have to do is get rid of the HP Way." When Perez protested, any slim chance he had was dashed.

Even the board's choice for a headhunter to drum up candidates was controversial. Without even inviting better-known recruiters to bid, HP handed the job in late March to Jeff Christian, president of Cleveland-based Christian & Timbers. Christian's firm had emerged from relative obscurity in the late 1990s, when the explosion of new start-ups created huge demand for recruiting services. Although he had done a number of lower-level searches for HP, Christian had never handled a major CEO search. Grumbled one rival headhunter, "It's like giving an intern permission to do triple bypass surgery."

Christian cast a very wide net for possible recruits. He contacted the usual suspects, whose names were mentioned whenever a CEO spot needed filling—people such as current IBM CEO Sam Palmisano, former Oracle Corporation president Ray Lane, Intel Corporation's heir apparent Paul Otelini, and Sun's Zander. He also called former HP executive Rick Belluzzo, and even tried Microsoft CEO Steve Ballmer, Cisco CEO John Chambers, and Michael Dell. Other than Microsoft's Bill Gates and General Electric's Jack Welch, Christian says, "I called just about everybody you could think of."

There was little progress, however. Daichendt, John Chambers's number-two person at Cisco, was ecstatic when he first got Christian's call, but two things that Christian told him about the search bothered him. First, he was told that HP was looking at 10 to 20 candidates. That would take time to sort out, which raised the chances that the names would leak, making things uncomfortable at Cisco. "I didn't want to get into any beauty contest," he said. Then, when he heard that Platt was taking a lead role in the search, Daichendt pulled out. He says he admires Platt, but also knew their styles were so different that it was inconceivable that Platt would want to bring him on board. "I admire Lew, but I disagreed with the search process they adopted. I don't think I would have made it through the first round of interviews," he says.

Christian's style also alarmed some of the chosen executives. "It was one of the most bizarre phone calls I've ever had with a recruiter. I think he's in over his head," said one candidate. Another complained that Christian would call, overcome with urgency, and then not call again for weeks. A third says Christian repeatedly missed phone appointments, and he feared that Christian had leaked his name to the *Wall Street Journal* in an effort to win publicity for himself. Christian denies this and suspects sour grapes.

Carly Fiorina was also among Christian's first group of candidates. He only knew her by reputation, but what a reputation! Lucent was one of the hottest companies on the planet. Also, Lucent was in the communications business. Fiorina would be able to help HP sell gear to the telecommunications giants that were quickly wiring the world, and her gender would make for great press. Hiring a woman as CEO would be a perfect fit with HP's values. She would be a walking example of the board's devotion to the progressive views of the company's founders. That could come in handy in helping her get all those HPers to change their ways.

She wasn't the perfect choice, it was true. She'd never been a CEO, for starters. She'd never run her own division successfully. Despite these weaknesses, Christian decided he wanted her on his short list. He repeatedly tried to reach her for almost three weeks, sometimes calling several times a day, he says. Finally, he left a voice mail telling her the job was CEO of HP. "I really think you want to talk to me. You should want to talk to me," the message said, she recalled.

Once she knew the nature of the job, she returned the call. She'd grown up in HP country and had worked with the company for years. When she studied HP in advance of the Lucent spin-off in 1996, she'd admired the company's ability to post double-digit growth despite its huge size. However, she'd since met with HP executives three or four times a year in an effort to forge business partnerships, and she'd grown frustrated by the company's seeming inability to make any decisions, says Dick Sadai, a Lucent colleague who accompanied her on some of these visits. Still, for someone who had made a career of seeking out challenges, the opportunity must have seemed irresistible. She agreed to meet Christian for lunch on April 7 at a Hilton near Lucent headquarters in Murray Hill, New Jersey.

Christian was blown away by the person he met during the two-hour lunch. "She is one of the most focused people I've ever met. She had this quiet intensity. It was one of the most impressive interviews I've ever done." Particularly refreshing was her honest analysis of her own attributes. While many CEO candidates try to camouflage their weaknesses, Fiorina was straight up. She admitted she wasn't a technologist or a computer industry expert, but she was a leader, a team builder, and a fast learner. She'd always been able to skirt her deficiencies in the past, and she could do it for HP.

When Christian mentioned her name to Platt and Ginn, they were enthusiastic. Part of the reason may have been that Christian was making negligible progress with other candidates. Some, like Sam Palmisano, weren't interested. Others were too expensive. Dell second-in-command Kevin Rollins owned $300 million in Dell stock, and would require that HP compensate him for that. HP didn't want to go beyond $100 million. Belluzzo, despite receiving e-mails almost every day from HPers who hoped he'd return as CEO, believed there was no going back. Also off limits were other Lucent executives, such as Pat Russo. HP's board had decided to limit itself to one candidate per company. To go after more seemed too much like a raid, un-HP-like behavior that could also hurt business relations with Lucent, says Christian.

Zander, the number-one candidate at first, wasn't sure he wanted to be CEO of a company that competed directly with his beloved Sun. He also grew frustrated after he'd been through four or five interviews, but still hadn't gotten any clear sense from HP's board of its plans. Finally, Zander issued an ultimatum: He told the board to call him when it was ready to make an offer. Instead, he got a call back from Christian, who said the board wanted him to take a battery of psychological tests designed by Hagberg. Somewhat insulted, Zander took himself out of the running.

Oracle's Ray Lane also had some concerns about HP's search process. When he first met with Christian at a Boston hotel, he agreed to think about HP's top job. Lane even told Oracle CEO Larry Ellison, who advised him to consider the post. "Ray, if IBM called me, I'd talk to them, too," Ellison said, according to Lane. "There are certain companies that if they call, you talk to them."

Lane then met with Platt at the Garden Court. Much of the conversation centered on the board's desire to reinvigorate the HP Way. "They felt they needed an outsider who knew that the strength of HP was the HP Way, but accepted that it had tired out," Lane said. Lane knew these were difficult marching orders. "It is a culture that will probably eat you alive if you are too extremist," he thought. Besides, culture wasn't the only problem, by a long shot. The PC business was in need of major repair. HP Labs, despite lots of promising work, wasn't delivering technologies that helped HP's bottom line. Maybe most important, the company faced a daunting strategic decision. Since the mid-1990s, the company had buddied up with Microsoft and Intel. That had caused its own proprietary computers to lose momentum. Lane figured it was too late to turn back now. That meant competing with Dell on far more accounts—a scary prospect. Lane figured that it would take at least five years to accomplish the board's goals. That would make him 60. His father had died at 43. Though running HP would be an honor, it was time to be with his family. "He wanted to kick back, not kick it up a gear," says a friend.

The last straw came when Platt called and asked Lane to take Hagberg's psychological tests. Candidates first were asked to fill out a 340-question online survey, in which they were asked to respond to statements such as "I don't try to keep up with the Joneses" and "I seldom feel like hitting anyone." Then, they were required to go to Hagberg's offices for a three-hour interview by two psychologists. Lane wanted no part of it, and initially refused. "I thought it was a silly thing to ask a CEO candidate to do," he says. Ultimately, Platt convinced him to take the tests, but a few days later, he took himself out of the running. "I really don't want to do this job," he told Platt.

"I really wish you'd stick it out. We're down to a really short list," Platt said.

"I'm sorry, Lew. I have to be honest. I'm really not serious about this."[1]

As candidates began to fall off the list, the board—particularly Dick Hackborn—grew worried, say two board members at the time. "The search was not going very well," recalls Gimon, "and the search committee was embarrassed that they weren't coming up with more good names." By late May, says Christian, Carly Fiorina was considered a front-runner.

From Fiorina's perspective, the timing was certainly good. Lucent's stock was trading at around $60, up from a split-adjusted $5.83 on the day of Lucent's IPO in 1996. At that rarified price—

unless the most bullish Internet hype came true—there was nowhere for Lucent's stock to go but down.

From the time Fiorina decided she wanted the job, she played her cards masterfully. She met with Platt, each member of the search committee, and HP's human resources chief, Susan Bowick. All were impressed. "She stood out like a sore thumb" in terms of her vision, charisma, and understanding of HP's potential, says Keyworth. "Hackborn thought he'd died and gone to heaven," says one industry headhunter familiar with the search. Jeff Christian wasn't surprised. "With some people, you feel their presence the minute they enter a room," says Christian. "When Carly leaves a room, you still feel her presence. She will always be the candidate that is the most memorable."

From the start, Christian had the sense that Fiorina was managing the process every bit as much as Platt or the search committee. "I had this strange feeling that she was the CEO before she became the CEO," he recalls. "She knows how to put the pieces in place, before anyone else knows what the pieces are." Fiorina carefully managed what information they received, to make sure they only heard from her fans. When Ginn called Lew Golm for his opinion, Fiorina gladly gave her old boss from AT&T clearance to respond.

However, Fiorina also worked to keep the board from talking to her critics. When she learned that Christian was calling references she hadn't provided to him, she icily warned him to stop. "I thought we agreed I would provide the right references at the right time," she told him. "She wanted to manage everything she could," says Christian. Other executives might have taken a laissez-faire attitude; better for the board to find out everything, to make sure it was a good match. Not for Fiorina—for her, it was about winning.

She also quickly picked up on the political winds that were blowing within HP's boardroom. As Ginn got up to show her out after meeting with her in late April, she suddenly stopped him, says Keyworth, who heard the story from Ginn.

"Sam, I would really like to take this job," she told Ginn. "This is the job of a lifetime. But I'll only do it if Dick Hackborn will be chairman of the board while I get my feet wet."

When Ginn reported the story to the full board, Keyworth recalls thinking: "She passed the ultimate IQ test." Not only had she been smart enough to request the most admired person on the board to be her mentor, but her request to have Hackborn as chair would solve the board's "Lew problem." It would give the board cover to usher Platt into retirement.

As for Hackborn, she had little trouble winning him over. The pair met twice, for about six hours, Fiorina recalled in an interview. The first meeting was at a posh eatery across the street from the New York Stock Exchange in Manhattan. They shared their perspectives on HP, on the future of the industry, and on management. "We come from totally different places. But it was one of those things where you just click with somebody. I think both of us were kind of surprised by it. There was just a surprising chemistry, there was a surprising common sense."

The second meeting was at the Hilton, at O'Hare Airport in Chicago. With the nicer restaurants filled up with tourists, they went to the Gaslight Club instead—a steakhouse with a Roaring '20s theme and waitresses decked out in skimpy costumes featuring fishnet stockings. Sitting in a booth behind a fringed curtain, the pair talked over salads and pitchers of iced tea. "It was lovely, but kind of surreal," Fiorina says. The more they talked, the more they hit it off. Finally, she made her pitch: "Dick, you represent so much of what is the true soul and spirit of HP." The two of them would be a powerful combination—his insider's perspective coupled with her outsider's view. Plus, he wouldn't have to be very active, or deal with Wall Street, the press, and such—all of the activities that had prevented him from taking the CEO job himself years before. Who knew? Maybe she wouldn't need him for very long at all.

"I guess that's right," Hackborn responded. Less than a year before, he'd decided to quit the board altogether before Platt talked him into staying a while longer.

"Come on, Dick, you can't tell me there's a better person to do it. There is no better person to do it," she said.

He agreed. "It was her first turnaround at HP," Hackborn says.

Many of Hackborn's friends would come to see it differently. "I think she sold him a bill of goods," says Doug Carnahan, a longtime

HP executive who helped Hackborn build the laser printer business. "I think Dick got snowed." When she was asked to take Hagberg's psychological tests, Fiorina didn't hesitate. It was blazingly hot on the morning of Saturday, June 20, and the air conditioning in Hagberg's Foster City office didn't work. They tried moving to the courtyard outside, but the wind coming off San Francisco Bay was blowing too hard, so they headed to the lobby in Hagberg's office instead.

As with all the top candidates, Hagberg showed Fiorina the cultural evaluation he'd prepared on HP. He wanted to warn her. HP had a collective culture that would revolt if faced with drastic change. Like antibodies attacking a foreign agent, the results might be deadly. "They are going to come after you, and you'd better be ready. And because you're a woman, the antibodies may come after you harder than they would otherwise," Hagberg told her. Hagberg says Fiorina got it. "She had a very good grasp of what needed to be done—and what would come," he recalls.

Fiorina passed the test, but not everyone on the board had made up their minds. As the weeks passed, Platt was becoming convinced that HP was awakening on its own. Since he had announced his plan to retire that March, the stock had risen 34 percent, thanks to the e-services push and crisper execution. Growth had rebounded to a respectable 12 percent in July, from just 1 percent— the lowest since 1954—in early 1999. "There's a lot of positive momentum in this place," he said. At one point, he even suggested that Ann Livermore be given the CEO job, with him as chair. She ran a business comparable in size to the one Fiorina ran at Lucent, and she knew the HP Way, both its strengths and weaknesses. If the company was serious about building on what the founders had created, she would be a good fit—especially with him providing support as chair. Livermore liked that plan. When Platt called to suggest she pull together her press notices to show to the board, she agreed, says her publicist at the time, Atchison Frazer. By then, it was too late for Platt. He was the odd man out. According to one attendee of a board teleconference in early June, Fiorina was pretty much a done deal. In the end, even Platt enthusiastically supported her. Says Jeff Christian: "Carly just looked and felt more like a CEO than Ann. If Ann had Carly's personality and salesmanship and communication skills, she probably would have been hired."

In the end, Fiorina landed a blockbuster deal for a novice CEO. She would get 290,000 shares of restricted stock and rights to 290,000 more in the future. That was worth $65 million at the time—enough to compensate her for options she left on the table at Lucent. Then there were options to buy 600,000 shares at HP's price at the time, $113 per share. To the extent that she lifted HP's shareholders' fortunes, so would she lift her own. Then there was her $1-million salary and an annual bonus of $1.25 to $3.75 million, depending on the company's performance, not to mention the $3-million signing bonus, the $36,343 in mortgage assistance, and the relocation allowance of $187,500.[2] That included the cost of moving Fiorina's 52-foot yacht from the East Coast to San Francisco Bay, says Gimon. Her package was clearly a huge departure from anything any HP executive had ever received. In some ways, it even stood out among the obscene compensation plans that were being handed out to executives at the time. The contract specified, for example, that Fiorina was not only permitted but *expected* to use company aircraft for personal use, says Nell Minow, who runs a Web site about corporate governance called the Corporate Library. "There are very, very few companies that have that. It's the Rolls-Royce of aircraft provisions," says Minow.

Through all of this, Livermore continued to believe she was a serious candidate. She and her publicist, Frazer, thought their campaign to raise her chances, code-named Dark Horse, was going just fine. Frazer had even prepared a press plan for when the great day came. "Ann was quite confident she was going to get it," says Frazer.

However, her day never came. On July 16, he says, Frazer got a call from Anthony Effinger, a reporter with the Bloomberg business news service. Effinger was going to break the news that Fiorina was about to be named HP's CEO. Shocked, Frazer gave a quick "no comment" and raced to Livermore's conference room. Livermore was being made up for a photo shoot for an upcoming profile in *BusinessWeek*. "You're just not going to believe this," Frazer said.

"Bloomberg is going to say that HP is preparing to name Carly Fiorina as CEO."

Livermore's face went blank, says Frazer, and she stared at him for what seemed like a minute. Her instincts were to keep fighting, he says. Finally, she said, "Look, I always thought Carly was on the list." Indeed, Livermore had known Fiorina. She had been the HP executive assigned to handle HP's dealings with Lucent. According to Frazer, then Livermore said something shocking.

"You should tell Anthony to check her background really well."

"Why's that?" Frazer asked.

"Because I have all the files on how Lucent is organized, and she may not have as senior a position as I do. And her position may not match up with the way it had been described publicly."

Livermore denies that this interchange ever happened, or that she knew much about Fiorina's background. Either way, the deal was done. On Friday, July 16, Fiorina agreed to take the job, and she left New Jersey for Palo Alto that evening. Other than the search committee, she hadn't even met the members of the board, including Hewlett, says Christian.

Given the search committee's resounding recommendation, there was little chance the board would stand in the way of her appointment. Before driving over to HP headquarters, Fiorina swung by the old offices of Marcus & Millichap, where she'd worked after dropping out of law school. "I sat in my car, and I felt humbled by a great sense of responsibility for a great legacy," Fiorina would say in her Stanford commencement speech in 2001. "I thought about the uphill battle that lay ahead if I took the CEO job at HP. I had no illusions about the magnitude of the challenges in leading a company that had a great past, but was now searching for its future. I knew that I was an unexpected choice for the position, and I knew that with this job would come a fair bit of scrutiny and criticism . . . But I didn't feel afraid. I had recently watched my mother confront death with bravery, and I learned what choosing to be brave really means. And I left fear behind."[3]

When the news broke that Fiorina had been chosen as HP's CEO, many of the people who'd known her were shocked. Childhood friends who remembered the quiet girl couldn't believe it. A college pal says, "My jaw dropped to the floor."

Business colleagues wondered how she'd risen to such heights so quickly, and worried. "She was certainly in the right place at the right time. But I thought it would have been good for her to have had more experience," says Alan White, the associate dean of MIT's Sloan School. "To have her go directly to the CEO job at HP was a surprise," says Dan Hesse, Fiorina's old pal from her Sloan School days. "It was a huge job in a different industry. I'm not aware of any high-profile CEO job being given to someone who was both from outside the industry and who hadn't already been a CEO." Former AT&T CEO Bob Allen thought, "That was a really big step. If I could have scheduled her career, I would have had her do some other job on the way to that."

In Silicon Valley, the power brokers wondered at HP's choice of someone with such a scant track record. "I've got vice presidents of sales with more experience than she does," sniped one executive who'd been considered for the post.

Nowhere was there more surprise than over at Lucent. Most people were sad, and concerned that such a valuable executive was leaving the company, though many wondered if she was up to it. Lucent chair Henry Schacht, though a huge fan of Fiorina, told one former colleague: "Carly's fantastic, but she needed one more job—a five-year stint where she was running something on her own." Schacht explains it differently. "When Carly asked for my advice, I asked her if she wanted to think about getting a COO experience before she tackled a CEO experience of this magnitude," says Schacht. When she came back and said it was the opportunity of a lifetime, he told her "If that's the way you feel about it, then you should go for it. My bet's on you."

As for Walter Hewlett, he was unconcerned. She seemed the perfect choice to carry out a rather simple job, in his mind—to reinject energy and passion into a company that had grown tired in recent years. A few days after her hiring was announced, Hewlett ran into a friend who lambasted HP's choice for its new leader. "That was the most dumb-ass thing HP has ever done," said the person.

"No, no, no," Hewlett responded calmly. "We need a shock to the system."

7

AN EVENTFUL HONEYMOON

She was our rock star. Sun had McNealy, Microsoft had Bill Gates. We had Carly.
— ROBERTO MEDRANO, FORMER HP EXECUTIVE

As a balmy California Saturday unfolded in July 1999, a handful of staffers nervously awaited Carly Fiorina's first visit to HP as its new CEO. Lee Bonds, in internal communications, told her staff to get in early and to dress to make a good first impression. The press clips said Fiorina favored Armani and Chanel, so the typical HP weekend wear wasn't going to cut it. "No Bermuda shorts or flip-flops," Bonds advised.

Just a few days before, many people at HP's corporate office hadn't even heard the name Fiorina. When word leaked that the new CEO was likely to be one of two women from Lucent—Fiorina or Pat Russo—the race began to find out everything possible about them. Insiders were thrilled when Fiorina got the nod. The *Fortune* cover, published nine months before, said it all. She was everything that HP wasn't—charismatic, bold, even glamorous. She had proven herself beyond all doubt at Lucent, a feat that had made her the most powerful woman in business. Now, HP had her.

Fiorina arrived alone on that first day. After meeting with some executives, she sat down with a small group of staffers at a table in the Japanese garden outside Lew Platt's office. As they got acquainted in the quiet setting, they discussed how to make a big splash with her hiring. By the time the session ended, the staffers couldn't believe their good fortune. Fiorina was a great communicator. She picked her words carefully, exuding an unflappable, calm confidence. While pleasant and quick to laugh, she was also decisive and strong. She notified the group that her gender should not be played up for feel-good stories in the media. Her success was due to talent and hard work; to suggest anything else smacked of sexism. Other than that, she was open to ideas. When someone recommended that she do a videotaped question-and-answer session with Platt to be posted on the company intranet, she willingly agreed.

Fiorina had come prepared for her new job. She'd read Dave Packard's book, *The HP Way* (Boston: HarperBusiness, 1995), five times, deepening her understanding of the company's legacy. As a longtime HP customer, she understood HP's potential—and how frustrating it could be to deal with. Best of all, she could accurately convey what the company was all about. Leaders before her had embodied the HP Way, and knew why it was so special, but like jazz fans trying to convince the world of Coltrane's genius, they often failed to find the right words to explain it. Fiorina had that gift, and she knew it. Everyone at the table knew she could be high tech's new superstar. "She's going to be worth 40 or 50 cover stories in the first year," enthused one staffer. "Who is going to turn her down?"

Fiorina's debut came off like a dream. The media blitz started with a press conference at 6:00 A.M. California time, when the East Coast stock analysts and reporters were just getting to work. By late morning, hordes of photographers began arriving at HP headquarters for a noontime photo opportunity. She aced interviews from outlets ranging from CNBC to the *Wall Street Journal*. "It was a deliriously good time to be a public relations person," recalls one handler. "It didn't matter how hard the question was. She could charm anyone."

There were a few small dustups. When asked during the press conference what her coronation meant for women in the workplace, she responded firmly: "I hope that we are at a point that everyone has figured out that there is not a glass ceiling. My gender is interesting, but really not the subject of the story here."[1] Women's rights advocates cried foul, accusing her of ignoring cold, hard facts: Women made up just 10 percent of senior managers in Fortune 500 companies and were almost nonexistent in the CEO's seat. "Yes, the times are changing. Yes, Carly Fiorina made it through. But when you look at the patterns you see that gender bias is still widespread," Simmons College professor Joyce Fletcher told the Associated Press a few months later.

Any minicontroversies quickly died away. CNET's News.com online news service declared "Fiorina's HP Win Is a Loss for Lucent." Investors agreed. That day, HP's shares rose 2 percent to $116.25, then an all-time high.

Toward the end of the afternoon, Fiorina took time off from her frantic schedule to be photographed for a cover story in *Business-Week* that would be titled "The Boss." Sitting in the dark, as the photographer's strobe light flashed, she allowed herself a moment of reflection. "I wish my mom could see me now," she mused to no one in particular, say two people who were there.

Although the media loved Fiorina, HP's employees didn't know what to expect. Most had figured that HP's board would hire yet another 50-something white male with the predictable computer industry resume. This was different—and that was a good thing. For years, HP, a company that prided itself on firsts, had employed high-ranking female executives. Now, it would be the first Dow 30 company with a female boss. At 44, Fiorina was younger than most of the company's executives, more in step with the energy of the times—and with Hackborn as chair, she'd have the closest thing to Bill Hewlett or Dave Packard at her side. "How do you stop the antibodies from rejecting an outsider? By making Dick Hackborn chairman," said former HP executive Bob Frankenberg.

Still, Fiorina's track record was unsettling in some ways. She was a marketer coming to an engineer-dominated company. Her media stardom was also a mixed bag. Everyone agreed the company needed a more visible leader, but self-promotion was still a mortal sin in the HP corporate religion. Others raised eyebrows when details of her huge pay package were released. "People looked at that and thought 'She better be able to walk on water,'" said Richard O'Brien, HP's economist at the time. The company deflected the questions, pointing out that $65 million of her pay was to compensate for options she'd walked away from at Lucent. What's more, huge paydays were a sign of the times. In 1999, AOL CEO Steve Case's package was worth $159 million, while Intel Corporation's Craig Barrett's came in at $116 million; eBay's Meg Whitman, the only superstar female CEO to make *Forbes* magazine's list of highest-paid executives, earned $43 million to run a far smaller company.[2]

Mostly, there were questions about her intentions. Did she intend to just add spice to HP's image, or truly shake up the place? Given HP's zooming stock price since late 1998, even the top brass seemed in favor of the former. Just weeks before Fiorina arrived, Chief Financial Officer Bob Wayman said that the new CEO was not being hired "to come in and undo everything that has been done here." Human resources chief Susan Bowick, who, like Wayman, would become a key ally of Fiorina's, agreed. "This is not a company in crisis," she said.

Fiorina knew she was bound to run into resistance, but was sure she could handle it. "I don't have any concern at all that I won't be accepted here," she said in her first extended in-person interview, sitting by the Japanese garden with *BusinessWeek* the day after her debut. "I think I'm really good at reading people and reading organizations. Now, I absolutely acknowledge that I could do some really stupid things and cause them to say, 'We thought we were going to accept her, but now we're going to reject her.' But I don't intend to do that."

One of her first steps was to try to win over Ann Livermore, who had been passed over for the CEO position. Livermore was upset and toying with the idea of leaving. Fiorina needed to make her stay. Livermore was head of the only division within HP that seemed to get the Internet. That first Saturday, her first day on the job, Fiorina told Livermore the company needed her and promised to make it worth her while if she stayed. Livermore would receive 64,066 shares of stock worth $2.7 million if she stayed for three years—so-called time-based restricted stock. She and other executives received transition agreement awards; she got 42,590 shares worth $1.6 million.[3] Fiorina also promised to mentor her so she would be a better CEO candidate down the road. "Carly is not easy to resist," says an HP staffer, who spoke with Livermore soon after her two-hour conversation with the new boss. Livermore says she's "learned a lot from Carly," but didn't decide to stay based on one meeting.

As Fiorina met with more employees, her conquest continued. On her second day on the job, she visited the people least likely to embrace her: the engineers at HP Labs. For years, the members of this nerdy clique had been upset over their increasingly marginalized role within the company, as HP focused more on lower-end PCs and printers. Making matters worse, many of their colleagues had just left for Agilent, on the premise that those who stayed behind would be stuck at a company with no real commitment to technical innovation. The appointment of Fiorina—a salesperson with a history degree—might mean those departees were right. "There was a lot of skepticism," says Stan Williams, head of a project to build chips out of molecular particles.[4]

Much of that skepticism faded after Fiorina's visit. Addressing the engineers from a makeshift podium on a patio at the labs, she said all the things they needed to hear. Just as Bell Labs had been crucial to the success of Lucent, their contributions would be crucial to her plans for HP. The company had to get back to its reliance on breakthrough inventions. She wanted them to start thinking big again—to come up with big-bang inventions to restore HP's reputation as a top innovator.

Fiorina's body language spoke volumes. After just a few seconds behind the podium, she grabbed the mike and wandered into the group, establishing eye contact with attendees and confidently taking all questions. This was quite a difference from Platt. "Lew was a great manager, but his personal style was . . . the deer caught in the headlights," Williams says. "He looked like Al Gore."

Fiorina, however, was Clintonesque. She had an electric presence, and an ability to adapt to any audience. It all sounded so right. She understood what employees knew in their bones—that the company had somehow lost track of what had made it great. "Well, there's a few more converts," she'd say on returning to the office after an appearance. Her first speech to the entire Palo Alto staff, held in a clearing on campus near some trees called Packard Grove, left some shocked by her eloquence, some to the point of tears. "I turned to the person I was with and said, 'This woman is going to run for president,' " says Bojana Fazarinc, HP's former branding chief. Adds software manager Roberto Medrano, who also has since left the company, "Sun had McNealy, Microsoft had Bill Gates. We had Carly." So far, at least, the HP antibodies were staying put. The company embraced Fiorina with open arms. After four days of non-stop press interviews, Fiorina slammed the door shut on the media extravaganza. She sent the makeup artist packing and dove into the job of learning HP from the ground up. It was time to get to work.

She had a lot to learn, but Fiorina already had big plans for HP. In that first interview with *BusinessWeek,* she spelled out an ambitious to-do list.[5] She would light a fire under HP Labs. She'd call for a marketing makeover. The old joke about HP's hopelessly dull marketing—"If Hewlett-Packard had invented sushi, they'd have called it cold, dead fish"—wasn't funny in an age when a hot brand was worth billions. HP's pay practices, which stressed salary and profit-sharing checks, were an anachronism in an industry in which 20-somethings were becoming millionaires off stock options.

Most critically, HP had to define an overall corporate strategy to turn its gaggle of businesses into one powerful whole. HP had the products, the technologies, and the financial might to be a unique Internet powerhouse. No company, not even IBM, could match the breadth of its product line. No company was as strong with both consumers and corporations. By tying it all together, HP could make the Internet far more useful—for a salesperson who wanted to print a personalized brochure with the latest pricing before visiting an account, or for a kid who wanted to zip Grandma a digital photo of the fish he just caught. Platt had broken his pick trying to figure out how to make it all work. In the end, he'd given up and told his four top executives to run their own businesses. Fiorina wasn't ready to give up.

Fiorina decided to unveil her plans on August 9, at the company's annual strategic review in Monterey Bay. In the days of Hewlett and

Packard, executives came in fear to these meetings. The cofounders wouldn't think twice about killing a business that wasn't performing well. That had changed in recent years; the meetings were now mostly information-sharing sessions, where plans for the coming year were almost always rubber-stamped. This time, Fiorina ordered HP's general managers to come prepared to justify their businesses' existence, and show how they fit into HP's overall plan. There were tough questions to explore. Selling barely profitable PCs might be a great business for lean-and-mean Dell, but was it really essential for HP? The CapShare handheld scanner was James Bond cool; traveling executives could use it to scan articles with the flick of a wrist. There was no way the company was going to fund the huge marketing push to make it a winner, though. "This is a company that can do anything, it is not a company that can do everything," Fiorina concluded. It was time to get tough and play to win.

Many of HP's managers met Fiorina for the first time at a dinner the evening before the meeting started. Until then, she'd been mostly out of sight, studying the company. The group didn't know what to expect, but she quickly soothed their nerves. "Everyone was a bit twitchy at first, but she was the life and soul of the party," says e-services marketing chief Nick Earle. Fiorina went from table to table, chatting easily with the managers, sharing personal stories. "It was like barroom talk," Earle says.

However, HP's top brass saw a different side of Fiorina the next day. Unix server chief Bill Russell was in the middle of his talk. After discussing his division's falling fortunes, Russell began talking about his plans for the upcoming year when Fiorina broke in. "Let me make something very clear," she told him, according to numerous people who were there. "You will make your numbers. There will be no excuses. And if you can't make your numbers, I will find someone who can."

Russell, a member of the so-called British Mafia that was running much of HP's computer business, stood speechless at the front of the room. "I'm a pretty tough guy. That's my rep around here," he later told a colleague. "But I've never been so humbled in my life."

Fiorina wasn't there just to put fear into her executives. She also had sweeping changes in mind. The biggest: She wanted to undo the decentralized approach that had been in place almost continuously since 1957. Rather than 83 independent businesses, each selling a particular kind of product, she wanted to collapse them into just a handful of units. There would be two so-called back-end divisions that would be responsible for designing, manufacturing, and distributing HP's products—one for printers and one for computing products. Then there would be two front-end organizations that would market and sell those products—one to consumers and one to corporations. That way, customers would only have to deal with one sales team, rather than many. "You couldn't miss how silly it was the old way, if you were part of the wide-awake club," said Scott Stallard, a vice president in HP's computing group. "A parade of HP salesmen in Tauruses would pull up and meet for the first time outside of the customer's building." In Fiorina's scheme, only one Taurus would pull up—and that salesperson would be able to give clear direction so all of HP's product teams could collaborate to satisfy the customers' wish list. Many in the room were in shock. HP's success had always relied on the idea of autonomy—that the best way to run a company was to help business unit managers set attainable goals, then get out of their way and let them deliver. As such, generations of HP managers had dreamed of becoming general managers of these divisions, making them mini-CEOs, in a sense. In the new structure, the top managers would not run their show, but would have to depend on peers from around the rest of the company. "Everything that these folks had designed their careers around was going to change, so there was tremendous pushback and fear," Wayman recalls.

It wasn't just fear of losing authority that caused the managers to worry. They believed Fiorina's plan would fail. Fiorina wanted Livermore's e-services effort to be a cornerstone of the company's new strategy. Trouble was, almost everyone in the room believed e-services was a joke—a nice concept, but little more than a collection of slick marketing ads. More important, many feared Fiorina was being naïve. A front-back setup might work for companies with a narrower scope—say, Cisco or Dell—but HP sold far too many products in too many markets. How could the heads of these four new sweeping divisions possibly give enough attention to each and every product line, and make the thousands of quick decisions necessary to beat more focused rivals? And who would be responsible for financial results? If profits came up short, was it because the back-end folks spent too much money on R&D, or because the front-end folks didn't do a good enough job of selling? It could kill HP's culture of accountability, and make it easier for managers to point fingers or say "That's not my problem."

Fiorina was way too smart to try to shove her ideas down the team's throat. Instead, she engaged the group in long debate, challenging their assumptions and prodding them to think out of the box. In the end, she won the day. Her performance left some in amazement. "She's able to set goals that most people don't think are achievable," Wayman later said. "Even if [we] came up short, it would be more than HP would have done otherwise. It was a classic team-building exercise. I thought it was masterful."

Others smelled danger. They sensed that most of the people in the room weren't really on board. Almost everyone wanted to support their new CEO and give her ideas a chance. That was the HP Way. Veteran managers had seen big changes before, and didn't discount this one out of hand. It just didn't look like it would work. Though some tried to explain their concerns, it didn't much matter. A roomful of reticent HP executives, told for years they were hopelessly out of step with the times, were no match for Fiorina's forceful personality. "I don't know anyone who was in favor of it other than Carly. She just did it," says a former top executive who was there. Says another former top executive: "She came in with a recipe, and come hell or high water, she was going to use it."

Fiorina wasn't done. After the general session, she called a meeting of the executive committee to talk about HP's long-term growth targets. All the signs suggested that HP could never approach the 17 percent annual growth it had averaged for decades. The company was simply becoming too big and unwieldy.

That wasn't how Fiorina saw it. So long as its rivals were zooming along at double-digit growth rates, HP should be able to match them—and only by setting aspirational goals was HP going to think bigger. In the windowless executive boardroom around the corner from her office, she told the executives that she expected HP to grow at least 15 percent in the year that would end on October 31,

2000. Going forward, she set an aspirational goal of significantly higher sales and profit growth. "Stuff doesn't just happen. It never just happens," she said later, reflecting on the meeting.

The plan was too hot for HP's pragmatic executives. Firing up the sales engines was one thing, but doing so while simultaneously attempting the biggest organizational change in the company's history was begging for trouble. Besides, HP had not grown that fast in years, and it was best not to push the business faster than it could go.

That was all Fiorina needed to hear. Suddenly, she was on her feet at the whiteboard, asking the executives what their growth rates were compared to those of their top rivals. In each of its businesses, someone was leaving HP in the dust—Dell in PCs, Sun in servers, and IBM in services. The executives requested a compromise. They asked if she would scrap or delay the reorganization if they could come up with business plans that hit her growth targets. Fiorina agreed to give them a few weeks. Of the four divisional chiefs, inkjet printer chief Antonio Perez came in with the highest, with a plan to grow his business at roughly 16 percent. The others came up short. That was that. Her plan would go forward, as she had known it would.

In an interview, she sounded smug in victory. "They went off and did what they could, and they didn't get there," she said. "That was not a surprise to me, because you can't achieve different results by doing the same thing over and over." So why didn't she just veto their deal and get on with her plan? "Because the art of leadership is about balance . . . [of knowing] when to push and when to back off. When to teach, and when to let people make a mistake. Because to get systemic, long-lasting change, people have to really understand it and they have to own it," she said.[6] Trouble was, not everyone was understanding or owning it. Many were simply giving in.

In late 1999, HP employees were treated to nothing less than a Fiorina-palooza. Glowing stories about her appeared in the in-house magazine, *Measure*. In September, the new CEO embarked on a "Travels with Carly" tour that included stops in eight HP sites in the United States and five each in Europe and Asia. An internal Web site chronicled her every move. She held countless coffee talks to connect with hundreds of employees at a time. Her message contained both carrots and sticks. On one hand, HP was a great company with unlimited potential, not to mention a proud legacy that she vowed to maintain. On the other hand, the company had badly neglected that legacy and become inwardly directed, cautious, and slow. She urged employees to "Preserve the best, and reinvent the rest." She ended one coffee talk by asking the audience to send her a list of "The 10 stupidest things we do." "I'll read it," she told them, according to an article in *Forbes*.[7]

She made an extra effort with employees she thought had particular potential. In late October, she met with 60 programmers who were working on a promising technology called e-speak. For years, e-speak inventor Rajiv Gupta had been frustrated by HP's inability to get serious about the Internet. Fiorina's visit was like a gift from the corporate gods. "I'd heard about e-speak, and at first I didn't believe it," she told his team. "But now I do, and this could be the next big thing. The future of HP rests with you." Then, before leaving, she said: "If any of you are thinking about leaving, come see me. I want to talk you out of it."

Many of those who worked directly with Fiorina were bowled over by the new CEO. She could work nearly around the clock, often waking at 4:00 A.M. and working until 10:00 P.M. She was a shockingly quick study. She was too busy for much chit-chat. She usually took her lunch in her office because there wasn't time for mixing with workers down at the cafeteria, Lew Platt-style. However, she was quick to give a thank you or a hug for a job well done, and if she almost always won debates, she was also a great listener. "She would watch people's facial expressions, and read that, too," says Brad Driver, an investor relations manager at the time. "Having an executive at that level who can hear your thoughts is pretty special."

Within weeks, an almost Kennedy-era idealism spread among her immediate team. "The company had been coming to terms with the fact that it wasn't Camelot anymore," says consultant Rich Hagberg, who had done the cultural assessment for Platt just months before. "It was in a period of depression. But then she came in and said: 'We can do it!' "

Others wanted to believe, but were unconvinced. Some veteran executives, particularly those in HP outposts away from Palo Alto, thought she came on too strong with her criticisms of HP's past performance. "If this company is so screwed up, how did we get this far?" said one current high-ranking executive. Some of her rhetoric was over the top. When she referred to HP as "an e-company with a shining soul," many employees groaned. "She just grates on HP ears; it just sounds icky," recalls one engineer.

She also got a mixed response on her new "Rules of the Garage." Developed by one of HP's ad agencies for use in newspaper ads, they were supposed to be a kind of hip, updated version of Hewlett and Packard's original corporate objectives. To many HPers, they came off sounding trite—not the pragmatic brilliance of the founders, but the precious musings of marketers. The rules were:[8]

- Believe you can change the world.
- Work quickly, keep the tools unlocked, work whenever.
- Know when to work alone and when to work together.
- Share—tools, ideas. Trust your colleagues.
- No politics. No bureaucracy. (These are ridiculous in a garage.)
- The customer defines a job well done.
- Radical ideas are not bad ideas.
- Invent different ways of working.
- Make a contribution every day. If it doesn't contribute, it doesn't leave the garage.
- Believe that together we can do anything.

Some of the managers in the trenches, running the businesses each day, never took to her. At a coffee talk in San Diego, some of them relished watching Fiorina try to respond confidently to detailed questions to which she couldn't possibly know the answers. As the event let out, one attendee made a passing comment as he passed a top executive in the hall. "Well, I guess your new boss is one of them."

"One of what?" the executive responded.

"An eloquent idiot," the staffer said, using one of the favored digs reserved for the know-it-alls back at headquarters. "She speaks very well, but she has no idea what she's talking about."

Fiorina knew that many of her reforms might take months, even years, to implement. She didn't expect everyone to make the journey. "Many people here are very conformist in their thinking patterns," she told Stanford professor Robert Burgelman in early 2000. "It takes shocks to the system to change these things. I think that 20 percent of our people won't come along, either because they don't want to or won't be able to change their thinking patterns."[9]

Branding was one area where Fiorina believed she could make quick changes. It was one of HP's obvious weaknesses. In nationwide focus groups, people asked to describe what HP personified painted a ho-hum picture: a white, affluent, church-going, suburban male—nice guy, but boring as a stump. Reliable, but not much else.

HP's ads hadn't helped. While rivals took scathing, often entertaining shots at one another in ads, HP stayed above the fray. In the past, a low-key approach had worked fine. It was a perfect match for a company that was admired for its reliability and integrity, but in the middle of a Net boom, HP could no longer sit quietly. Since IBM launched its witty e-business campaign in October 1997, Big Blue's stock had dramatically risen. Sun's "We're the dot in dot.com" had done wonders for it, as well. "HP is one of the most revered and admired brands in the world and yet, it perhaps is in danger of feeling a bit old-fashioned," she said. Her goal: "to make sure it is fresh and updated and represents the next century as well as this century."[10]

Fiorina moved quickly to do so. She cut the number of HP's ad agencies from dozens to just 2. She would shift much of HP's $300-million-plus ad budget from countless forgettable product brand names, and pump up the HP name itself. She agreed to change the company's familiar logo. Rather than the name of the founders, it would consist of the initials *HP* over the word *Invent*. Though it normally took months to pull together a TV spot, she told her team in September that she wanted one ready to go by early November. She had arranged to give a keynote speech at the huge Comdex trade show in Las Vegas, where techies converged each year to ogle the latest products and hear from luminaries such as Microsoft's Bill Gates and Intel's Andy Grove. There, with all of the press, analysts, and rival CEOs watching, Fiorina wanted to debut the new HP.

What should the ad be? For certain, it should hark back to the founders to drive home the theme of invention. But it couldn't come off as nostalgic. It had to point to the future.

The ad team passionately dove into the project. Ad executive Rich Silverstein started with some old footage of Hewlett and Packard that had been used in a promotional video for the state of California a few years before.

When Silverstein showed his first crack at the ad to Fiorina, she was thrilled, according to people who attended the meeting. "I love it, I love it, I love it," she told him as the clip ended.

Still, Silverstein had an idea to make it really stand out. "How would you feel about appearing in the commercial?" he asked the CEO.

She considered the question. "It depends on whether you think it would make it better."

This was dangerous territory. Other than Wendy's Dave Thomas, Chrysler's Lee Iacocca, and a few others, CEOs rarely appeared in their companies' ads. Even Steve Jobs, who initially did the voice-over for Apple's "Think Different" ads, decided to use actor Richard Dreyfuss instead. He didn't want the ads to appear egotistical. But Fiorina agreed to do it.

The spot began with grainy black-and-white footage of young Dave Packard and Bill Hewlett puttering around the garage, and Packard, in his best suit, putting a product into the trunk of his car. A woman narrated the ad, as soothing acoustic music played in the background: "This is the workshop of radicals. A one-car garage, where two young men with $500 in venture capital invented an industry. Their idea was simple: Invent something useful and significant, or it doesn't leave the garage. The idea was so simple it was radical."

The spot ended with a woman leaning against the garage, arms folded confidently. It was Fiorina, whose name was never mentioned. "Today the company of Bill Hewlett and Dave Packard is being reinvented," she said. "The original start-up will start acting like one again. Watch."

Later, she would be criticized harshly for appearing in the ad. Longtime HP employees, executives, and admirers were offended that this newcomer would stand in front of Hewlett and Packard's garage—actually, a mock-up set near Packard Grove—as if she had anything to do with it. Although meant to sing the founders' praises, it seemed a cheap attempt to cash in on a legacy that had despised hero worship or hucksterism. "With her, everything is a marketing event," sniffs former HP executive John Russell. Even longtime supporters worried that making such a public and bold promise left her nowhere to go but down. Management experts questioned her judgment. "I fear the campaign may ultimately backfire within HP," wrote corporate psychologist Steven Berglas, at UCLA's Anderson School of Management. "No one is granted access to the inner circle of entrepreneurial teams without first passing muster, which means demonstrating practical, hands-on worth. . . . You just don't relate the [founding] myth like some campfire tale."[11]

A few months later, Fiorina would say in a speech to employees: "I did not stand in front of that garage for fortune or fame. I stood in front of that garage to say to you, and to say to the world, that I stake everything on this company. Because the people of this company are worth betting everything on." At least for the time being, most employees believed her.

From the start, timing was not on Fiorina's side. On July 20, her second day on the job, HP's stock took a dive and wouldn't recover to that level again until early 2000. Pointing to the stock slide, Fiorina would later say she was denied a honeymoon. That's a stretch. It's true the spotlight shone more intensely on her because she was a female CEO in a male-dominated job, but most of the feedback was positive in those first months. Glowing news articles cast her as HP's Wonder Woman, swooping in to save the Internet laggard. Despite the stock swoon, Wall Street analysts praised her efforts to shake up the company, casting its 83,000 employees as the obstacle causing the trouble. There was almost no mention of her relative lack of qualifications for the CEO job. Few asked questions about her role at Lucent, which had begun its headlong fall by early 2000.

Fiorina did little to evade attention. Her supporters point out that she refused far more media opportunities than she accepted. That is undoubtedly true, but the woman who once told *Forbes* that

"Leadership is a performance" clearly sought out the limelight. "People are excited to see a woman at the head of a big company, so I'm going to be using my image for publicity," she told a group of retirees who gathered at Bill Hewlett's home in November for lunch. "I am going to use every bit of it that I can, because I think it's good for business," recalls former HP executive Al Bagley, who attended. Her approach stood in stark contrast to that of another closely watched newcomer during the 1990s, IBM chair and CEO Louis V. Gerstner Jr. From the time he took over IBM in 1993, Gerstner ducked the media. Asked about his vision, he responded famously in his first press conference: "The last thing IBM needs right now is a vision." He quietly set about building up IBM's lucrative consulting business, which eventually turned the company into a $90-billion powerhouse—not through acquisitions, but by changing the culture from the bottom up. In the meantime, he made low, achievable promises to investors and shrugged off criticism from Wall Street regarding the company's slow, single-digit revenue growth. In contrast, Fiorina promised in November 1999 that the company would grow at 12 to 15 percent a year. It wasn't inconceivable, as HP posted 12 percent growth in the quarter that ended October 31, but publicly stating a higher goal was dangerous. Fiorina arguably set herself up for trouble, if not outright failure.

Fiorina has always insisted that killing the culture was the last thing she wanted to do, but very little about her personal style fit the HP Way. People with offices near Executive Row, used to seeing Platt or John Young roaming the halls most days, wouldn't see Fiorina for months. She didn't socialize much with employees outside of work, preferring to spend time with her husband and on remodeling their home in Los Altos Hills. When she arrived, she paid lip service to driving a Taurus, to be at one with HP's other managers. But that lasted only until her car, a sporty convertible, arrived from the East Coast, say former HP managers, that was it for the Taurus.

Fiorina also had no intention of flying coach. Platt had run himself ragged for years, logging 200,000 miles a year or more on commercial flights. HP did have planes, but most of them ran on a constant schedule between HP cities such as Corvallis and San Diego. They were more of a service for the rank-and file than an executive perk. Just prior to her arrival, Wayman and Platt had decided to sell off two of the nicer planes. They were cramped affairs that would never rate mention on *Lifestyles of the Rich and Famous*. The bathrooms smelled, and the drink of choice on board was screw-top wine. But with profits shrinking, it was felt that even these were luxuries HP could do without.

Soon after Fiorina's arrival, that plan changed. Instead of paring down its fleet, the company bought two Gulfstream IV jets and decided to greatly expand its hangar at San Jose International Airport. Also, the company reduced the number of commuter runs; the planes are now used more by higher-level executives, says one source within HP's aviation department. All this made financial sense. It's probably more cost-effective to use the planes to get the most out of highly paid executives, rather than keep nearly empty commuter flights in the air.

Still, the planes would become a flash point as Fiorina and HP got to know each other—a symbol that raised fears of an imperialist among HP's egalitarian masses. Her personal security arrangements also raised eyebrows. Bodyguards were unheard of at HP before Fiorina arrived, but given her gender and the great scrutiny she would be under, she hired a former Kennedy family bodyguard named John Viggiano, who had worked for her at Lucent, say former HP managers. A stocky man with a thick New Jersey accent, he persuaded her to stick to her treadmill rather than take her cherished early morning runs. He sent an HP staffer to Las Vegas two days before Fiorina's keynote speech, with orders to drive the routes her limo would take and check out the safety of the parking garages where she would be getting in and out of the car.

The increased security was a big shift from HP's trusting, open atmosphere. Until Fiorina arrived, HP executives' telephone numbers were listed in the phone book, a custom that benefited mildly enterprising reporters and thoroughly furious customers. Sometime after Fiorina arrived, executives were ordered to get unlisted numbers.

What's special about a CEO having a bodyguard, a plane, or an unlisted phone number? Not much. But other CEOs don't preside over HP, nor did she share HP's heightened—some say over-the-top—sense of humility. If former HP bosses expected to be treated like everyone else, she expected to be treated with the deference due a big-time CEO. One night during the Telecom 99 trade show in Geneva, she and former HP Labs chief Joel Birnbaum were waiting in the train station for the famous Orient Express, on which HP was to hold a soiree for big customers. Bob Lucky, a vice president of Telcordia Technologies, came up to say hello to Birnbaum, an old friend. Not sure who the woman was standing with Birnbaum, he made small talk. "So, how is that new CEO of yours?"

Fiorina gave a chilly smile, says Lucky. "Well, why don't I leave so you can tell him," she said curtly, and walked off.

Fiorina soon earned a reputation around Silicon Valley, as well. Dan Warmenhoven is a former HP executive who runs an influential computer storage firm called Network Appliance, Inc. "There are only a few people who have the size ego she has and can get away with it. Larry Ellison comes to mind," says Warmenhoven. "She won't meet with me. My company is too small, I guess. I could get on the calendar of Larry Ellison or Scott McNealy or Craig Barrett a lot easier than I could get on Carly Fiorina's calendar."

Fiorina never apologized for being who she was, or for not fitting someone's stereotypical definition of an HP executive. She was there to change things, after all. Perhaps she was just too different. As 1999 drew to a close, a backlash began to build. Myths about "Queen Carly" proliferated. Talk of opulent marble bathrooms began to make the rounds, as did rumors of a full-time, HP-employed hairdresser, and a king-size bed in her custom-designed plane. In one story, she ordered trees at HP's campus near Paris destroyed, to make room for her helicopter. The truth? Her handlers decided that the helicopter was the only way she could have kept all four of her appointments that day. No one knew trees would have to die. In fact, Fiorina hates helicopters, and wasn't happy when she heard that 12 small saplings had had to be removed because of her, according to an in-house newsletter. "I am reliably informed that the trees have been replanted," she said tongue-in-cheek in the column devoted to debunking "Carly myths." "If not the exact same saplings, some saplings very similar."[12]

Young and determined: Bill Hewlett and Dave Packard forged their lifelong friendship as undergraduates at Stanford University. Hewlett is pictured mountain climbing in 1930; Packard, an excellent athlete, was on the football team. *(Photos courtesy of Agilent Technologies)*

Father and son: Bill Hewlett fishing with Walter Hewlett, age 7. They shared a love of the outdoors, music, and technology. Walter would later tell a fellow HP board member: "The privilege of my life is to be my father's son." *(Photo courtesy of Walter Hewlett)*

Corporate Camelot: Bill Hewlett and Dave Packard, in a company skit in the late 1960s. HP was fast becoming famous for its huge profits and progressive HP Way. In the skit, they played two strangers who get adjoining seats on an airplane—and proceed to brag that they both run the world's best company. *(Photo courtesy of Agilent Technologies)*

An unremarkable start: School picture of Carleton Sneed. Long-time friends say HP's charismatic leader was quiet and studious until after she graduated from college.

Following legends: Former HP CEOs John Young, left, and Lew Platt struggled to maintain the HP Way as the company made the transition from instruments to computers. *(Photo courtesy of Agilent Technologies)*

The birthplace: Packard and Hewlett in front of the garage where they founded the company, on the company's fiftieth anniversary. *(Photo courtesy of Agilent Technologies)*

Old guard, new guard: Fiorina with Lew Platt on her first day at HP. After only a few weeks, she would stop seeking his advice. *(Photo © DA SILVA PETER/CORBIS SIGMA)*

The honeymoon: Fiorina and Michael Capellas on September 4, 2001, the day they announced the merger. By the time the event had finished, the company's stock had begun to drop. *(Photo © Reuters NewMedia Inc./CORBIS)*

Power behind the throne: Other than Bill and Dave, no one has had more impact on HP than board-member Dick Hackborn. He built the gold-mine printer business, blessed Fiorina as CEO, and championed the Compaq merger. *(Photo copyright © 1991 Peter Sibbald)*

Nervous but hopeful: Walter Hewlett entering the courtroom with his wife, Esther, by his side. *(Photo © Reuters NewMedia Inc./CORBIS)*

A legacy ends: Walter Hewlett waving at end of his press conference on the day HP shareholders narrowly approved the Compaq merger. He joked that he looked forward to returning to his life as "a musician and an academic." *(Photo courtesy of the San Francisco Chronicle)*

Victory: A soon-to-be triumphant Fiorina entering the courthouse. Her bravura performance would win over the judge, whose strongly worded opinion in favor of HP would silence many of her critics. *(Photo © Reuters NewMedia Inc./CORBIS)*

Why such an active rumor mill? To some extent, it was because Fiorina was threatening the status quo. For decades, HP employees hadn't had to worry about keeping their jobs. Now, she was threatening to expose HP's dirty secret: The place had protected legions of warm bodies, people who showed up every day but who left at 5:00 P.M. and rarely contributed a useful new idea. One perennial joke around Silicon Valley was, "My husband's retired. He works at HP."

Fiorina's message to them: game over. During Fiorina's first conference call with Wall Street analysts, she warned that the company had fired 250 "nonproductive" salespeople in HP's computer business. She also changed the way those salespeople were paid. Rather than salary, she weighted their pay more heavily toward commissions, the way other tech firms did it. The upshot: Salespeople could make much more than they had before, if they performed; otherwise, they would earn less. She even dumped the Taurus program, which was a screaming symbol of mediocrity when other tech salespeople drove BMWs and Ferraris. "Clearly, we mean business," she said during the call. "It's part of the new HP environment, where underperformance is not tolerated."

The board also okayed new compensation policies, similar to the one she'd helped develop at Lucent. A "pay for results" plan rewarded 200 top managers with a small bonus for hitting Fiorina's financial targets—and a much bigger one if the company hit her loftier aspirational goals. These targets were tied in to how HP did relative to its competitors in each of its key businesses—Dell in PCs, IBM in services, Lexmark in printers, and Sun in servers. The program, which would be expanded to the top 2,000 managers in the year that followed, meant that HP could no longer just measure itself against itself.

If Fiorina was making waves inside HP, they seemed to be the right ones at first. In her first full quarter on the job, HP posted 10 percent revenue growth and 7 percent earnings growth. Still, Fiorina was not content. "We're simply not delivering the kind of performance we're capable of," she told employees in an all-hands voice mail to discuss the results. "We need to be faster in all kinds of ways—faster to decide, faster to choose, faster to act."

She also wanted HP to be more daring, even in how HP communicated with investors. Her approach made some company veterans nervous. For years, HP used a very simple process to report the quarterly results. A group of corporate staffers and the heads of the businesses would spend a few hours summarizing exactly what had happened that quarter—where the growth and profits were, and where they weren't. Wall Street, if sometimes frustrated by a lack of detail, knew it could count on HP's numbers as an accurate reflection of the health of the business.

Those end-of-quarter meetings changed after Fiorina arrived. During one of these meetings, Steve Brashears, an assistant controller, noted that HP's accounts receivables were higher than usual, suggesting a high amount of unpaid bills. Lew Platt would have taken action to bring it back in line as soon as possible, and urged the sales force to make sure their customers paid up. Fiorina, on the other hand, stared at Brashears and said, in a dismissive tone, "But that's a good thing, right, Steve?" according to participants in the meeting. Even if the unpaid debts might have to be written off at some time in the future, the sales could be booked that quarter. "Accounts receivable was not high on the list. She was more concerned with showing revenue growth and good earnings per share," said one attendee.

Later in the meeting, Fiorina grabbed the group's attention again. Wayman was reading the draft version of the earnings release, when Fiorina suddenly stood up and, with a big smile, belted out a refrain from an old Harold Arlen song: "Bob, you've got to 'accen-tu-ate the positive'," she sang as she swayed, arms out in show-tune fashion. "I felt as if I had unwittingly stepped into a Julie Andrews movie," says one attendee.

Some of those in the room were amused, and relieved. HP, they knew, had a reputation as the gray lady of Wall Street. Almost every other high-tech company used its end-of-quarter release as a marketing opportunity to some extent. So long as no untruths were told, a bullish quarterly release could catch the eye of investors and give the stock a nice bump—and the higher the stock, the more confidence corporate buyers might have. It was simply smart business. "[Fiorina] meant nothing more than 'Let's tell 'em the good things we're doing,' " says Brad Driver, the former investor relations manager, who later went to work for handheld computer maker Handspring Inc. "We all kind of laughed. It was just a different approach, a different energy, from Lew Platt."

Others worried that Fiorina's approach might erode HP's spotless credibility with investors. Those worries increased in later meetings, when Fiorina repeated the performance. It was always done in a good-natured way, and she never ordered anyone to say something they felt was unsupportable. Usually, she'd aim this prodding at Wayman, a 30-year veteran who personified HP's sterling reputation. "Come on, Bob, put more hope in your voice!," she'd say, as he sheepishly argued to tone down the language in a release. "I know, I know," he'd say, and the group would proceed until everyone was comfortable.

As quarters passed, Fiorina would put still more of her stamp on HP's investor relations. In the past, all the division heads would come in to work out the end-of-quarter release. Fiorina believed this was a waste of their time. Moreover, rather than Platt's quick once-over, she and a small group would take a day or more to scrub the numbers. Some executives would complain about reading their financial goals in the press. In addition, while Platt had left it to Wayman and his crew to do the quarterly call with Wall Street analysts, Fiorina took the lead role on the call, as most high-tech CEOs do.

Did Fiorina's aggressive new approach help? No. In mid-2000, some analysts accused the company of some low-level trickery. Analysts such as Sanford C. Bernstein's Toni Sacconaghi claimed HP hit Fiorina's growth and profits targets only by sneaking some one-time gains into the mix. "It wasn't the blow-out quarter they tried to say it was," says Sacconaghi, who calculated actual revenue growth at 14.5 percent versus Fiorina's goal of 15 percent. "It sounds nitpicky, but it makes [me] wonder what to believe. . . . It's unfortunate, because it wasn't a bad quarter."

Some of HP's rivals noticed a change in HP's financial announcements, as well. "I grew up with HP calculators, but they don't work right anymore," joked Sun Microsystems' Ed Zander in early 2001. "Everything they mention seems to be growing 50 percent, but the company as a whole only grows 10 percent." Asked for comment at the time, Fiorina insisted that HP's financial reporting was accurate. "The calculators still work fine," she said.

What would Bill Hewlett and Dave Packard have made of the woman running HP? It's an imponderable question. Packard had been dead for years. Hewlett was confined to a wheelchair, and his speech was very hard to understand. As with many stroke victims, it was hard to know at all times how engaged he was with the world around him—although it was clear to all that he was very frustrated by his confinement. His greatest daily joy was being driven around in a specially equipped van with his wife, a friend, or one of his nurses.

Fiorina did meet Hewlett once, at the luncheon at his house that November. A group of retirees and old friends was sitting in the garden, sipping wine and talking, when Fiorina and her husband arrived. After admiring the view, according to one attendee, Fiorina set a chair down in front of Hewlett, leaned down and quietly said something like: "I just wanted to tell you how much I admire the company that you and Dave built. It's a company with a shining soul. You should be very proud. I'm going to try to take care of it for you."

Hewlett's reaction is subject to debate. Fiorina says "He managed a few words, but it was a struggle. . . . His wife thought he understood. He had a look in his eyes that he understood." In a company video shown on the day Hewlett died, Fiorina would say that "his eyes shone with the light of interest, compassion, pride in his company and that wonderful inventive spirit that inspires the people of HP today."

Two people who were at the luncheon saw it differently. They say Hewlett mumbled something, at which point his wife said "Bill wants to go for his ride." Hewlett might not have known who Fiorina was or what she was saying, but Al Bagley, who was there, says, "I don't think Bill was impressed with her."

8

UNRAVELING

Wisdom is an understanding of what can and cannot be accomplished.

— Former HP executive Phil Faraci

The stars appeared to be lining up neatly for Carly Fiorina by November 1999. Wall Street had punished HP's shares in the months after her arrival. Now, the mood had shifted. The strong revenue growth posted for the quarter that ended on October 31 suggested that she was going to be able to light a fire under the moribund company. On November 18, she got a lucrative windfall with Agilent's triumphant initial public offering. Because HP still owned most of the new company, HP's shares jumped 16 percent when Agilent's soared 49 percent on its first day of trading. The good times would roll for another six months. After years of sitting out the bull market, HP's stock would ride the wave alongside other highfliers through mid-2000.

Still, HP was a company on the cusp of radical, painful changes. Confident that HP was only scratching the surface of what it could be, Fiorina set in motion plans to change almost every aspect of the company. It would be organized differently, market its products differently, do R&D differently, set strategy differently, deal with customers differently, and reward its employees differently. Rather than take on one or two of these areas at a time, Fiorina intended to tackle them together, to bring the company into what she called "holistic" alignment. When done, the company would be ready for anything. Paraphrasing Darwin during an interview, she argued, "It is not the most intelligent of the species that survive, or the most powerful. It's the most adaptable to change."[1] The idea was to retain as much of the underlying HP values as possible. One way or another, the company would chip away at the bad habits that had grown like barnacles over Hewlett and Packard's old HP.

In diagnosing HP's weaknesses, her plans were dead-on. HP had to be easier for customers to do business with. It needed to be more aggressive. Its employees needed to pull together to help the entire company, not their own little fiefdoms. From all appearances, it was inspiring, clear-eyed leadership. This reinvention would take three years, and there would be tough patches, she warned. It would be like sailing: "You don't get to your destination in a straight line. You know where you are going, but you adjust your course as necessary to fit the times."

If the transition were done right, Fiorina envisioned a company that would be ambidextrous—able to dominate in existing businesses while creating new ones. In an era in which the most successful technology companies were laser focused on a particular business, she expected HP to do it all—be as cutthroat as Dell and as innovative as IBM. If Fiorina had her way, the company would do all of this while maintaining double-digit growth.

Some argued that what Fiorina wanted to do was like trying to change the engine of a 747 in midflight. No company had ever figured out how to manage such diverse businesses and maintain such growth, says Stanford business professor Robert Burgelman. "No one has tried to solve the problems she is trying to address," he said in an interview.

Perhaps most remarkably, she would do it almost entirely on her own. CEOs brought in from the outside to shake up a company almost always bring along a cadre of longtime allies to help them—at the least, a chief financial or operations executive to handle the hatchet work. Fiorina came with no one other than Dan Plunkett, an executive coach from Mercer Delta Consulting whom she'd worked with at Lucent.

She sought little counsel from many of HP's top executives. After the first month or so, Fiorina stopped talking to Lew Platt altogether, he says. He'd read about her moves in the newspaper. "I think someone on the board told her, 'Don't let him throw any cold water on any of your plans,' " he says. Fiorina didn't visit with the other old-time HP executives, such as former CEO John Young, who still kept offices at an HP building down the street from headquarters. "She never even went down to have cup of coffee with them," says Dan Lynch, a Silicon Valley entrepreneur and friend of Platt's. "That's just dumb."

Fiorina did consult a few old-timers, including Dick Hackborn and retired HP Labs president Joel Birnbaum, but insiders say she seemed to rely most on a loyal group of corporate staffers and outside consultants. Within months of her arrival, consultants from Bain & Company, Boston Consulting Group, and Stone Yamashita were hard at work on major projects. Bain was so involved in helping Fiorina craft a companywide strategy that one executive joked, "Am I allowed to go to the bathroom without asking Bain?" The hand of Keith Yamashita, a hip, pony-tailed ex-Apple employee, defined the look and feel of the new HP. The 30-person San Francisco company helped write Fiorina's speeches, HP's annual reports, and reams of expensive, jargon-filled brochures and posters intended to rally the troops. Fiorina loved him; HP would pay the firm more than $1 million a month, sources say. However, more than a few HP employees were baffled by Yamashita's abstract cyberbabble, such as that found in one 70-page booklet with the cryptic title "Shape." One can only imagine what Dave Packard, who chewed out managers who dared even to use color graphics in internal communications, would have said.

By the end of the year, many managers began to worry about the scope and speed of Fiorina's reforms. At a senior leadership meeting of HP's top executives that December, Fiorina continued to bang the drum for her approach. First, she showed a video in which many of HP's biggest customers railed at the frustration of dealing with the fragmented giant. They were sick of the horde of

HP salespeople who showed up at their doors, all haggling to win their piece of the pie. Customers thought of HP as one company, and wanted it to act like one. "We were on a slow-glide path to mediocrity—not falling off a cliff but very slowly losing our aggressiveness, our competitiveness, our hunger to succeed," recalls former executive Neil Martini. "Carly made everybody realize how we were viewed from the outside."

Then, she laid out more details of how her reorganization would solve the company's problems. The two back-end groups would be responsible for making innovative, profitable products to keep HP competitive over the long haul—everything from R&D to production and distribution. Two front-end groups would be responsible for making the quarterly numbers—setting and hitting sales forecasts, setting prices, and such. Those front- and back-end groups would share financial accountability. That part of the plan scared managers. How, for example, could a product team design a product to be profitable if it didn't control pricing? "Everybody owned everything and nobody owned anything," says former printer division executive Phil Faraci.

The new scheme also turned HP's internal pecking order on its head, favoring Fiorina's sales force. Fiorina had already put in place lucrative commission plans, and this new structure would give salespeople far greater authority. "She was hero-worshipped by the field. She was Princess Diana," recalls former HP marketing executive Nick Earle.

The operations chiefs and product engineers who had held power for decades saw that they would not only lose their independent fiefdoms, but would be recast as lackeys of a sort to these newly empowered salespeople. Snide jokes about the "back end" being for donkeys and asses began to circulate. "She was attacking the very heart of the beast before she had much support," one executive recalls thinking at the time. "The girl's got balls."

Even Hackborn, who attended the meeting to lend his support, mentioned some concerns, say numerous people who were there. He argued that the only way Fiorina's plan could work was if everyone supported it fully. That didn't sound like "a 100 percent endorsement" from Hackborn, says one attendee.

After the session, many managers still believed Fiorina's plans were half-baked. Other than a few people who were appointed to specific high-level jobs, it was unclear who was supposed to do what under the realignment. There was no playbook or training manual to help employees figure out what Fiorina wanted. "There was violent opposition. Everyone told her it was going to be an unmitigated disaster," says Lee Caldwell, a former IBM executive who joined HP as technology chief of the printer business that October. Many understood what Fiorina was trying to accomplish, but thought she was simply overoptimistic and rushing ahead too fast. Salespeople who'd only been asked to bring in the orders and not spend too much money to do it were suddenly expected to balance the nuts-and-bolts details to hit a profit margin. "Carly, I'm not opposed to this. I just don't know how to do it," one top executive told her. "You can't wish skills on people who have never had them."

Certainly not everyone was souring on Fiorina, nor would they. Reality may have set in since her arrival, but many employees and managers remained inspired by her leadership. Even if she didn't have all the right answers, she was making decisions. That was the most important thing. The new work environment "is energizing, it's fast, and it's fun," said Susan Bowick, senior vice president of human resources.

For much of April, a special task force holed up in a conference room near HP's headquarters. Shuttling back and forth to Fiorina's office for real-time approvals, it had come up with a long list of recommendations to slash spending, revamp HP's Web site, and improve the way HP set strategy. All were great ideas, and some worked. The company consolidated the computer systems of countless divisions. It racked up huge savings by centralizing procurement of everyday supplies to get the best volume discounts. It came up with more efficient ways to package and ship HP's products. All told, the company came up with more than $1 billion in savings.

Much of the enthusiasm came from within Building 20, HP's headquarters in Palo Alto, where a clique that many came to refer to as the "Cult of Carly" began to develop. No formal group, the Cult of Carly was an ever-shifting mix of HP veterans and newcomers. As a group, its members seemed to share common traits that stood in contrast to those of the old HP. Some of them—young, aggressive, and relatively lacking in operations experience—were more like eager dot-commers than bland, archetypal HP managers. They believed in the power of buzz and embraced quick action over thoughtful deliberation.

Many company veterans sensed the changing of the guard before too long. With Fiorina, a consummate polished salesperson, at the helm, some employees who had never thought twice about what to wear to work suddenly felt the need to run out and buy a designer suit. The change went far beyond Armani versus Dockers. In the past, HPers believed they had an open dialogue with management. Increasingly, "It became a one-way flow of information, and you couldn't question why," says former economist Richard O'Brien. Many felt that loyalty and a willingness to work long hours, not candor, was what earned points. One person who worked closely with Fiorina's group, former investor relations manager Brad Driver, insists there was nothing nefarious going on. "She was just trying to find people with lots of energy," he says. "She wanted people she could really rely on. She wanted a trusted team."

At first, Fiorina's closest ally was Debra Dunn, according to many current and former HP staffers. Dunn had a mixed operating record, in a host of marketing and administrative jobs. She'd helped Lew Platt oversee the spin-off of Agilent, then became Platt's key aide in managing the details of the CEO search. That gave her plenty of face time with Fiorina, and the two women hit it off. Both were smart and ambitious. Before long, Dunn had an office on Executive Row, just a few long strides from Fiorina's office. When she was named senior vice president for corporate operations, many of her peers felt it was a testament to her political skills, not her qualifications. Says a former top-ranking HP executive: "Debra was one of the most political people you could ever meet. Don't turn your back."

Dunn's run as palace guard ran out after a while. Some say she was replaced in that role by Allison Johnson. Johnson joined HP in 1999, after helping IBM establish its successful e-business branding campaign a few years before. Working closely with consultants, she quickly helped pull together HP's own e-services campaign. E-services turned out to be far more hype than substance, but it did lift the stock for a time. In late 1999, Internet browser inventor Marc Andreessen invited Johnson to join his start-up, LoudCloud, Inc. To keep her, Fiorina counteroffered with a bigger job in the corporate office. "Allison was blown away by Carly," says Nick Earle, her boss at the time.

The feeling would become mutual. Soon, Johnson was put in charge of HP's communications and branding efforts. In her new role, she was a fearsome protector of Fiorina's image. Internally, her power went far beyond her job description, say many current and former managers. "After a while, the only person that Carly seemed to listen to was Allison," says one former executive. "She was the prime minister at HP," says another. Says another current employee: "They feed off each other. It's like 'You're so great—no, you're so great.'" In many ways, Fiorina and Johnson were kindred spirits. HP insiders say Johnson, who would be a key advisor during the proxy fight with Walter Hewlett, was the only one who could match Fiorina's astounding capacity for work. The two women also shared a sometimes ruthless determination to win. Throughout her career, Johnson converted conference rooms into round-the-clock "war rooms" to win some marketing battle or other. Former colleagues say she gives total loyalty to her causes and expects the same of others. "There's an Oliver North quality that I've always found unsavory," says a former colleague from IBM. "She's a true believer." Indeed, Johnson once told this person: "I don't just stir the Kool-Aid. I drink it."

Like most cultural revolutions, the one taking hold at HP had a nasty aspect to it. Some long-term staffers were pushed out unceremoniously. Others couldn't get on Fiorina's calendar for months, and found they had to go through multiple layers of handlers. Some once-proud HP veterans even stopped talking about the old days. "It wasn't seen as a sign of loyalty," says one former manager. "It was seen as a sign that you were a loser who couldn't get a job anywhere else—and you were suspected of being a Lew [Platt] lover." CFO Bob Wayman would become one of Fiorina's key allies in the Compaq fight, but the word at first was that "Bob doesn't get it." Fiorina rarely sought his advice in her first year on the job, say friends he complained to.

Some found that money played a bigger, different role in the new HP. HP people were always well paid by most standards, but they knew they could earn more at other tech companies. They stayed at HP for the camaraderie and the unique culture, and out of loyalty. Even Bill Hewlett and Dave Packard never paid themselves more than $125,000 per year, according to one article.[2]

In part, Fiorina's huge pay package ended that. HP's other top executives got big raises and stock awards to bring them into balance with the CEO, and to compel them to stay with the company. Others, particularly those loyalists at headquarters, were also offered sweeter deals. When she heard that Brad Driver was thinking of leaving the company, Fiorina offered him an 80 percent raise that bumped his pay to $180,000 and at least that much in stock, says a coworker. Fiorina's big bonuses, even when they paid off in a good way, had some unexpected effects. "I didn't work for money until I worked for Carly. I was being converted into a short-term, pay-me kind of person," says Faraci, who argues that her plan was unfair to lower-level employees, who didn't benefit equally. "HP became classist," he said.

HP changed in other ways, as well. In the past, it had a reputation for fairness with the press, often refusing to dish exclusives or demand special treatment from the media. Now, an imperial egotism crept in. Soon after Fiorina took the helm, the late reporter Tom Quinlan of the *San Jose Mercury News* insisted on answers to some tough questions in an interview with her, say former HP press people. Afterward, HP public relations sent out the command that Quinlan would no longer be granted interviews. The message: "We will not allow reporters to be rude to Carly," according to one former HP publicist.

The attempt to control the coverage continued. The author's own experience with similar treatment came after writing an article posted to *BusinessWeek*'s Web site on the day before the shareholder vote.[3] The article cited sources on the team overseeing the Compaq merger who feared that the merged company would not be able to hit its financial targets—information that was later verified in court. Unhappy with the article, HP demanded that a new reporter be assigned to cover the company and stopped granting interviews to the author. It also went on what sources describe as a "witch hunt" to track down the anonymous sources.

Inside HP, Fiorina made it easy for her detractors to leave. In March 2000, she offered retirement packages that were nearly too good to resist to anyone older than 55. Often, the package included immediate vesting of all options. For those who believed HP's fortunes were sinking—and there were many—it was a no-brainer to leave quickly and cash out. "The moment they said we could retire, it took me five minutes to find the form, five minutes to fill it out, and five minutes to submit it," says Carl Snyder, HP's former head of procurement. Some of HP's most proven executives would leave in the exodus. Antonio Perez, head of the inkjet printer business, left in early 2000. "Cash and fear, that's how she operates," he complained to a friend. LaserJet chief Carolyn Ticknor would leave a year later. Colleagues say Ticknor was uncomfortable with Fiorina's growth-at-all-costs mentality, and that both she and Perez felt Fiorina refused to listen to them. HP says Ticknor retired and Perez left to pursue other interests.

At Lucent, Fiorina was known for a management style that had a heavy dose of showmanship. She earned the same reputation at HP, as she and outside consultants tried to win support for her changes. In July, the company held an event at a Monterey hotel to rally support for the reorganization of HP. Fiorina recruited HPers to stand up and relate how the reinvention had touched them. Vyomesh Joshi, head of the back-end printer group, talked about his initial fears about sharing responsibility for his division rather than running his own show. He said he'd come to realize how much more HP could be under the new approach. Another speaker said he felt as if he had found a new extended family, and that he could grow stronger by learning from others' missteps. It was emotional and moving, say attendees, but left some wondering if it was too much style and not enough substance. With Fiorina emceeing, "It became like Oprah. It was like being in the audience at a TV show," says one attendee. Fiorina, for her part, felt it was effective. "They understood that they were the leaders of the reinvention, not me," she said. "And they saw six months of progress."

To outsiders, Fiorina's reinvention of HP seemed to be right on schedule as of mid-2000. In the quarter that ended April 30, the company posted 15 percent revenue growth and 17 percent profit growth. "This quarter's terrific result is linked directly to our reinvention efforts," Fiorina enthused. "I don't know of any other company that could have gone through the magnitude of changes that we've gone through, and posted the results that we did."

She was riding high. In May, Fiorina appeared on a cable news program to announce that HP had snagged a big contract with online auctioneer eBay away from Sun Microsystems, only to have eBay announce days later that it was sticking with Sun. Though a momentary embarrassment, it was no big worry. Weeks later, the company announced a large deal with Amazon.com. In July, Fiorina shared the dramatic story of her reinvention efforts with the likes of Microsoft's Bill Gates, Berkshire Hathaway's Warren Buffett, and AOL's Steve Case at media mogul Herb Allen's powerfest in Sun Valley, Idaho.

A high point may have come on June 1, when HP sold off its remaining holdings in Agilent. In an event dubbed "Welcome to the New HP," Fiorina laid down an evangelizing challenge to employees: "This company has always done good, but we were not living up to our full potential. . . . We looked in the mirror and saw a great company that was becoming a failure. . . . We have an opportunity to lead in a way that none of our competitors can touch. Is it ambition? You bet. But it suits the capabilities of this company." That day, thanks to the sale of its Agilent stake, HP's stock rose almost 6 percent to $142, up from $116 on the day Fiorina joined the company. Even rivals were taking notice. Sun Microsystems made a video spoofing the company, just as it had other companies over the years. The video, shown inside Sun and at other events around Silicon Valley, features a model standing in front of a flimsy looking garage, which falls down as she complains to the photographer about the cheesy production values. "At some level I was quite flattered," Fiorina told *BusinessWeek*. "They are totally fixated on us. They know we're coming—and they know that if we get our act together, we're dangerous."

nside HP, the distance between perception and the reality of Fiorina's reinvention effort was widening. It had started well enough, but the execution fell down in key areas. One problem was the marketing reinvention. Because HP was so decentralized, it had a ridiculous number of marketing people compared to rivals. Everyone knew this and understood that there had to be a better way. Processes were designed by a marketing reinvention team to do just that. For example, one marketing manager would be assigned for each line of products, rather than one for every single new model. When the company said in early 2000 that the changes would mean the loss of 1,600 marketing jobs, there was almost no outcry. Fiorina even received e-mails from staffers saying they would understand if they were laid off, if HP finally improved the way it handled marketing, say managers involved in the effort.

Then months passed and the cuts weren't made, leaving thousands of people in limbo. Fiorina was furious. Since the marketing managers had failed to follow orders, she laid down an edict in late summer that none of them were allowed to run ads for their products without her okay. It was a year before any significant layoffs occurred, however. By the time the layoffs were made, the economy had begun to decline, and deeper cuts were necessary. "I remember sitting at my PC reading the e-mail, thinking "I can't go through this again," says Allison Graves, who worked on printer marketing. The worst part was that the company hadn't really changed the way it handled marketing. "It just felt like a layoff. People starting getting cynical after that," says one HP executive.

Under the weight of all Fiorina's changes, HP's corporate machinery nearly ground to a halt in late 2000. Normally, salespeople would have their sales quotas by October, so they would know what products they needed to sell to earn their commissions in the new fiscal year. Due to the chaos around the front-end, back-end reorganization, some quotas weren't set until spring, say many managers. Phil Faraci, a member of the reinvention team and one of the speakers at the July leadership meeting, quit around this time. "Lots of us felt Carly was very charismatic, very strong-willed, very quick, and very intelligent—but not very wise. Wisdom is an understanding of what can and cannot be accomplished." HP's board did not share that opinion. On September 22, the company announced that Dick Hackborn was resigning as chair, and that Fiorina would take that mantle. This put her firmly in control of the board. Most of the old-timers with connections to the Hewlett and Packard families were gone. Soon, the only family member still on the board would be Walter Hewlett. Also, Covad Communications Corporation's Robert Knowling, her old customer from Ameritech and US West, had joined the board. Knowling made his allegiances clear in an interview soon after he joined the board. "I didn't join HP. I joined Carly. If she left tomorrow, I'd resign tomorrow. I have a tremendous belief in this person."

By the time she became chair, Fiorina had attempted her biggest move yet. On September 11, 2000, HP admitted it was in discussions to acquire the management consulting arm of Price-waterhouseCoopers (PwC) for as much as $18 billion. This was right in line with her overall strategy. By adding PwC's 31,000 consultants to its own 6,000, HP could focus less on hawking low-margin computers and printers, and more on landing lucrative corporate contracts. The company still wouldn't be a match for IBM, which "filled the skies with wingtips" with its 86,000 consultants—but it would be closer.

It might have been a great idea, but investors hated it. Analysts feared that many of PwC's consultants might leave to work for other consulting firms rather than stick with HP. Then there was the price. To make that $18 billion a good investment, those consultants would have to stick around and bring in huge amounts of business. Indeed, IBM also looked at buying the company around this time, and it concluded that the consultancy was worth roughly half as much as Fiorina was thinking of paying, says an IBM insider. IBM ended up buying PwC for just $3.5 billion in 2002, providing fodder for critics who say Fiorina would have overpaid.

It's easy to see why Fiorina wanted to make a big move. She had successfully lit a fire under the sales force. The company was growing in double digits again, just as she had promised. It had beaten Wall Street's expectations in every quarter she'd been at the helm.

However, she hadn't really addressed the company's strategic problems. In a way, they were worse than ever. The company still wasn't developing many new businesses to speak of, and more than half the growth was in home PCs and laptop PCs—two cutthroat markets in which HP was not going to be able to grow forever.[4] The situation was worse than it looked, because some of HP's key businesses had been "channel stuffing." A salesperson would offer a discount or some other perk to get a retailer or distributor to buy more of HP's product than they would otherwise order. That way, HP could show big sales for that quarter.

However, this is a smoke-and-mirrors tactic, because it essentially robs sales from the next quarter, resulting in an artificial one-time jolt that only serves to raise investors' future expectations. It first occurred in late 1999, the first full quarter on Fiorina's watch, and it reached a peak in the autumn of 2000, say multiple sources who were involved. Because much of the channel stuffing involved ink cartridges, by far HP's most profitable product, the practice propped up HP's bottom line as well as the top line in 2000. "It was totally short-term and short-sighted. It was ridiculous," says one former executive.

Fiorina didn't tell anyone to channel stuff, but she had created an environment where it could take hold, and, according to one executive, she didn't discourage the practice. "She said that channel stuffing is a technical term," says another former executive.

Indeed, at Fiorina's former job, she could always pull off end-of-quarter miracles to hit her goals. At Lucent, the majority of sales came from a few giant phone companies. She could usually hammer out a multiyear deal with one of them in a pinch. That approach doesn't work when selling to thousands of retailers. "The hardest thing to teach Carly when she arrived was that you couldn't just will it at the end of the quarter. We told her 'You really don't want to do this,' but she insisted. She was on a real hubris kick at the time," says one HP executive.

When the fall came, it came quickly. On November 9, Fiorina was advised by HP's financial team that the company was coming up far short of its earnings goals. Sales looked fine, but profits would miss by 25 percent, or $922 million, for the quarter that ended October 31. Many factors contributed to the miss, some of which did not reflect well on Fiorina's management. Despite her calls for spending cuts HP had hired 1,200 people in October alone. Poorly designed sales commissions rewarded the sales force for bringing in any and all orders, regardless of their profitability. Although product went out the door, more of it was low-margin gear such as PCs than management had expected. It was the biggest, most damaging miss of Fiorina's career.

In an emergency meeting with the board a few days later, she apologized, took full responsibility for the miss, and told the board she had ended talks to buy PwC. She even asked that the company keep a $625,000 bonus she was entitled to receive for the latter half of 2000.[5]

Breaking the news to the public would be no picnic. She was scheduled to speak at Comdex on the morning of November 13. Her advisors told her she would need to announce the company's bleak earnings at the trade show. At first, Fiorina was angry that she was going to have to step on her own keynote address, says Drew Brown, a managing director with HP's investor relations firm, Citigate Sard Verbinnen: "It was quiet anger that moved quickly to, okay, what are we going to do about it?"

She handled it in typical Fiorina fashion, working through the weekend and arriving in Vegas on one of HP's jets at around midnight on Sunday. At 2:00 A.M., she went down to rehearse her keynote speech. Then, she and advisors ran through possible questions she might be asked by stock analysts during the teleconference that had been arranged for that morning. At 6 o'clock, she hosted the call from her room at the Bellagio Hotel. "She was fresh as a daisy," says George Sard, her investor relations advisor. "She's just able to move on. It was remarkable."

She performed very well, but investors seemed past caring. The problem wasn't just the size of the loss, but the circumstances. It took the company two weeks after the quarter's end to realize it even had a shortfall, in large part because Fiorina had ordered a massive new computer system to track the newly reorganized company. "They had absolutely no idea what was going on with their business," says Mark Specker, a stock analyst with SoundView Technology Group. "She needs to be real careful that she doesn't get into a bad run. She will be judged on a very, very harsh scale if she does."

Fiorina would dig herself an even deeper hole. In early December, a few days before an all-day presentation with Wall Street analysts, she held a meeting for HP's top brass and asked for their best estimates for the upcoming year. According to one HP advisor, the consensus was that HP was going to be able to post 22 to 25 percent growth in the future. Dubious, Fiorina asked if they were sure. Ironically, by this time, some of her executives had bought in to her go-for-broke mentality, and were simply giving her numbers they thought she would like to hear. "This was the opposite of a CEO browbeating people into committing to a number they weren't comfortable with," says an advisor who was there.

In the end, Fiorina decided to increase HP's growth target for 2001 from 15 percent to as much as 17 percent. That was lower than her executives' estimates, but still high given that the economy was starting to sputter. Her thinking went like this: Although it was clear that HP's home PC and printer boom would not continue forever, she figured her efforts to fix HP's high-end computing businesses were about to pay off.

She may have thought she was being conservative, but that was not how the world took it. Usually, investors cry bravo when CEOs raise growth targets. This time, they openly questioned her judgment. "The 15 percent scenario is an everything-goes-right model. The sun is out, the birds are singing, and there are no unforeseen problems," says SoundView's Specker.

Instead, Fiorina's HP was racing into an everything-goes-wrong scenario. Over the coming months, many CEOs repeatedly revised their financial targets as the economy went into a recession. Some critics began publicly calling for Fiorina to name a chief operating officer to help run day-to-day operations. Scott McNealy had Ed Zander. Bill Gates had Steve Ballmer. Asked if she would consider hiring a chief operating officer, Fiorina said icily in an interview: "I'm running the company the way I think it should be run."

Her handling of the downturn would in fact be better than some—she slashed her growth target for the year to just 5 percent in January, long before many other executives had given in to the somber reality—but her credibility seemed damaged beyond repair. Unlike Steve Jobs, Larry Ellison, and the others, she had not earned the benefit of the doubt from investors. She'd earned many doubts. "I'm somewhat sympathetic," says Sanford Bernstein analyst Toni Sacconaghi, who'd been a critic. "She's making bold moves, and bold moves arouse stronger reactions." Said Fiorina in an interview: "It's not the end of the world. These things happen. You can't change a 60-year-old company without pushing—and there's going to be mistakes. Am I frustrated? Of course. But I didn't come here thinking it would be an easy job. I came in with my eyes wide open."

Internally, workers were tiring of Fiorina's habit of blaming the company rather than questioning her own approach. Many were angered when she pushed out longtime corporate controller Ray Cookingham days after the profit miss. "She used him as a scape-goat," fumes one former executive. In some ways, Fiorina's spell was wearing off. "Everyone wants to like her. She's so warm, and so approachable," says one current manager. "But enough people have been burned."

Fiorina recognized the falling morale, and did her best to rally the troops. She even argued that the earnings miss could be a "gal-vanizing event because it takes away options that we might think we have. When things are going well, you can convince yourself that change isn't as necessary as you thought it was." On December 12, she gave an impassioned speech to employees. "The heartbreak of this quarter is that so many things went well," she said. "We hit a speed bump—a big speed bump—and none of us like the price of the stock. Does this mean that, gee—this is too hard, that we're not capable? No. We're going to double down. In blackjack, you double down when you have an increasing probability of winning. And that's exactly where we are right now." Then, invoking the names of Dave Packard and Dick Hackborn, she urged her employees onward. "If any of you thought this would be a smooth trajectory to the top, you were sadly mistaken. I never had that illusion. It is going to be tough—but that is what greatness is made of. If we stop and look in the mirror, what we just went through can turn out to be a good thing."

As she spoke, many employees who had believed in her fidgeted nervously or looked at the floor. Says one: "I started thinking, 'This gal is in the wrong profession. She should be running for office.'" Her words had begun to ring hollow to some.

Fiorina's mistakes in late 2000 would prove far more long-lasting than anyone could have known. Her failure to take her foot off the growth pedal in late 2000 would create a nasty collision as HP ran into the worst downturn in tech industry history. Over the next six months, HP's workers would pay the price. In December, the company imposed a pay freeze and asked all employees to take five days of unpaid leave. That was fine—well in keeping with HP's "all-for-one" credo. In January came the second round of marketing layoffs. Another 1,700 people lost their jobs.

As sales kept plummeting, the cuts kept coming. In April, the company issued bans on cell phones and air travel, and announced that 3,000 people would be let go. In June, management told employees they would need to sacrifice more to pull the company through. Human resources vice president Susan Bowick said that some executives wanted to do another layoff, but Fiorina insisted that the company give workers some options. "We've asked a lot of them already," Fiorina said.

The employees came through. Roughly 86 percent of them signed up to take either a pay cut or time off worth 10 percent of their salary through October 31, saving HP $130 million. A memo went out saying that the voluntary cut didn't mean escape from a layoff. Still, when the company announced it was cutting 6,000 jobs in July, many felt betrayed. It was the biggest layoff in HP's history. "Either she's gotten remarkably bad advice, or she's trying to anger people," says one worker at HP Labs.

Other companies were slashing their payrolls, too, but angry HP employees railed at how the cuts were made. The HP Way had always been for managers to look employees in the eye and tell them why they were being let go. This time, word came down from above. Many employees were convinced that names had been chosen not to cull poor performers but to make sure that the layoffs were imposed across the board—as if the company were more concerned about preventing lawsuits than keeping good people. "It was the first of the drive-by shootings," says one person who left around that time. "It's getting to be like Chainsaw Carly," says another. "Winning e-companies with shining souls don't lay off 6,000 people." HP denies that the cuts were made to avoid lawsuits, but does admit that the process could have been handled better.

Many remained fiercely loyal, but a sense of loss set in as people felt management slipping. One staffer in Roseville, California, had asked to be laid off so he could get the severance package. When his manager refused, he was put into a job he had no idea how to do. His division was so chaotic that he found he could work just two days a week, and no one noticed. "I used to work 80 hours a week. Now, it's like early retirement. A lot of higher-ups think things are okay, but they're broken left, right, and center." Said another Roseville worker: "I think she lost most people a long time ago. Nobody really listens to her anymore. They hear her speak, but if there's no execution, you can say all you want, Carly."

Part of the anger was financial, no doubt. In late 2000, Fiorina replaced HP's profit-sharing plan with a "total rewards system." The plan would have paid HP employees as much as a 15 percent bonus if the economy had held up and the company hit her financial and market share targets. Instead, employees got nothing—which was a far cry from the 2 to 9 percent profit-sharing check they'd grown used to in the past. It was just another backfire. Rather than light a fire under employees, her pay policies demoralized them.

By mid-2001, some employees were in no mood to hide their anger any longer. The company had to close down an internal message board that some workers were using to lob obscenities at Fiorina. That only made matters worse, fueling Fiorina's "let them eat cake" reputation. The site was temporarily put back up, but soon closed again. Sources close to the issue say Allison Johnson demanded that the site be taken down or "heads would roll."

9

COMPAQ COMETH

The visual I see is a slow-motion collision of two garbage trucks.
—Sun Microsystems CEO Scott McNealy

In early 2001, Walter Hewlett was in mourning for his father. The end had not been easy. His father's health had taken a turn for the worse in 1998 when he suffered another stroke. Then, in mid-November 2000, while Walter and his wife were celebrating their anniversary in Carmel, California, he got horrible news. A fire had ripped through his father's Los Altos Hills home. Firefighters who rushed to the scene had evacuated the 87-year-old man from a second-floor balcony off his bedroom.

In the ensuing weeks, his ailing father had stayed in Walter's small living room. Usually filled with books and musical instruments, the room was overtaken by the nursing staff and medical equipment. Just a week after they found a permanent apartment for him, on January 12, Bill Hewlett died.

Walter Hewlett had always known his father's death would be hard. He'd once told fellow board member Jay Keyworth that "the privilege of my life is to be my father's son." As letters from former HPers and others poured in, he resolved to answer them all, and not with just a signature and a thank you. For the next few months, he spent hour upon hour writing heartfelt return notes to some 300 well-wishers. "He is not a letter writer," his wife Esther explains. "Maybe it was part of the healing process. It was as though these people were family to him."

On May 2, Hewlett made a $400-million gift to Stanford—at the time the largest gift ever to a university. It was a fitting last honor to Bill Hewlett, who along with Dave Packard had given more than $300 million to the university where they had met so many years before.

There were no outward signs of trouble between Walter Hewlett and Carly Fiorina as of early 2001. However, Hewlett had his concerns about her and about the board, which he felt would not stand up to her. He says he protested when the board made her chair, arguing it should not hand over so much power to the new CEO.[1] At one point in early 2001, with the stock price falling, he says she asked the directors to make public statements of support for her. Hewlett says he refused, although he did not tell the board or Fiorina his reasons.

"I personally felt it was an inappropriate thing for an employee of the board to do," he says. "She works for us. I didn't do it—and it wasn't because I didn't support Carly."

However, Hewlett hoped that Fiorina would change her ways after the November financial debacle. In the emergency board meeting, she'd talked about the need to tighten operations. Confident that Fiorina had scuttled all talk of megamergers, he even invested about $7 million to buy 200,000 HP shares later that month. His assumptions were wrong. By early January, Dick Hackborn was already mulling the idea of merging with Compaq. At first glance, it appeared that the companies' computer businesses were mirror images, but Hackborn found there was far less overlap than he'd thought. Compaq had muscle in corporate PCs, storage, and handheld devices. HP was strong in home PCs and Unix servers. "He clearly saw the fit," says Carolyn Ticknor, who talked with him about an HP-Compaq merger at the time. When Keyworth called Hackborn some weeks later to discuss merger ideas, Hackborn again mentioned Compaq. In March, Keyworth met with Fiorina in her office, and explained Hackborn's thinking.[2] "She was not surprised," says Keyworth. Indeed, she told him that Capellas had called her recently. "He's coming to see me."

As the economy continued to tank, support for a big merger rose. On April 18, Fiorina lowered her financial targets for the second time that year, warning that growth would be flat in the next two quarters. As usual, printers were carrying far too much of the profit load for the company. Unless other parts of the business pulled their weight, the company would be forced to cut back investment in its printing business, too.

In May, Fiorina hired the prestigious consulting firm McKinsey & Company to look into HP's strategic options, including a possible acquisition. Various dance partners were considered, including Xerox Corporation. In the end, McKinsey recommended five possibilities. HP could go it alone. It could pare back anything not related to the printer business. It could sell off the troubled PC computer business or, alternatively, spin off the printer division to unleash its full value. Buying Compaq was not among McKinsey's recommendations, say insiders. That was ironic, considering the later deal, but not surprising. HP might be sick from its exposure to the PC business, but Compaq was in intensive care. It had long since lost its market share crown to feisty Texas rival Dell Computer. All told, the company was stuck in a miserable cycle of cost-cutting and layoffs.

It hadn't always been so for Compaq. Like HP, its creation was the stuff of high-tech legend. In 1982, after IBM had just introduced the first PC, three managers from Texas Instruments, Inc., scribbled a design for a "luggable" PC on the back of a paper place mat as they sat in a Houston pie shop. Two years later, sales had rocketed to $111 million, making Compaq the fastest-growing start-up in American business history. It wouldn't stop there. By the mid-1990s, Compaq was the unquestioned champ of the PC market, from laptops to home PCs to back-office Windows-based servers.

By 1999, those days were a distant memory. After firing CEO Eckhard Pfeiffer in April 2000 amid mounting losses, the company tried in vain to attract a new outside CEO. When it came up short, the job fell to Compaq executive Michael Capellas. A native of the working-class mill town of Warren, Ohio, he was a self-described geek who had worked his way up to become Compaq's chief technology officer in 1998. Known for his operational skills and regular-guy management style, Capellas did what he could to get the company back on track. Within a year, he tightened up operations and finally began making headway on selling PCs directly over the Internet, like Dell did.[3]

Over the next two years, Capellas and Fiorina's careers would follow an eerily similar course. They were named CEO within three days of each other. They arguably had the two toughest jobs in the computer industry—two first-time CEOs foisted on troubled companies, where they tangled with powerful veterans such as Jobs, Gates, and Dell. Before long, Fiorina and Capellas announced nearly identical Internet-based strategies, neither of which earned many kudos.

They met in mid-2000, when they joined forces to help launch a consortium of companies that were going to buy one another's products in an online e-marketplace. The CEOs were smitten with each other. "We agreed on just about everything," Fiorina said later. In fact, they even joked at that first introduction that maybe they should do a merger. "It was like spontaneous combustion," says George Devlin, then Compaq's vice president for operations.

Their joke took its first step toward becoming reality in May. Fiorina first mentioned the idea to the full board at its May meeting, say Hewlett and another board member. "She said that Capellas wanted to sell the company," the other board member said. Fiorina called Sonsini to ask for his services on May 17. By then, the companies were in "very early preliminary stages" of negotiations, Sonsini says. According to HP, the talks didn't really start until June 22, when Fiorina called Capellas about licensing some of HP's computer software. He quickly suggested that HP just buy Compaq outright.

From the start, the two sides were intent on getting the deal done, says Sonsini, who was a key player in the negotiations. Unlike many mergers, HP wasn't looking to squeeze Compaq for the best price and send its executives packing, he says. On the contrary, HP wanted something akin to a "merger of equals" to ensure that

Compaq's executives and other employees stuck around to help HP change its ways. Compaq had a more aggressive sales staff, a huge customer base, and a faster decision-making process. To protect the deal, the lawyers added a number of clauses to make it hard for either side to walk away. There would be a $675-million breakup fee if either side terminated talks without a better offer. There was no "collar" on the stock price; no matter how much either stock rose or fell, there was no renegotiating price.

Fiorina and the board liked many aspects of the deal. Financially, it looked solid. Even if the merged company sacrificed some sales while focusing on the integration, it would be able to cut up to $3.9 billion a year by 2004, mostly by slashing 15,000 jobs. Those savings alone would give investors a $5 to $9 bump on the stock price. It also seemed like the best strategic alternative. Compaq's direct-selling capability could boost PC profits. Adding Compaq's computer services business would give HP another reliable cash cow, alongside printers.

Indeed, HP and Compaq would prove many skeptics wrong by putting together by far the most detailed, comprehensive merger plan the industry had ever seen. From the start, HP's board took a hard look at the areas where other companies typically trip up—by failing to eliminate overlapping product lines or ignoring customer service during the transition, for example.

Early on, they assigned respected executives to run an elaborate postmerger integration process. It was comprised of 23 separate teams that attended to details on everything from computer systems to human resources. Together, they comprised a so-called clean-team operation that worked solely on the integration. Because they would become intimately involved with the other company's data, such as forecasts and pricing schedules, clean-team members left their day jobs to avoid antitrust violations. To avoid endless bickering over which products would survive, they took an "adopt-and-go" approach. Whatever problems low-level managers couldn't resolve on Monday were kicked up to the next level, ultimately going to a six-person committee that included the two CEOs. The goal was to have as many details as possible finished by the day the merger was launched, right down to making sure a Compaq employee's paycheck had the HP name printed on it. "We can always improve the boat, but it's got to float when you launch," says Webb McKinney, a 33-year HP veteran in charge of integration on the HP side.

However, there's no guarantee that even the best merger plan will fly—and Compaq and HP's track records in that department were as dismal as that of the 1962 New York Mets. Capellas's management team had learned a lot from cleaning up the Compaq-DEC merger mess. Tandem Computer, while doing well, was operating almost as independently as it had before Compaq bought the company, say sources. As for HP, it had almost nothing to show for its few large deals. Its defensive 1989 purchase of Apollo Computer had done little to slow the rise of Sun Microsystems. In May 2001, Fiorina had sold off what remained of VeriFone for pennies on the dollar, just two years after Rick Belluzzo had purchased it. Then there was Bluestone Software. HP paid $467 million for the 500-person company in October 2000, promising to use Bluestone's product to become a leader in Internet software. Instead, most of its executives jumped ship as Bluestone got lost within HP's chaotic structure. "I thought it was botched from day one. I don't think HP knows how to integrate companies," says one Bluestone executive. In July 2002, HP discontinued its effort with Bluestone.

None of management's arguments made much of an impact on Walter Hewlett. He had more general reasons for hating the Compaq deal. It didn't really matter how many numbers or studies the McKinsey or Goldman Sachs advisors showed him. The deal was too big, disruptive, and illogical. What sense was there in sharing HP's printer business in order to double up on the size of its PC business? "I'm a mathematician. I know all about numbers," says Hewlett. "You can make numbers say anything you want." In the end, HP would simply be a gargantuan company struggling to churn a profit in lousy businesses.

Nonetheless, talks heated up. By early July, Hewlett was getting the impression he was being isolated—easy enough to do, as he was a minority of one. He missed a teleconference on July 10, when he was in the Sierra Nevadas. Each year, he hosted 100 or so HP and

Agilent employees who rode in the annual Markleeville Death Ride bicycle race at the Hewlett place on Lake Tahoe. He says he'd left word where he would be, but a secretary had misunderstood his directions and only left messages for him at his home. He says that because no one ever reached him, the board should have tried his Stanford lab or the secretary who oversaw Bill Hewlett's old office. "They had other numbers, and they never tried them," he charges.

Fiorina and Wayman told the directors at that meeting that the board would take a closer look at the merger at a two-day meeting to be held on July 19 and 20, according to government filings. Keyworth says board members had also been told at the May meeting that the July meeting would be crucial. Hewlett says that meetings had been scheduled and then cancelled numerous times in the interim, and that the board knew he planned to miss the Thursday session to play in a concert at Bohemian Grove on the first day. He'd missed that day of the meeting the previous three years for the same reason, he says. "Nobody ever said 'We know you go up to Bohemian Grove on that day, but you have to be at the meeting,'" says Hewlett.

This time, in his absence, the board spent the day in deep debate. Hackborn demanded to know why management was confident it wouldn't lose more sales. Sam Ginn questioned why HP would want to increase its PC exposure. The board would later consider another McKinsey report that suggested this tech merger might work where others had failed. Because the industry was maturing so quickly, this was more akin to a merger of consolidation—the tactic that had helped GM, Exxon-Mobil, and SBC become giants in their respective fields. Other directors, such as Ginn and Phil Condit, who had been through the AirTouch–Vodafone and Boeing–McDonnell Douglas mergers, respectively, found it useful.

By the morning after his concert, Hewlett was the only director who opposed proceeding with merger talks. He was overruled, and Goldman Sachs was hired to start pulling the deal together. During a midmorning break, Hackborn asked Hewlett to join him in a cubicle to chat about the previous day's events. Hewlett believed he was having a private conversation with a longtime friend. He said he told Hackborn that the merger was "a terrible idea." "I don't think I am going to be able to recommend it to the [Hewlett] Foundation," he added.[4]

After the meeting ended, around noon, Hewlett approached Keyworth on the patio just off the boardroom. "What's the crisis here, Jay?" he asked, according to both men.

"I don't think there's a crisis, Walter," Keyworth responded. "But we have a big problem, and we need to fix it. Now it's time to close ranks, Walter. You've had your say. We have to pull together."

"No, Jay, I think this is just the wrong thing to do. I think it's an incredibly bad idea," Hewlett said.

Keyworth was exasperated. "That's what kids [say]. That's not a dialogue."

Just then, Fiorina came storming onto the patio, and made a beeline for Hewlett. "I assume you're not talking about the weather," she said to the two board members.

"No, we're not talking about the weather," Hewlett says he responded, smiling.

Then he noticed her tone. "Walter, you are a director of this company, and this is inside information. You are obligated not to talk to anyone about this," she barked, according to Hewlett. Hewlett was insulted at the accusation, but more surprised at Fiorina's demeanor. "It was the first time I'd ever seen her that mad. She was quite aggressive," he claims.

Then Hewlett put two and two together, recalling his comment to Hackborn about not being able to recommend the merger to the Hewlett Foundation. He thinks Hackborn must have shared that information with Fiorina.

From then on, he assumed that no conversation he had with a board member was private. "I realized that this former friend was no longer someone I could trust," he says.

Hewlett would miss one more meeting, on July 30. There was no good excuse this time. He was climbing Mount Whitney in Southern California with his wife and daughter at the start of what would be a 17-day cross-country road trip. Hewlett had no regrets about missing the meeting, which was held via phone. "It was just an informational meeting," to give an update on the talks, he says.

What to make of all these missed meetings? It's easy to see why

Hewlett's colleagues were frustrated. "Walter did not work as hard as other board members to analyze the situation and decide how to go forward. I feel he was obligated to talk it through. He absolutely refused to do it," says Keyworth. "He reminds me of a medieval crusader, he was so self-righteous. It was blatantly obvious to everyone that Walter did not and never had acknowledged the need for a fix."

Other insiders who have known Hewlett over the years aren't sure they buy his story, either. "Walter is an academic guy who very much wants to do the right thing," says former CEO John Young. "But he's kind of distracted. It doesn't surprise me that he chose to play cello rather than be at that board meeting."

However, that hardly absolves Fiorina or her board for the onerous clash with Hewlett that came their way. People who have known Hewlett paint a similar picture. He tends to be quiet, analytical, and collaborative. "Walter is not the type to try to grab control of a board or twist arms to force his opinion on anyone," said Agilent board member James Cullen, the former president of Bell Atlantic Corporation. In a sense, that may have led Fiorina to underestimate his willingness to pick a fight. Conversely, everyone has their limit—and the board should have known that a grumble from Hewlett was like a rant from someone else.

In the coming months, HP would vilify Hewlett for taking them on after voting for the Compaq deal in the boardroom. Most experts think the company deserves the blame for planting the seeds. "Either they failed to persuade him, or they ignored him," says Charles Elson, director of the Center for Corporate Governance at the University of Delaware.

Says Ralph Ward, editor of the *Boardroom Insider,* an industry newsletter, "It's a faux pas when a director opposes a deal; when it's a family member, it's hari-kari time. The family members should have been on board, or it should have been a nonstarter."

From the start, Fiorina knew the Compaq acquisition would be controversial. She says that she and Capellas talked freely about how "the market is going to hate this deal." "Are you sure you want to do this?" a Goldman Sachs banker asked Fiorina, according to one advisor. After a quick analysis, the bankers advised Fiorina that

HP's stock would take a 10 to 15 percent dive as investors got used to the deal, versus the typical 5 to 10 percent on most others. The deal made sense, the bankers advised, but it was going to be a rough ride.

The deal almost didn't happen. On August 5, Compaq called off the talks. "It was a necessary pause," says Sonsini, who says talks were getting bogged down in details. One factor was the future role of Michael Capellas. Initially, HP envisioned him running a division or possibly taking the role of chief operating officer. That wasn't good enough for Compaq. Says one HP advisor, "I don't think HP wanted to offer Capellas the big job unless they had to."

It turns out that Capellas, who declined to comment for this book, was also exploring options. Sometime during or about the 10-day hiatus when the deal was on hold, Michael Dell invited Capellas to discuss a possible merger of the two Texas PC giants. Dell would probably have shut down Compaq's PC business and tried to expand Dell's high-end computer business, selling servers, storage, and the like to big corporations, says one Dell insider.

Dell wasn't much interested, it turned out, especially once it became clear how far down the path Compaq had been with HP, says the source. Once talks between HP and Compaq resumed in late August, there was no turning back.

Hewlett believes there was never enough honest debate about the deal, partly because the board never met without Fiorina present.

"That's a corporate governance no-no," says Harvard Business School human relations professor Jay W. Lorsch. "Directors are reluctant to oppose management when they're in the room. It's a law of the boardroom. Then again, if I were Carly, I would have wanted to stay."

Hewlett also fumed when he heard that Fiorina sold 87,817 shares, worth $2.3 million, on July 17, with the Compaq talks under way. "She knew she had inside information," he said later. "I would have loved to sell some of my shares, but it would have been completely improper. It's unconscionable that she would do that." The company points out that Fiorina sold shares to cover taxes due on a huge restricted stock grant issued that day, per her employment contract. Hewlett says that's no excuse. "It may be legal, but it's not ethical. Being an insider can be inconvenient."

All this led up to one penultimate board meeting at Wilson Sonsini's offices on August 30. That was when Hewlett says Larry Sonsini told him he had a duty to vote with the board—even if he wanted to vote his shares against the deal later.

After that meeting, Hewlett and his wife made the three-hour drive to their mountain cabin. That weekend, he struggled over what to do. He says he did not want to vote for the deal, but he feared that if he opposed it, Compaq would demand a higher purchase price. Then he briefly settled on a third course: to resign. It didn't last. "I've been involved one way or another with this company for 50 years," he says. "For me to pick up my marbles at this critical juncture just didn't seem right. Out of respect for the employees, I decided to stick with it."

That Monday, the board met to take its final vote. Hewlett decided to okay the deal, to maintain the board's unanimity—but he says he made it clear that he did not like the deal. "We're still very early in this process, and there's a lot that we don't know," he claims to have said. "But knowing what I know now, I'd vote my shares against this merger if the vote were today."

His colleagues insist he did not say that he planned to vote his shares against the deal. They say Hewlett did not give the appearance of being a few months from waging a proxy war against them. "I really believe Walter didn't know at the time that he was going to lead an opposition fight," says Sonsini, who thinks Hewlett later succumbed to the falling stock price, pressure from friends and relatives, and concern for HP's future. "I'm not sure it wasn't just fear of change."

While Walter Hewlett was obsessing deep in the Sierras, an army of executives, bankers, handlers, and lawyers were in New York pulling together final preparations for the biggest computer merger in history. Hewlett may have thought the only remaining detail to be negotiated was price, but there was still tons to be done—organizational details of the new company, postmerger pay packages, and the like. "I was up from Saturday morning through Tuesday night," recalls lawyer Marty Korman. "If price were the only thing on the table, I could have gone to sleep."

Getting off to a good start with such a controversial deal would be crucial. That Sunday, Goldman's bankers asked Fiorina to run the script for the press conference past its influential computer industry stock analyst Laura Conigliaro. The tough-minded Conigliaro warned Fiorina against overselling the deal. Rather than wax on about the new company's shining future, she should acknowledge the huge integration challenges, Conigliaro advised. Fiorina listened intently as Conigliaro told her that she was already viewed as "over-promotional." Based on the input, the companies moved up some slides in their presentation that pointed to the risks of the deal.

The Mike and Carly show came off well enough. On the evening of Labor Day, public relations put out the word. The next morning, the two CEOs took the stage to make their pitch as Sting's optimistic "Brand New Day" boomed on the sound system. By the time they exited, a tide of scorn was rising. Investors absolutely despised the deal. At day's end, the stock had dropped 18 percent—more than even Goldman had feared. Within two days, HP would fall another 3.5 percent. Even Compaq's already depressed shares fell, as investors knocked $13 billion off the value of the two companies. Investors competed for the best insulting metaphor to describe the deal. "It's like taking two stones and tying them together to see if they float," said one.[5] Others talked about two drunks trying to hold each other up, or how the deal was a cross between a turkey and an albatross. Rivals seemed especially happy for the newlyweds. "The visual I see is a slow-motion collision of two garbage trucks," Sun Microsystems' Scott McNealy would quip.[6]

The company recruited powerful friends to stanch the bleeding. The day after the deal was announced, Oracle Corporation CEO Larry Ellison and Intel Corporation CEO Craig Barrett were asked to call the author as *BusinessWeek* put a story to bed. Both liked the deal on paper, but were hardly gushing with confidence. Said Ellison: "The great thing about HP is they have a very strong culture—and the worst thing about HP is that they have a very strong culture. She will still have to make the company into a more aggressive selling machine." Barrett opted against sharing an opinion about whether the companies could execute such a behemoth merger. "Those are fun things to speculate about, and in two years from now we'll know the answer."

10

THE NOVEMBER SURPRISE

*I became a public figure because I had to. It was not part of my
plan. It was my lot in life to fight this battle.*

—WALTER HEWLETT

When Wall Street opened for business on September 4, it
took only minutes for Walter Hewlett's worst nightmare to begin. Investors dumped HP shares in droves,
driving the stock south 18 percent. By the end of the day, the $1.9-
billion Hewlett Foundation lost more than $100 million, and the
$3.5-billion Hewlett family trust lost more than $350 million.
Hewlett lost a bundle, as well—he owned 439,000 shares. No other
board member owned more than 18,000, save Fiorina, who'd been
given nearly 900,000 shares and options by the board.[1]

For Hewlett, the stock plunge was a horrible vindication of his
views. The world was screaming its disapproval of the merger. The
pundits were making many of the same arguments he had made.
That weekend, Hewlett had his first opportunity to talk with anyone
other than his wife about the deal. It was the weekend of the annual
deer hunt at the San Felipe ranch. The founders' old weekend
haunt was still coowned by the two families. Hewlett had kept up the
annual tradition of a September deer hunt with friends, including

many HP old-timers. Among them were Arjay Miller, a former HP board member, and Jim Gaither, a Hewlett Foundation trustee and longtime friend. Sipping drinks on the patio under the stars, Hewlett asked his friends to share what they knew about mergers. Gaither had plenty of experience as a corporate lawyer and venture capitalist. Miller had been the president of Ford Motor Company before becoming dean of Stanford's business school in 1969.

Both were pessimistic. Gaither said HP's cheerful explanations for the deal sounded far too similar to Compaq's initial reasons for buying DEC, and everyone knew how that had worked out. Miller, fearing the integration morass of putting the companies together, agreed. "Your chances of succeeding are not good," he said.

"I think I have an obligation to say how I feel," Hewlett said.

The next week, Hewlett began to act. One of his first moves was to visit with Gaither. As Hewlett recounted his summer of misery, Gaither grew furious. He was dumbfounded that HP would have made such a controversial deal without first getting the support of the Hewlett Foundation, the Packard Foundation, and the founders' children. HP advisors claim that in not courting the families, the company was only following the wishes of the foundations to be treated like all other shareholders. If the foundations wanted to buy and sell shares without concern of breaking the law, the board had to keep insider information from them.

Bunk, Gaither thought. This wasn't just any old acquisition. This was a risky, bet-the-farm move by an unproven CEO that would fundamentally change the character of the company. In deals this controversial involving such huge shareholders—particularly when there were powerful founding families involved—companies always locked up support up front, or they didn't do the deal. Even if HP's board hadn't sought this support, he found it puzzling that Compaq's advisors wouldn't have demanded voting agreements to make sure the families were on board before proceeding with the deal. Still, this was no time for rash action, Gaither advised. There were so many questions to consider. Was there anything Hewlett could do to realistically stop the deal that he had voted for? He was cotrustee of the vast family trust, all of which was earmarked for the Hewlett Foundation over time. Could he vote the trust's shares as he wished, or should the foundation make that call? The next step, Gaither said, was to get legal advice. With so many roles in this developing drama, almost any move Hewlett made could have legal consequences. For help, Gaither suggested that he call Steve Neal, the current CEO of his former employer, Cooley Godward.

Hewlett also decided to contact Laurie Hoagland, the Hewlett Foundation's chief investment officer, and ask him to do an objective analysis of the deal. If Hoagland agreed the deal was a loser, his analysis would validate Hewlett's pessimism. His report would also advise the foundation on how to vote its shares. If the foundation's trustees agreed the deal was wrong-headed, Hewlett could go public, representing not only his own shares but those of the family trust and the foundation, as well.

In mid-September, Hewlett met with Hoagland at the Hewlett Foundation, tucked away in a pine grove in Menlo Park. Hoagland, who had run Stanford's huge endowment fund before coming to work at the foundation, knew what he thought. When he'd heard the news on September 4, he'd scribbled down a list of "top 10 reasons to hate this deal." But he promised Hewlett he would launch an objective analysis. Hewlett said that if Hoagland recommended the deal, he would probably vote the family trust shares in favor, too.

Clearly, the David and Lucile Packard Foundation, HP's single largest shareholder, would be the wild card. It owned 10.2 percent of HP's stock, versus 5.2 percent for all the Hewlett interests. If it refused to join Hewlett's crusade, his opposition might well be a toothless, symbolic gesture by a lone-wolf board member. Unless the families put up a united front, Hewlett could do more harm than good by setting off a divisive fight that could hurt the stock and morale within HP. "I don't want to do anything proactively until we know which way the Packards will come out," Hoagland told Hewlett.

Both men knew the Packard clan would be hit hard by the stock's swoon. While the Hewlett Foundation had been diversifying its holdings for years, the Packard Foundation still had 85 percent of its wealth tied up in HP and Agilent stock. Still, getting them to join him in a public protest would be tricky. David Woodley Packard, Dave Packard's eldest child, would be no problem. The first time Hewlett spoke with him, a few days after the merger was announced, the former Latin teacher had made it clear that he despised the deal. That meant Hewlett could probably count on the shares of his Packard Humanities Institute, which owned 1.3 percent.[2]

That was a nice chunk of support, but nowhere near the Packard Foundation's stake. As such, Packard's opinion was not one of those that mattered most. Those belonged to his three sisters, none of whom was looking for a fight. Julie Packard, a vice chair on the board, ran the Monterey Bay Aquarium. Her husband, Robert Stephens, also on the board, was an environmentalist who ran a nursery. Marine biologist Nancy Packard Burnett was also a vice chair. However, it was Susan Packard Orr whose support was most important. The Foundation's chair, she had always taken her father's advice to let the professional managers do the managing; that was a main reason she'd stepped off HP's board in 2000. But how best to influence her views? Her brother was probably already bending her ear about the Compaq deal. Complicating matters was the fact that Orr liked Carly Fiorina, and the two women kept in touch. Hewlett decided he would be better off letting Hoagland's report do the talking.

As Hewlett was preparing to leave, Hoagland, a soft-spoken man with a runner's build, had a final question. "Have you thought about where this could all be heading?" he asked. "I don't know how close you've ever been to a proxy fight, but have you ever taken the time to read those full-page ads you sometimes see in the papers? They tend to be pretty expensive, and to get pretty personal and vitriolic. If it gets to that, you better be prepared for some real unpleasantness."

Hewlett didn't make much of a response. "He just took it on board," said Hoagland.

On the morning of September 23, Keith Flaum was looking forward to coming to work. Flaum, a 38-year-old partner at Cooley Godward, was going to meet Walter Hewlett. Like most at the firm, Flaum knew little about Hewlett beyond his famous last name. Now, the mysterious scion, who had voted with HP's board in favor of the Compaq merger less than a month ago, wanted them to help him oppose it.

This was going to be a fascinating case, Flaum believed. It was a chance to work on one of the biggest deals in high-tech history and to represent a member of one of Silicon Valley's royal families. It was also a chance to undo a deal that had been put together by Cooley Godward's more famous archrival, Wilson Sonsini.

Hewlett arrived around 10:00 A.M. that day, wearing his usual khakis and buttoned-down shirt. Flaum and Neal showed him to a tiny conference room. As Hewlett told the lawyers his story, he could peer out the window to see HP's headquarters looming down the road. For four hours, Hewlett talked nonstop. Often closing his eyes and clenching his jaw in frustration, he recalled the times he had told boardmates of his opposition, and recounted in detail lawyer Larry Sonsini's advice to him before the acquisition was announced. "Walter was hugely emotional," says Flaum. "I felt from then on that Walter had been treated unfairly. He was clearly a considerate, nonmanipulative guy."

Hewlett described the weird web of interlocking relationships that was at work. Dick Hackborn, Fiorina's key supporter, sat on the board of the Hewlett Foundation. Former HP CEO Lew Platt and one-time chief operating officer Dean Morton were on the Packard Foundation. Hewlett said he had no idea what the Packards thought of the deal, but made it clear that he was not prepared to do anything that would pit the two families against each other. "It's always been a great relationship," he warned. "Whatever happens, you have to keep that in mind."

The lawyers quickly saw that Hewlett was on treacherous legal ground. They warned him against telling David Woodley Packard too much about his plans. If the two men cooperated in opposing the deal, they would have to file a document with the Securities and Exchange Commission declaring themselves a voting bloc. That would force Hewlett to go public before he knew his course of action.

Still, the lawyers began to chew on what Hewlett's opposition might mean for HP. Wilson Sonsini might have designed the merger to withstand many challenges, but what about a challenge waged by a rogue board member? The merger agreement included a battery of provisions to make it nearly impossible for either company to back out of the deal. Were they all legal, if they prevented a board member from acting on a sincere belief that the deal would hurt shareholders? Might Hewlett be sued by shareholders or by the company if he successfully scotched the deal, and HP incurred the $675-million breakup fee? There were many such questions for Flaum and Neal to ponder as Hewlett headed home.

By mid-October, after 10 or so meetings, the bare outlines of a strategy took shape. Hewlett would wait for Hoagland's report and see whether the Hewlett Foundation wanted to oppose the merger. He would also hire his own financial expert to advise him on how to vote the family trust's shares. Then he would wait for the Packard Foundation vote. If the Packards voted down the deal, the management at HP and Compaq might be forced to see the writing on the wall. Rather than fight the inevitable, the companies might work out a deal to go their separate ways.

For a financial advisor, Gaither suggested that Hewlett call San Francisco–based Friedman Fleischer & Lowe (FFL), a private equity firm. It wasn't an obvious fit, because private equity firms make money by buying out-of-favor companies, but FFL would be able to do the hard-bitten financial analysis of the Compaq acquisition— and most big investment banks wouldn't want to risk ruffling the feathers of HP, a huge potential customer. Gaither knew FFL CEO Tully Friedman, who ran the company's offices from an elegant office overlooking San Francisco Bay. Gaither also knew Friedman did not think much of the Compaq deal. Friedman had said as much at a board meeting of Levi Strauss & Company, where both men were directors.

When Friedman got the call about Hewlett from Neal, he hesitated. Friedman smelled a public fight, and he wanted no part of it. During his long career as an investment banker and deal maker, he knew there were far easier ways to make money than to get embroiled in a corporate catfight. Besides, he didn't know Walter Hewlett from Adam. Friedman insisted on meeting Hewlett in mid-October to make sure he wasn't just some disgruntled, meddling family member.

After meeting Hewlett, Friedman, a bearish man with a cutting sense of humor, quickly changed his mind. He was impressed with

Hewlett's understanding of the business issues at hand, and with his story. Friedman agreed to do a financial analysis of the Compaq deal, which to him felt roughly akin to a public service. After all, this wasn't just a corporate deal. If FFL helped to kill the Compaq deal, he felt, it would be serving the needs of the Hewlett Foundation and Packard Foundations and their good works, too. The money wasn't bad, either: a flat fee of $500,000 for what would likely be a three-week project.[3]

By late October, Hewlett had decided he was going to have to publicly declare his opposition to the merger. HP's humiliation on Wall Street was intensifying, and Compaq's declining fortunes were making the merger look like even more of a loser. On October 23, the company reported absolutely abysmal results for its third quarter. Mergers are valued based on a company's future earnings potential. Hewlett thought the initial deal had been far too generous to Compaq shareholders. Now that Wall Street had slashed its earnings estimates for Compaq by 70 percent, it looked like an even bigger rip-off. "I became a public figure because I had to," Hewlett later said. "It was not part of my plan. It was my lot in life to fight this battle."

Because the HP shareholder vote was expected to be held in early 2002, Laurie Hoagland figured he would have until at least January to finish his appraisal of the merger. However, as the stock languished and the chorus of criticism continued, Walter Hewlett decided to act sooner rather than later. HP was pouring time and money into setting its new course for the future. If he was to stop the deal, the sooner the better. He asked Hoagland and the team at FFL to finish their analyses in time for HP's next board meeting, scheduled for early November.

Emotional pressure was also building. Family members and HP old-timers were encouraging Hewlett to do something. David Woodley Packard was all but demanding it. An emotional man with his father's forceful nature, he'd quit HP's board in protest of the Agilent spin-off in 1999. He'd done his best to distance himself from the company, but in recent months he'd come to despise Fiorina. He'd loathed her garage ad, which he felt was a shameless marketing effort that his father would have never dreamed of doing. The last straw came when he heard that the Compaq merger would require 15,000 layoffs. With that, he'd read through 12 boxes full of Fiorina's speeches and other public comments. "She loved quoting my father, but it was almost always out of context," he says. "She has no idea what my father was like, but the way she talks you'd think she were his favorite daughter."

As weeks passed, Packard repeatedly prodded Hewlett to go public with his concerns. "I've got to wait," Hewlett would tell him. At every meeting with his lawyers, Hewlett would ask "Can I announce yet?" recalled Flaum. Again and again, lawyers walked him through the myriad legal and strategic reasons to wait for the analyses to be finished, and Hewlett would back off. "Yes, I under-stand," he'd say.

There was other planning to be done. In case Hoagland and FFL gave the merger a thumbs down, Hewlett would need to pull together a team to help him make his case to the world. HP had dozens of lawyers, financial analysts, press relations people and support staff, not to mention outside consultants and private planes. Hewlett had a fax machine in his closet at home. He didn't even use e-mail much.

To get started, Tully Friedman hired Wachtell Lipton Rosen & Katz, a premier firm known for helping companies stave off hostile takeovers. Wachtell lawyer Steve Cohen assumed that this tiff could be heading for a full-blown proxy fight. He knew HP would hire every Wall Street expert it could think of to prevent them from working for Hewlett instead. He called proxy solicitor Dan Burch, president of MacKenzie Partners, one of a handful of firms that specialize in helping companies manage the usually mundane paperwork involved with shareholder votes. In a proxy fight, in which a disgruntled shareholder gathers votes in opposition of management, the proxy solicitor is like a campaign manager in a political election. If Hewlett wound up in the middle of a proxy battle, Burch's job would be to know which investors owned how many shares, and how to get their votes. It's a job that requires a huge Rolodex, a politician's gut instincts, and the broad organizational skills to keep banks of telephones and fax machines rolling to get out the vote. Burch, a big, jovial Irishman, had a reputation for his role in hotly contested merger fights. He not only knew all the key contacts at the big institutional investors, and probably their kids' names, but he'd be willing to spend weeks on the road visiting them with Hewlett.

Next, Hewlett needed to lock up a good investor relations firm. Whatever her faults, Fiorina was a master marketer, and a vicious competitor. With her back up against the wall, she was not likely to hold back in an advertising war for support. Kekst & Company, the world's best-known publicist for such do-or-die situations, was already working for Compaq. Hewlett's team thought Joele Frank might be just the ticket. The former biochemist had a reputation on Wall Street for her attack-dog aggressiveness. "She's creative, dedicated, and relentless," said Cohen.

Frank agreed she'd work for Hewlett, if need be. A few weeks later, with Hewlett's advisors almost finished with their reports, she got the call to prepare a short press release.

Sure, she said, and she handed the job to Dan Katcher, a cofounder of her company. They had no idea of the soap opera they had just walked into. When a colleague walked by his office, Katcher flagged him down: "It looks like we've got a few days of work to do on this HP–Compaq deal. This could be fun."

By the end of October, both FFL and Hoagland had decided the deal was a bomb.

Hoagland's team gathered opinions from a wide range of sources, including Wall Street analysts, institutional investors, and so-called arbitrage firms that make their living by trading on wild stock swings that accompany merger talks. Few had anything good to say about the deal. On October 30, Hoagland sent his final report to the four members of the committee that would decide how the foundation would vote. Hewlett was not on this committee. It had been set up to make sure family members had no say on investment decisions involving HP and Agilent stock. HP would later say that Hewlett forced the foundation to vote against the deal. Committee member Irv Grousbeck denies it. "It was a fairly easy call. There wasn't anyone on the committee who was in favor of the deal."

When the foundation's full board met on November 5—trustee Dick Hackborn never got word of the meeting, although Hewlett says he left him a message—it agreed to support Hewlett's decision to publicly oppose the deal.

That same day, FFL vice chairman Spencer Fleischer got a case of the jitters as he, Tully Friedman, and a colleague drove down Highway 101 to meet with Hewlett. They were going to present their findings about just how bad the merger looked to them. Their analysis, which would become the foundation for Hewlett's campaign to kill the deal, was scathing. First, the merged company would have a less desirable mix of businesses than HP had on its own. The deal would do little to help HP's money-losing computer business, but would dilute HP's lucrative printer business from 43 percent of the company to just 25 percent. It was like giving Compaq shareholders a big share of a gold mine, in exchange for their garbage dump. If Fiorina's plan to improve the gigantic combined computer business didn't pan out, the company would be forced to siphon off even more profits from the printer business. "Yes, that's what I've been trying to tell them!" Hewlett exclaimed at one point.

Then, there was execution risk. Most mergers didn't pay off. A survey of 7,000 mergers and acquisitions done by Sanford Bernstein & Company, showed that stocks of the acquiring company fell by an average of 11 percent in the two years after the deal. In big deals in which the initial investor reaction was negative, such as this one, the dip had been closer to 14 percent. Also, HP and Compaq both had miserable records with mergers. The most destructive had been Compaq's troubled purchase of Digital Equipment Corporation in 1998, and this deal had too much in common with that one. Friedman finished off the presentation, arguing that the merger would probably hurt HP shareholders for years to come. "In my opinion, this is not a close call."

Hewlett sat impassively listening for most of the two-hour presentation, but it was all he needed to hear. With both FFL and the Hoagland team confirming his views, he decided to act.

The next morning, everything was in place. Hewlett's team of advisors assembled in Cooley's conference room. The plan was clear: Hewlett was not going to criticize Fiorina, and he wasn't going to try to take control of the company. He was simply announcing his opposition to the deal. Hopefully, it wouldn't even come to a proxy fight.

They had debated how much notice, if any, to give HP before springing the news. Hewlett, at one point, had thought about giving Fiorina a few hours' heads-up, as a courtesy. That idea had been quickly shot down. If she was given a head start, Fiorina would have tried to discredit Hewlett before he could tell his story, and they wanted an untarnished view of investor sentiment. If HP's stock didn't rise on the news, it would show that investors did not share Hewlett's views, and that further protests were pointless. The decision was made: give Fiorina 30 minutes' notice. HP's side would say it was an unfair surprise attack.

When the appointed time came, someone faxed a copy of the press release to Fiorina's office. Moments later, Hewlett went to an adjoining conference room and placed the call to Fiorina. He told her he would be putting a press release out a half-hour later, at 10:00.

"I wish you wouldn't do that. I wish you would have called me earlier," Fiorina responded. After Hewlett briefly explained his actions, she said "Please don't do this. Could you give us some time?"

"No, Carly, I've thought about this for a long time. We're going to announce it," Hewlett told her.

After returning to the conference room, Hewlett phoned fellow board members. He also called David Woodley Packard, pleading with him not to put out his own release opposing the deal. He feared that Packard's emotional defense of the HP Way would discredit his arguments. "Walter begged me not to," says Packard, who could not be restrained any longer. That night, Packard leaked the news that he'd vote his shares against the deal to the *San Jose Mercury News*.[4] Now it was Fiorina's turn to see a nightmare come true. Minutes after his press release went over the wires, Hewlett began a round of interviews with national media. He had practiced for hours the night before, doing mock interviews with his wife. Now, sitting before a table covered with Post-its listing key talking points, he more than held his own. "With this transaction, we get what we don't want, we jeopardize what we already have, and we compromise our ability to get what we need," he said in one interview. Asked whether he was dissatisfied with Fiorina, he said "This is really not about Carly. I want to emphasize that I am a supporter of Carly. I supported her selection as CEO of Hewlett-Packard, and I have supported many of the things that she has done. I simply do not support this deal."[5]

It was a total blindside. Fiorina had figured she'd have another three months to appease investors about the deal. From the start, the deal had been a hard sell. Then came the September 11 attack, which had rattled investors, delayed their road show to sell the deal, and contributed to Compaq's horrible quarter, which ended on September 31. Now, she could do nothing as Hewlett ticked off all the concerns that thousands of investors had been worrying about. They apparently agreed with him. By day's end, HP shares rose 17 percent—giving investors back more than $5.7 billion of the losses her deal had cost them.

Hewlett's top advisors began placing bets as to how Fiorina would respond. Joele Frank figured the CEO would announce that HP was considering Hewlett's action, and would take the night to come up with a carefully conceived retort. No way, said Neal. He figured Fiorina would fire back immediately. Sure enough, the following press release hit the wires about an hour later:

> While we regret very much the Hewlett family's decision, we are not surprised. The HP Board of Directors and HP and Compaq remain fully committed to the merger and expect shareholder approval.

This was a mistake on HP's part. The phrase "We're not surprised" sounded smug, arrogant, and condescending, and it raised far more questions than it answered. If the company knew Hewlett had concerns about the deal, how could it have let this happen? Whether he was right or wrong, his name was Hewlett! And had HP let Compaq's board in on Hewlett's concerns, before that company agreed to sell itself and risk this kind of nightmare? Watching HP's release come over the wires, Steve Neal leaned over to Hewlett and said, "I bet Compaq is on the phone right now, saying, "What the hell do you mean, 'You're not surprised?'" One of HP's own advisors also thought it was a misstep. "I was surprised by the 'we're not surprised', because I sure was surprised."

Actually, Compaq already knew. While enjoying a dinner with customers in Paris, Compaq CEO Michael Capellas was interrupted by an aide. "Carly needs to talk to you," he recalls the aide saying. "I know Carly pretty well. Carly would not take me away [from a dinner with customers]. My first thought [was] 'My God, a plane hit one of our plants.' And that's when she told me. And my first reaction was I felt very bad for her. My first reaction was empathy." Capellas said he believed HP's board had no idea of the depth of Hewlett's opposition to the deal. "The guy did vote for it. At the end of the day, he voted for it."[6]

HP's corporate machinery set out to get Wall Street's top fighters on its side. It quickly realized that it was making its calls too late. HP called Dan Burch three times that night, only to be told the next day that he was working with Hewlett. A few days later, an HP lawyer called Joele Frank. If he'd looked, he would have seen her name at the bottom of Hewlett's press release.

Hewlett's announcement made him an instant celebrity in business circles—as much a lightning rod for controversy as Carly Fiorina had ever been. Some industry titans maligned him for double-crossing the board after going along with a unanimous vote. "That, to me, is unpardonable. It's a sin," retired General Electric chair Jack Welch said. "It's corporate governance at its worst. And I feel for the CEO."[7] However, aside from CEOs who liked their boards loyal, most corporate governance experts came to Hewlett's defense. "He's a symbol of investor capitalism at its best," said Charles Elson, director of the Center for Corporate Governance at the University of Delaware. "Rather than rolling over and playing dead, he was willing to challenge management." Said Nell Minow, who runs a Web site on corporate governance called the Corporate Library, "The moral of this story is be nice to your shareholders, or they won't support you when you need them."

Hewlett's news hit HP like a thunderbolt. In one California

plant, excited cheers broke out. Quickly, pent-up emotions about the deal and about Fiorina began to pour out. Over the next few days, message boards on Yahoo! and on CBS Marketwatch lit up with flame mails aimed at all things Fiorina. Some were nostalgic odes to the HP Way. Others were fierce attacks on the new CEO, labeling her "the bitch" or "Chainsaw Carly."

Walter Hewlett was suddenly a corporate savior. Few thought he knew HP's business well enough to have real answers to what ailed the company, but a victory for Hewlett was an irresistible two-fer to many employees—an opportunity to kill the merger and get rid of Fiorina to boot. An example, in part, from wysche23, on November 10:[8]

> Amazingly, (Walter) has given me a new energy simply by mak-ing his announcement. I pray that he gathers enough support to nix this deal, and hopefully, Carly can be swept under the rug along with it.
>
> Thank you, Walter, for standing up for what your Dad and Dave had created, even though the decision to do so must have been difficult.
>
> The employees of Hewlett Packard are behind you.
> Blah,
> Wysche

Not everyone shared these views. Scores of staffers wrote to Fio-rina to express their support. Stan Pluta, an engineer who had lived through the consolidation of the aerospace industry in the early 1990s, wrote: "I was with Northrup when it merged with Grumman, and there are so many parallels. I remember everyone chastising Kent Kresa at Northrup, but he's still there—after almost ten years of acquisitions." He explained the support for Hewlett this way: "I don't think it's a large number, but there are people who don't real-ize the world has changed. HP has to change to fit the world."[9]

Still, HP's executives knew they had a serious morale problem— one that was snowballing by the day. While 84 percent of HP em-ployees polled by management said they supported the Compaq pur-chase as of November 5, that fell to just 55 percent after Hewlett's announcement. "We were on good track" in winning support until Hewlett's announcement, said Susan Bowick, HP's head of human resources. "Because he's on the board and has the name Hewlett, people don't know what to believe. . . . The [morale] statistics . . . are lower than we've ever seen."

In response, HP's top executives went into damage control mode. Bowick addressed an auditorium full of managers in Palo Alto. Ann Livermore held a teleconference with her managers and set off on a worldwide series of talks that would put her in front of 30,000 employees in seven countries. Her message: "This isn't Carly's deal or the board's deal. It is our deal."

Fiorina also hit the road, visiting HP sites to shore up support. On November 28, she and Livermore held an hour-long coffee talk at HP's site in Roseville. When asked to explain why Hewlett did what he did, Fiorina tried to stay above the fray. "He's handled this so poorly," she said, noting the 30-minute warning he gave management. "He needs to work more closely with us and the board."

According to company surveys, these efforts helped enormously. "Confidence goes up tremendously after a couple of hours of explanation," insisted Bowick. "Once you walk them through what it means if the deal doesn't go through, they get it."

However, the surveys didn't seem to reflect the larger mood. By now, a deep-seated cynicism had set in. Many employees doubted the integrity of the employee surveys. The questions seemed to be weighted to give a positive view of management and the Compaq deal.

Moreover, despite management's claims of employee support, some attendees of these coffee talks don't remember a feel-good mood. During a question-and-answer period at a coffee talk in Corvallis, Oregon, on December 10, a low-level engineer approached the microphone. Visibly shaking, he took out a piece of paper to read his question. "When is this going to start feeling like HP again?" he asked.

"When we start making our numbers again," Fiorina answered.

"I thought, 'Oh my god,'" recalled a high-ranking executive at HP who was there. "This woman is a sales manager. That's what you tell your salespeople—not what you tell these people." Some of HP's efforts to reach out to employees didn't seem to make much of a dent. The company gave every employee a bonus worth two days' pay after it posted good financial results that October. One employee wrote a letter to David Woodley Packard summing up his thoughts: "I would gladly donate my 'Carly Bucks' to either bring back good people that were lost [to layoffs] or contribute to a fund to pay her off and get her out of here."

As reporters began to tap into this well of discontent, HP set out to find support for the deal. The company issued a video featuring Hackborn explaining his support. HP gave reporters a list of more than 70 employees and executives, with their phone numbers, who said they supported the merger. Ironically, some of those on the list would later come to oppose the deal, and one anecdote suggests that it wasn't so easy to find these supporters. Allison Kent, a veteran manager, was attending a training seminar with 40 other up-and-coming executives when an HP PR person asked which of them would lend public support for the deal. Kent says she was the only manager in the room who raised her hand.

After Hewlett's November 6 bombshell, all eyes turned to the Packard Foundation. With its stake, the foundation could likely deliver a death blow to Fiorina's Folly, as some now called it, but trying to guess which way the Packard Foundation would vote was nearly impossible. None of its board members would speak publicly. The press figured, correctly, that two former HP executives— Lew Platt and Dean Morton, who was chief operating officer when he retired in 1992—would be key, but their opinions were unknown.

In fact, some had not made up their minds. After Fiorina and Wayman made their pitch on September 14, Morton was inclined to support management. "She was moving decisively, if not always exactly correctly," Morton thought. Still, the trustees were not ready to take management's word for it. In late October, they hired the consulting firm Booz Allen Hamilton to outline the risks and rewards of the deal. The foundation also did its own investigation.

From the start, the Packard Foundation took a far different approach from that of the Hewlett camp. The trustees made the explicit decision not to join forces with Walter Hewlett, says Platt.

Hewlett didn't trust HP to disclose all the information his team needed to analyze the merger, but the Packard Foundation wanted Booz Allen to get its data directly from the company. HP's executives felt this was proof that Hewlett had made up his mind to kill the deal come hell or high water, while the Packard Foundation wanted only what was best for its shares.

The foundation's desire to stay out of the fray reflected the views of Susan Packard Orr. Like Hewlett, Orr was a Stanford graduate who loved technology, philanthropy, and her privacy. Yet Hewlett's vocal opposition put her on the spot. With the media hounding the trustees to learn how they would vote, the foundation picked up the pace of its analysis. When Hewlett's financial advisors went to make their case, they were struck by the formality and weighty mood in the room. Orr sat in stony silence, clearly not enjoying the position she'd been put in. "I'd pay a million to know what you're thinking," thought John Coughlin, one of Hewlett's financial advisors, who was sitting next to her. "You could just see the invisible shield around her." The others weren't much easier to read, but Coughlin did pick up critical body language clues from Lew Platt. "His head was nodding the whole time."

Later, the foundation heard a very different side of the story from Dick Hackborn. Pleasant and unemotional, he was candid about some of the criticisms regarding Fiorina and the Compaq deal. Morton asked Hackborn how he could support a bet-the-farm acquisition when for decades he'd believed in HP's old formula of steady growth from within. "I still do—but this is the exception," he responded. Much of the talk was about the complexity of the merger. Hackborn praised the planning that had gone into the integration effort. Others agreed that the integration planning *looked* great—but overall, there were still big questions. "It looked good on paper," Packard Foundation president Dick Schlosberg quipped. "But so did the New Orleans Saints' playbook last year."

As the Packard Foundation deliberated, Hewlett and HP's other board members struggled to find common ground. During the first board meeting after Hewlett's announcement, everyone was respectful and polite. As the meeting ended, Keyworth and Hackborn asked Hewlett whether he'd spend some time with them. They walked down the hall into Bill Hewlett's old office.

The three men had known each other for decades, and all cared deeply about HP. One of them said, "Look, we're friends, Walter. But have you thought this through all the way? We know you know what happens if you lose. But what happens if you win?" According to Keyworth, Hewlett turned ashen. Hewlett promised the men he would "go think about it" and quickly left.

Arriving back at Cooley Godward's office down the street, Hewlett shared the exchange with Neal. He said it sounded as though they wanted to maintain a positive conversation. However, when Hewlett told Neal that he had agreed to think about his position, Neal chided his client. "That was a mistake, Walter. Now, they're going to say you might change your mind. You're going to read about it in the morning paper."

Sure enough, the morning papers quoted "a source close to HP" saying that Hewlett might be reconsidering his opposition—evidently, a move to suggest Hewlett wasn't firm in his convictions.[10] Hewlett was furious. It was another example of the broken trust.

Of course, HP's top brass was furious, as well. They felt Hewlett's opposition was disingenuous and unfair. Despite talk of his tortured summer, it was about the stock, his family obligations, and his emotional ties to the HP legacy. Hackborn, for one, felt that Hewlett hadn't studied the deal enough and hadn't even engaged in real debate. "The thing that hurts the most is the self-righteousness," said Keyworth. For others, there was a grudging understanding. "Walter has a rational reason for preferring that we not do this merger," said Wayman, pointing out that the stock slide crimped the Hewlett Foundation's diversification efforts. "But there are also emotional issues. . . . If he's got emotional issues, he's got to look beyond them."

Wayman was also outraged when he read the report by Hewlett's financial advisors, which was made public on November 16. From where he sat, it was a pure advocacy piece, full of fallacious arguments designed only to kill the deal. The report cited Compaq's horrible quarter as proof that HP had paid too much, but dismissed the obvious impact of the post-September 11 slowdown. It pooh-poohed the strategic merit of the deal by pointing out that it wouldn't make HP the equal of IBM in services or a match for Dell in PCs, totally discounting the fact that HP could be more competitive in these areas. Wayman fumed that FFL didn't factor all of the expected cost savings into their calculation of key measures such as operating margins, net margins, and return on equity. "It finally got my dander up," said the normally restrained Wayman.

Until the Packard Foundation announced its intentions, HP officially stayed relatively quiet. Behind the scenes, however, HP's public relations machine was on the move. Within days, Hewlett's attendance record at board meetings made the rounds in the press. A source at one of the investment banks suggested that Hewlett was mad at the world for a variety of reasons. After years of playing nursemaid to his father, he found himself with no role to make him feel worthy. Others disparaged him for his lack of business and technology savvy, pointing out that he'd never even worked for the company—a slight stretch, considering that he'd worked there briefly on three occasions. At first, Hewlett did little to defend himself. All of his interviews with the press were expressly off the record. Reporters couldn't quote him without his advisors' clearance. This was partially because he was such a media novice; they couldn't risk a misstep that might rankle the Packard Foundation. To protect that relationship, Hewlett even surrendered the chance to ensure himself a place on HP's board. If he'd submitted his name to HP before November 29, he could have been a write-in candidate at HP's 2002 annual shareholders meeting. When that date came and went, Fiorina and Sonsini were shocked that he had passed up the opportunity. With so much stock and so much support from investors and employees, he could easily have won a seat

HP and its advisors were also feeling good about their chances with the Packard Foundation. According to two HP advisors, Susan Packard Orr had told Fiorina over the phone, "Don't worry, we're not going to make this decision on a political basis, but on an economic basis." The Booz Allen consultants had told HP's executives how impressed they were with the company's integration planning, as well.

By early December, the Packard Foundation was close to making its decision. It had heard from all parties. David Woodley

Packard had made sure that each of the trustees had seen the three-inch stack of letters that disgruntled, often emotional HP employees had sent him. Until the end, most of the trustees did not know which way they would vote. Hewlett met with Orr privately a few days before the vote, but insists he didn't try to sway her one way or another. "Boy, I guess you're really on the hot seat," he said.

"That's for sure," she said, according to Hewlett.

The Booz Allen report was far from definitive. It said that HP's cost-cutting goals were probably attainable, and suggested that HP's integration plans might just work. Sales were the biggest problem. The most likely scenario was that the combined companies would lose 9 percent of their sales to competitors—nearly double the 4.9 percent the company claimed. Based on one calculation, the foundation wouldn't be better off for at least two years—and that was if everything else went perfectly well.

Fiorina and Wayman visited one more time, and remained bullish when they left. Some of the trustees asked if there was anything they could do for HP. The executives said it would be helpful if the foundation made its decision quickly.

The foundation obliged. Its finance committee met for many hours on December 6. The next morning, the full board sat in on one last session. The meeting was held at Dave Packard's old house. Set atop a hill in the middle of an apricot orchard, it's now used to host conferences and such—and it was the perfect place to avoid the TV cameras gathered at the foundation's office. The board voted to oppose the deal. "In the end, there was no dissent," says a trustee. After the stock market closed for the day, Orr called Fiorina to break the news. Dean Morton called Wayman, a frequent dinner party guest and golf buddy over the years.

The HP executives and their advisors were shocked. They had been banking on a victory, says one advisor. When the news broke, the Packard Foundation put out a brief press release and did very little to explain its vote. HP argued that the foundation had special reasons for opposing the deal—that the trustees were more concerned about a short-term hit to the stock rather than long-term benefits. Foundation sources say that's not true. "We didn't want to say 'This is the dumbest goddamn deal we've ever seen in our lives,'" said one Packard Foundation trustee. "We just wanted to play it straight. We had some hope that they would throw in the towel."

So did many of the members of Hewlett's team. When the news of the Packard Foundation vote was announced, most of Joele Frank's public relations firm was at her Manhattan apartment, where she was throwing a Christmas party. Quickly, her team dashed off a press release thanking the Packard Foundation and asking HP's management to call off the merger. If it didn't, Hewlett would officially declare war. "If Hewlett-Packard and Compaq decide to put this matter to a stockholder vote, I intend to solicit proxies against the transaction."[11]

This was the moment Hewlett had been waiting for, the knock-out punch he hoped would win the day. There was good reason to think it would land. With 18 percent of the shares opposed, many governance experts would say Fiorina had a duty to consider walking away rather than subject the company and its shareholders to more pain. Clearly, it was a Rubicon for Fiorina. If she went ahead and HP lost the shareholder vote, she was almost certainly out of a job.

It wasn't over at all, not with Fiorina calling the shots. The afternoon of the Packard Foundation's decision, she met with her shell-shocked advisors in the same war room she'd used while negotiating the merger. At one point that afternoon, Fiorina was asked to take a step back and consider all of the HP team's options. They could continue on their present course—and try to overcome the opposition and win the vote, of course. They could try to reprice the deal, making it more favorable for HP shareholders. They could look into spinning off HP's PC business. The final possibility was to think about terminating the deal—calling it quits.

"Are you suggesting I throw in the towel?," an incredulous Fiorina said, according to one person who was in the room. "That is not an option. We don't want to do that. We will win this."

Before calling it a night, Sonsini said to Fiorina: "You know, Carly, in every great experience, there's an epiphany that occurs. Maybe this had to happen. If this proxy contest didn't happen, maybe you couldn't do all the things you were brought here to do. There's always a silver lining. If we win this, maybe we'll look back and say that this day was especially important. Maybe HP had to break away from the families and all those traditions—and maybe doing it all at once was the best way."

The next day, a relaxed Fiorina did an interview with *Business-Week,* before rushing off to host a Christmas party at her home for HP's top executives. Although disappointed with the Packard Foundation decision, she seemed as if a weight had been lifted from her shoulders. Now, she knew where she stood. "The foundation has to do what they feel they have to do to serve their own interests. And I have to do what I have to do to serve the interests of all of our share-owners and our customers and our employees. And I accept that those interests can differ."[12]

She was also confident the company could prevail, despite the setback. "We've done the numbers with and without the Packard vote and we can win this vote and so we intend to do so." Fiorina added that she was more upset with the feeding frenzy surrounding the merger than she was with the vote. "You know, the Packard Foundation decision is much less upsetting to me than some of the unfair characterizations of this company, the lack of fact based analysis around the progress this company is making, the bias that some people have."

As for Walter Hewlett, she was not so charitable. Asked why he opposed the deal after voting with the board, she replied that she didn't know. "There is a big difference between an individual managing his own personal assets and the assets of the foundation and a board member going out and actively soliciting against a board's decision," she said. "Walter's behavior publicly has been a complete surprise. And I think it is an insult to this board."

11

PROXY FIGHT

Sometimes the devil you do know is better than the devil you don't.
—MERRILL LYNCH ANALYST KEVIN RENDINO

Walter Hewlett's Palo Alto home, a functional structure that he designed and built with a contractor friend from college, suggests a man who is comfortable with the life he has led. It is just blocks from where he spent much of his childhood. Strands of Christmas lights remain up year-round over his front door. An old Volvo his father gave him, which he and his Stanford buddies covered in psychedelic 1960s style graffiti long ago, sits in the driveway. His red electric car, recharging in the driveway, sports an "Abandon Inertia" bumper sticker.

Inside, it's the quiet house of a middle-class academic. There are books lining the walls and a Steinway piano in the living room with some Schubert sheet music propped on a stand. The family's cats wander about. The only trace of Hewlett's famous dad, other than his Japanese prints and other family heirlooms, is a poster-size HP ad that has been sitting behind his favorite chair for months.

Hewlett bears a vague resemblance to his late father. His gaze is firm, but he lacks his father's mischievous twinkle. He wears his gray hair in a grown-out 1950s-style crew cut, and his large ears give him an almost elfin air. During interviews for this book, he'd sit cross-legged in his chair, wearing slightly rumpled dress shirts that seemed a size too big. Before responding to questions, he'd often go silent for a minute, remove his owlish glasses, and rub his forehead red before answering. Despite his shuffling gait, Hewlett is a dedicated athlete, a two-time all-American marathoner in college who once considered making a run at the U.S. Olympic team. He still prepares for six months each year for the Markleeville Death Ride, tinkering with his bicycle training regimen as if it were a science project. Even his diet is unconventional. Long before the Zone regimen became popular, Hewlett was eating venison and eggs most mornings. The high-protein diet, he believed, kept his energy up for the entire day.

For the battle to come, Hewlett would need all the energy he could get.

After the Packard Foundation came out against the merger, conventional wisdom was that Carly Fiorina's bid to buy Compaq was doomed. With the vote already stacked against her, Fiorina would have to win more than 60 percent of the remaining vote to get the majority required by HP's bylaws, but Fiorina had never been one to put much stock in conventional wisdom. Based on what her advisors told her, she knew what HP's employees, investors, and others didn't. She knew she could win.

The math was fairly simple. Of HP's 1.9 billion outstanding shares, the founding families and their foundations held 18 percent. Fiorina expected individual retail shareholders, who usually vote with management, to split down the middle because of Walter Hewlett's name recognition. That would make the tally roughly 30 percent for Hewlett, versus 13 percent for HP.

However, institutional investors such as big banks, mutual funds, and insurance companies held the key to victory. They owned the remaining 1.1 billion shares. To win, HP would have to capture around 75 percent of these shares. That sounds high, but institutions are even more likely to vote with management than are retail shareholders. As sophisticated businesspeople, they tend to trust in the judgment of other businesspeople, and they understand that boards have a legal duty to do what's best for shareholders. Also, if they

vote with their feet" by selling their shares,
hands of supporters come the shareholder
re may be more slippery reasons why they
management: existing or potential business
services companies do billions of dollars a
corporations like HP, whether by providing
vestment banking advice, or administering
being equal, it's a dumb move to vote against

were two things that could really deep-six
was if Mario Monti, the competition com-
ean Commission, decided to take a closer
iving his okay. He had shocked the business
General Electric's $47-billion merger with
likely he'd want to at least do a so-called
this deal, which might take four months.
y okayed the deal, that was a long time to
uncertainty surrounding it.
e involved an influential outfit called Institutional Shareholder Services. Based in Rockville, Maryland, ISS
advises institutional investors on how they should vote on proxy
questions. Roughly 23 percent of HP's shares were held by ISS
clients—and roughly 13 percent would automatically follow ISS's
recommendations. Bottom line: If ISS supported Hewlett, he could
add another big chunk of shares to his tally. With almost one-third
in the opposing camp and the retail vote likely to split, HP would
have to pretty much run the table on all remaining institutional
shareholders.

If HP could get past these two obstacles, the fight was its to lose.
HP could outspend and outstaff Hewlett, rich as he was. HP also
had a huge strategic advantage. As 2001 neared its end, Hewlett was
basking in accolades from corporate governance experts, the press,
and HP employees, but Fiorina knew that he had a huge strategic
problem. Hewlett wasn't offering investors anything to be *for*. If buying Compaq wasn't the right way to fix HP, what was? "If we stayed
true to our story, we felt we could win against 'We just don't like the
deal,' " said Larry Sonsini.

The fact was that Hewlett was in a box. He just didn't know it yet.

Walter Hewlett knew from the start that he faced an uphill climb to win a proxy war, but he, too, had reasons for optimism. Current events were on his side. Investors were fed up. Shareholders took a record beating in 2001, and massive layoffs, accounting scandals, and stories of the overarching greed of once-famous CEOs had served to deepen their mistrust. Almost all the problems were in high tech, where even the hottest highfliers had fallen after the binge spending of the Internet years came to a sudden stop.

The bad mood was just starting to gather steam as HP and Hewlett prepared to do battle. Government investigations claimed corruption by superstar stock analysts; in November, Merrill Lynch's Henry Blodget resigned in shame. On December 2, Enron Corporation, a shining light of the New Economy, shocked Wall Street by announcing it was bankrupt. It was the greatest corporate disaster in U.S. history, and more scandals were coming: Adelphia, Global Crossing, Tyco, WorldCom. It was in this apoplectic environment that HP would have to convince investors that buying Compaq made sense—that this tech megamerger, unlike all the others, would somehow work out.

Hewlett had other advantages. First, he was easy to like, a good foil to Fiorina, who had become high-tech's queen of controversy. Plus, the Packards' support was nothing to sneeze at, and sentiment was still moving his way. The proof was in the stock price: Every time something happened that cast doubt on the merger's survival, the stock rose. Indeed, as of mid-December, HP shares had returned to their premerger levels.

Even Compaq seemed to be getting weak knees. The company's board desperately needed the deal. Michael Capellas had all but publicly declared that Compaq could not make it on its own by selling the company at the low price he did. But on December 13, Compaq's board met in Houston to discuss its options if the company lost the merger. "Obviously at this juncture, Compaq has a Plan B," Compaq board member and former HP manager Thomas J. Perkins said.[1]

Even before the Packard Foundation rejected the merger, HP had begun its preparations to take on Walter Hewlett. A team of insiders started meeting with advisors from Sard, Goldman, and others at 9:00 A.M. a few times a week in the old boardroom at HP headquarters to strategize. Chief Counsel Ann Baskins took the lead in getting quick regulatory approval from the European Commission. CFO Bob Wayman worked with Goldman Sachs bankers. Fiorina's two closest advisors, say many sources, were Larry Sonsini and Allison Johnson. Sonsini was her voice of experience, a counselor on more than just legal matters. Johnson coordinated the day-to-day campaign. "She was the glue that kept it all together," said George Sard, who provided investor and public relations counsel for HP. Hewlett's core team was far different. Without the huge corporate machinery HP could bring to bear, his was a virtual network of experienced hired guns.

As the battle lines hardened, the two sides would come to loathe each other, at least for the duration of hostilities. It became more than just business. Hewlett's backers demonized Fiorina as a self-centered carpetbagger, surrounded by lackeys willing to say anything or even break the law to do her bidding. Fiorina's backers privately joked that Hewlett's team was a "lucky sperm club," dominated by a posse of Stanford grads and sons of well-connected fathers. Besides Walter Hewlett and David Woodley Packard, there was Jim Gaither, whose father was an old HP board member. Steve Neal's father was a respected lawyer and former Stanford professor. "There's a component of the Stanford Mafia here," said Wilson Sonsini lawyer Boris Feldman.

As each side dug in, longtime friendships suffered. As usual, it seemed, Dick Hackborn was at the eye of the storm. After years of garnering admiration, now he found most of his old friends simmering with anger at his support of Fiorina and the Compaq deal. On December 17, Hackborn resigned from the board of the Hewlett Foundation. It was painful for all involved. Hackborn had been appointed by Bill Hewlett himself, and he was greatly valued by other board members for his wisdom and easy sense of humor. Indeed, a few weeks later, after he issued a public letter defending Walter Hewlett, Gaither left a long voice-mail message at Hackborn's home.

"I'm sorry, but I felt I had to do this, Dick. We'll have a lot of fence mending to do when this is over." He never got a response.

Just before Thanksgiving, Walter Hewlett entered what he called his "alternate universe," a distasteful world of airports, never-ending business meetings, and mean-spirited corporate politics. He'd remain there until mid-March of 2002, spending most weeks traveling the country to visit investors, coming home only on weekends.

Hewlett, who typically spent his days either working on his family's philanthropic efforts or figuring out some new computer program at the music lab he'd started at Stanford, hardly seemed prepared for the ordeal. At first, he insisted on driving himself to the airport and flying coach. Though he had never even carried a cell phone and hated using e-mail, he soon was carrying not one but two Blackberry pagers so he could be in constant contact with his team.

Despite his inexperience, Hewlett warmed to the task. He was no natural speaker. Invariably, he'd begin meetings with investors stiffly, saying "Hello, I'm Walter Hewlett. I'm a director of Hewlett-Packard and I'm here as a shareholder. Let me tell you how we got to this point." But by the time he left, most investors were favorably impressed. "He knows this business," said Jeffrey Heil, head of equity investments for the regents of the University of California. Most came away trusting that his motives were what he claimed they were: to boost the price of HP's shares, rather than to perpetuate some nostalgic view of the company or to maintain his voting power. "There's no indication that he's voting solely to maintain the status quo," said Kevin A. Fujimoto, an analyst with Banc of America Capital Management, after a January 24 meeting. Fujimoto decided to oppose the merger after the meeting, and even a visit from Fiorina the following week couldn't turn him around.

Hewlett did present some problems for his advisors, however—particularly his unwillingness to adopt the cutthroat tactics that are typical in proxy fights. He refused to allow them to point out Fiorina's role in the Lucent debacle that was making headlines at the time. Until the final days of the contest, he wouldn't attack her in any way. He also refused to ask the Hewlett Foundation to alter its ongoing stock diversification program, which led to the sale of 5.5 million shares on January 4.

He imposed an HP-like sense of propriety in advertising that would have made his father proud, as well. At one point, someone suggested running a newspaper ad under the headline "Houston, We Have a Problem," the immortal phrase associated with James Lovell's report of an explosion and subsequent power drain aboard Apollo 13. Hewlett, concerned it would be disrespectful to the astronauts and their families, nixed the idea.

He also refused to play the nostalgia card. HP did everything it could to hitch its wagon to the founders' legacy, even calling its Web site "votethehpway.com." Hewlett refused to overplay his family connection. At one point, the hypercompetitive Dan Burch urged Hewlett to invoke his father's name more forcefully. "You should tell people that he would have been against this merger," Burch said.

Burch pressed the point over Hewlett's objections, until Hewlett got fed up and sounded off. "Darn it, I'll tell you something right now: if I thought my father would be for this deal, I wouldn't be here right now. But I'm just not going to do that. I'm just not comfortable with it." Though it could be frustrating, his advisors were also charmed and inspired by his principled approach. "He's one dimensional, but it's a very nice dimension," said Hewlett's media–trainer, Michael Sheehan.

Hewlett's ethical code did leave some leeway for hardball tactics, however. For the first few months of the campaign, his advisors kept HP on the defensive with a barrage of charges. They leaked the story of Hewlett's private boardroom conversation with Sonsini to establish Hewlett's claim that he'd been unfairly strongarmed into agreeing with the board in the first place. After Hackborn and Fiorina hinted they might quit if the merger failed, Neal sent Sonsini an angry letter demanding that HP notify regulators about exactly who planned to step down if that occurred—or to correct the record if it were not the case. Working the press, Neal painted the picture of HP's board as a bunch of sore losers. "It's unprecedented to see a board of directors quit just because they don't get their way," Neal said. Sonsini, convinced Neal was just manipulating the press with such charges, never responded.

If HP wasn't flat on the mat, it was playing a dangerous rope-a-dope by letting Hewlett throw so many punches. The company's first serious counterpunch came on December 19. In an effort to swipe Hewlett's emotional advantage, it ran full-page ads that sought to claim the founders' legacy in the *Wall Street Journal,* the *New York Times,* and other papers. The ads showed a photo of HP's original audio oscillator, with the caption "Even now, some suggest we might stop at printers. But HP's ambitions have always been much greater." Johnson added a closing line lifted right from Packard's book, *The HP Way* (Boston: HarperBusiness, 1995): "To remain static is to fall behind." The phrase would soon begin appearing on all of HP's proxy-related ads and other materials. That same day, HP also added considerably more meat to its case for the merger, with a 49-page report designed to counter the claims in the report from Hewlett's financial advisors. The report laid out the sources of the projected $2.5 billion in savings, and detailed exactly where it expected to lose revenues to assuage fears of a far greater top-line drop.

Still, Hewlett was in the catbird seat as 2001 came to a close.

After a short holiday break, Fiorina returned to work after the New Year, ready to go. That first week back, she called a meeting with the goal of turbocharging the company's defense. Starting at 8:00 A.M., 50 or so top HP and Compaq executives walked through every aspect of the campaign, from legal to regulatory to advertising. Key decisions were made. She, Wayman, and Capellas would immediately begin giving as much time as necessary to meeting with investors. "If we need to get on a plane to visit every shareholder five times, we're going to do it," she said. Fiorina also decided that she would take the day-to-day reins of the campaign, a task most CEOs would delegate. She and Capellas gave the team a critical morale boost, say two people who were there. Until that meeting, the companies' executives had eyed each other warily, uncertain if they were more friend than foe, but by getting the teams working in such a close way, the CEOs blasted through the mistrust—as well as the widespread fear of failure. "The world thinks we're toast," she told the group. "But we're going to fight this thing, and we're going to win."

Very quickly, HP's tactics grew more aggressive. On January 7, the company issued a letter, addressed condescendingly to "Dear Walter," that excoriated him on a variety of fronts. It blasted him for mischaracterizing his conversation with Sonsini. One of Hewlett's government filings had suggested that Sonsini had *told* him HP would pay a higher price if the board vote wasn't unanimous, when in fact Hewlett had only assumed this would be the case.[2]

"To suggest that you were pressured into approving the merger is inaccurate and inappropriate," the letter stated. "Quite frankly Walter, you have never offered an alternative strategy that we all haven't debated and rejected."

For a while, the HP team discussed whether Fiorina should challenge Hewlett to a debate. In the end, Fiorina rejected the idea. She would make such mincemeat of him that "It might backfire on us. It might look like were picking on him—like it wasn't a fair fight," recalled an advisor.

HP found another way to run into that trap, however. On January 18, Allison Johnson and ad executive Steve Simpson drafted a letter to shareholders intended to establish some facts about Walter Hewlett. The draft claimed he was an "academic." Reading that, one board member drew big laughs when he suggested they add "and musician" to the definition, according to an HP advisor. Everyone thought that was just priceless—and it was true, so how could you argue it was mudslinging? Some, such as Sonsini, feared it would make a martyr out of Hewlett. Nonetheless, the release went out.

Sonsini was right. Suddenly, powerful friends such as financier Dick Jenrette and former Harvard president Neil Rudenstine, who had both served with Hewlett on Harvard's board of overseers, rushed to his defense. "I was very offended," said Jenrette, cofounder of Donaldson, Lufkin & Jenrette. In a way, the dig belied the fact that many, if not most, investors and HP employees agreed with Hewlett. Joele Frank was thrilled. "HP should have won this proxy fight in a cakewalk. But they elevated Walter's status way beyond what it would have been."

HP figured Hewlett's time in the sun would begin to fade as its top brass met with investors. Capellas had earned big points with Wall Street for tightening up Compaq's sagging operations, and for his forthright, friendly ways. Wayman knew HP's business better than anyone, and earned credibility points for his gracious manner. He stood out among the combatants for his ability to put himself in Hewlett's shoes.

As for Fiorina, she'd been down this road before with the Lucent spin-off, and knew what buttons to push. She was likeable, and remarkably informed and eloquent when giving her pitch. At times, her ability to read investors was downright mystical. In a meeting with Fiorina, Brandes Investment Partners senior analyst Vinit Bodas wanted to quietly test Fiorina's willingness to break up the company. He'd simply asked for her general thoughts about the printer business. "Before I tell you that, I want to tell you that we're not going to spin the printer business off," she said. "And I know who has put that idea in your head. It was Walter."

Fiorina juggled her many responsibilities—including investor visits, strategy meetings, and at least a half-day on Thursdays on the integration effort—without breaking a sweat. Compaq executive Mike Winkler described her this way: "She's a woman of steel. She simply will not let herself or her operation fail. She's not mercurial or emotional in any way. It's that Maggie Thatcher constitution."

Toward the end of January, HP began to make headway with the investors that really counted: the biggest ones. The current quarter was going better than expected. The European Commission had just approved the deal—a major victory. What's more, the integration seemed to be way ahead of schedule, entering its third and final phase.

Fiorina decided to go on the offensive on February 4, when she was scheduled to speak at a Goldman Sachs conference for investors in Palm Springs. "It's great to be here this morning," she deadpanned. "I haven't had the opportunity to address a room full of institutional investors since, well, Friday. I was having withdrawal."

She then launched into a cogent explanation of the merger, but this time with a new tone. Rather than an offensive strike designed to transform HP into an IBM-like superpower, she emphasized the defensive nature of the deal. The computer business was going to settle into single-digit growth, and margins would keep falling as hardware became standardized. As such, buying Compaq was perhaps the only way for HP to remain profitable and strong. Fiorina, who had made a career by setting pie-in-the-sky goals, was now parroting the investment community's own dour sentiments about the industry's future. Having had to repeatedly lower HP's earnings or growth estimates for much of the previous year, she was getting good at this new game.

The timing of the deal was perfect, she argued. HP didn't pay a boom-time premium, and since customers were not buying much due to the tech recession, HP would have time to get through the merger unscathed. Walter Hewlett was offering only a dead end. Damning him with faint praise as a "good and decent man," she said, "Frankly, my problem isn't that our opposition is saying 'no' to the merger. The problem is that they are giving us nothing to say 'yes' to, because they haven't proposed any solutions to the challenges we face."

Before she finished, she made a concluding comment that had even more impact than the speech. "I come here today confident that we have turned the corner on this merger. The momentum is shifting," she said. In comments to reporters after her speech, she went even further, telling them that "We have the votes."

This was clearly a misstep, dangerously close to a violation of securities law. "The lawyers turned green. I don't think she was aware that it was borderline illegal," says one advisor. Frank, for her part, turned red when she heard about the comment. As news reports from the Goldman conference hit the wires, she hit the roof. "She can't say that!," Frank hollered. "It's an SEC violation!"

However, the damage was done. A day later, HP put out a release to say that Fiorina had not predicted victory, but only expressed confidence that HP's position would prevail. It didn't matter much. Many investors figured Fiorina wouldn't have been so bold if she hadn't known that things were tipping her way. "I figured the deal had less than a 50 percent chance before yesterday," Ray E. Hirsch, technology group director with American Express Financial

Advisors, said on the day of her speech. "Now, I give it a 65 percent chance."

Possibly not coincidentally, HP set the date for the shareholder vote that same day. It would be March 19. For everyone involved, it would be a very eventful six weeks.

With momentum starting to shift, the Hewlett camp had to come up with some answers. Its initial strategy—to go for the knockout blow—hadn't panned out. Now, it was time to pull out all the stops. His team raced to issue its proxy statement first, mailing out its document on February 5. This was significant, because many retail shareholders only read and respond to the first proxy statement they get in the mail. Hewlett's advisors were so anxious to be first that they mailed out the document before the SEC had given its final okay. Though not illegal, this was risky, because Hewlett wouldn't be protected against lawsuits if anything in the document was later deemed to be misleading. However, Hewlett was on a roll. It was not a time to hold back.

But Hewlett had bigger problems. Investors who just weeks before had been ridiculing the deal now seemed to be thinking differently. Rather than the damage the deal would do, they were growing more concerned with what would happen if Hewlett *did* kill it.

"What I don't like is complete uncertainty," said Merrill Lynch's Kevin Rendino. "If the deal is voted down, I don't know what I'm left with. I don't know if the board will stay, if management will walk out the door, or what the strategy will be. Sometimes the devil you know is better than the devil you don't."

Because investors were spooked that HP's board would quit, Hewlett met with former CEO Lew Platt for three hours in February. Platt told Hewlett that yes, he would lend his management help on an interim basis if it came to that—but only after all the smoke had cleared from the proxy fight. He wanted no part in the ongoing HP soap opera. He didn't want to return as CEO. However, Platt assured Hewlett that he didn't need to worry about the current board resigning. He was certain that the veteran executives would do the responsible thing and stick by their posts. There was still the question of whether to offer an alternative strategy.

Hewlett did not want to do so. Tully Friedman agreed. He was certain HP would have a field day the second Hewlett professed to know the computer business better than HP's entire board and management team.

Frank felt the momentum slipping away fast, and she was not one to sit by and let that happen. Repeatedly, insistently, she urged Hewlett's financial advisors to come up with something to give investors. The more she said it, the more the tension rose—but no one would take her on. Frank had earned her reputation as one of Wall Street's fiercest pit bulls. Her voice said it all. One team member stopped using his speaker phone at home during weekend conference calls to avoid irritating his wife, who complained of the sound of Frank's strident voice all the way from downstairs. "Her voice scared my dog," he said.

After the Goldman Sachs debacle, Frank insisted one time too many for Friedman. "What's our alternative?" Frank said, during one of their endless meetings. "We have to have an alternative!"

"Stop right there," Friedman bellowed. "Don't ever ask that question again."

Pause.

"I don't ever want to hear you ask that question again," Friedman continued.

Silence.

More silence.

More than a dozen people on the line waited in shock for what must have been a minute of dead silence. Friedman had finally done it. He'd shouted down Frank.

There was no lasting damage from the eruption. Frank, not easily hurt, named the new fighting fish in her office aquarium "Tully II" and moved on.

In fact, the exchange helped break the logjam within Hewlett's team. Over the next few weeks, the team decided to try a halfway step. They would offer broad outlines of a strategic plan, but nothing specific enough to give HP the ammunition it needed to discredit Hewlett.

The plan, announced on February 19, was called "Focus and Execute." It said what many investors wanted to hear, and what many insiders believed was the right course. Rather than double up on PCs and forever anchor itself to that miserable market, HP should focus on its most profitable businesses. It should concentrate time and money on expanding its "crown jewel" printer business, and on regaining strength in the high-end computer business, where margins were still reasonable. Where it made sense, the company should make "targeted acquisitions" to fill a particular need—say, in consulting. There was no point, however, in trying to take on Dell in lower-margin markets where me-too products would suffice. HP would never be able to match Dell's efficiency, especially while trying to also out-IBM at the high end of the market.

As predicted, HP jumped at the chance to disparage Walter the Strategist. The company argued that backing out of PCs was far easier said than done, and would require many layoffs and losses. And hadn't HP been trying to focus and execute all along? "It's not a plan," Fiorina snapped. "It's a press release." To some degree, she was right. A report from Hewlett's financial advisors boldly claimed his three principals could help HP add $14 to $17 per share, numbers that sounded as if they had been pulled out of a hat. The company also jumped on Hewlett's suggestion that HP consider spinning off the printer business—a move that would leave HP's investors with a collection of uninteresting, sickly computer businesses.

In the end, Focus and Execute would fail to do Hewlett much good. Many people felt the concepts were right. IBM had benefited hugely by backing away from the PC business in previous years. By selling PCs only to companies that bought more profitable products, it had stemmed its PC losses and improved its overall profits—just as Hewlett was suggesting HP do. Still, he was in a strategic limbo. Focus and Execute looked to many like a hesitant halfway step designed to win a proxy fight, not to fix HP. All that seemed certain was that if the Compaq merger was nixed, HP would need to find a new strategy, a new CEO, and maybe even a new board of directors. HP, it was becoming clear, had trumped Hewlett's Focus and Execute with an unstated strategy of its own: the chaos theory.

"HP did a great job of parading horribles," Friedman said. "It was like, 'after me, the flood.'"

Smelling blood, HP poured on the pressure. As February moved into March, the company stepped up its spending to record levels. When all was said and done, it would run many ads, some costing well over $100,000 per pop. It sent eight letters to HP's 960,000 shareholders, each mailing costing roughly $3 million. There were many spending firsts. In one case, HP paid for an overnight mailing to people with more than 2,000 shares, which cost a whopping $6 to $10 per person—a first in proxy-fight history. The company also used a billboard in Times Square that it had rented before the proxy fight.

Hewlett tried his best to keep pace; his team ran ads and sent out six letters to shareholders. The sheer deluge of paper became preposterous, with even small shareholders getting several mailings a day in the final weeks of the fight. One HP employee in Boise said employees were getting so many proxy cards with self-addressed stamped envelopes that they all had enough free stamps to last a month.

In the end, Hewlett couldn't possibly compete on the spending front. He says he spent nearly $40 million, including legal fees, far more than his advisors' initial estimate of $20 million. But HP, which has never formally announced the total, spent $70 million or more, say insiders. Indeed, Hewlett quietly seethed at the fact that the family interests, given their 18 percent ownership, were footing the bill for roughly one-fifth of that amount. All told, it was the most expensive corporate tiff in history.

The HP ads were more personal than Hewlett's, but Hewlett remained remarkably immune to it all. In late February, for example, the company ran a big ad that screamed "Flip-Flop." It slammed Hewlett for his many changes of heart, including his original vote switcheroo—which was exactly what Larry Sonsini had told him he could do. After reading the ad over breakfast that morning, Hewlett put down the paper. "Okay," he said, not reacting at all to the accusations. "Who are we going to see today?"

Michael Sheehan, Hewlett's media trainer, marveled that Hewlett never seemed to take anything personally. "It was more like a pleasant bafflement, like, 'I can't believe anyone would think this stuff is important.'"

The behind-the-scenes chatter was as interesting as what showed up in the ads each day. HP in particular played it fast and loose with the facts. HP put out the word that all its board members and top executives would quit. It wasn't true; Bob Wayman and directors Phil Condit and Sam Ginn said as much. HP insisted that the Hewlett and Packard families had conspired to oppose the deal; there was never any good evidence of this. When the Hewlett Foundation sold 5.5 million shares as part of an ongoing diversification program, HP sources claimed it had timed the sale to benefit from Walter Hewlett's initial opposition. "They know, to a person, exactly what the foundation has been doing for the past four and a half years," said Jim Gaither. "I find that pretty disgusting." When the *Financial Times* put out a story that Hewlett had met with Platt about coming back as CEO, the company happily put out a press release. "It was tone deaf for Hewlett's side not to realize that institutional shareholders thought Lew Platt had driven the company into the ground," said George Sard. "We were absolutely doing what we could to fan the chaos."

Some observers sitting on the sidelines grew frustrated with Hewlett's refusal to take a stronger stand or play dirtier. "Carly played to win. Walter played to tie," said Roger McNamee, founder of the influential Silicon Valley investment company Integral Partners.

Carly Fiorina was slowly winning the war for investors, but she was getting creamed on another front: relations with HP's employees. Inside the company, many had become openly hostile.

The company's assault on Hewlett embarrassed and pained many HP veterans.

As the proxy fight continued, a sense of weariness set in. Focused on wooing investors, management did a less effective job explaining the deal to employees. That lack of effort showed.

"It's not the layoffs," said one employee. "It's that nobody seems to feel bad about it." When the company tried to recruit staffers in Boise to be in a TV ad supporting the deal, only three people showed up, says one of the three. When the new-economy magazine *Red Herring* ran an article calling for Fiorina's resignation, a Boise employee left stacks of Xerox copies by the coffee stations in the building.[3]

News articles had hinted at the cancerous attitude growing among many employees, but David Woodley Packard confirmed it with three employee surveys. He hired Field Research Corporation to poll current and former employees in three big HP towns—Corvallis, Oregon; Boise, Idaho; and Fort Collins, Colorado. The results were strikingly consistent, and the conclusions were clear: Of 940 current employees, about 64 percent opposed the merger, and 67 percent said HP was a worse place to work than when they started working there.

HP claimed the results were biased and unrepresentative. The company insisted that its monthly polls, suggesting that two-thirds of employees supported the merger, were more accurate. What they failed to say was that many employees had grown so distrustful of management that they were afraid even to participate in company surveys. Evidence suggests that Packard's surveys were closer to the mark. Packard had insisted that Field Research send its results directly to the press, before even he saw them.

The most compelling evidence of employee disdain would arrive March 18, when Hewlett announced that 72 percent of shares held in a big HP retirement program had been voted in opposition to the merger.

Some key members of HP's so-called clean team, too, feared the worst. Some 600 people on this team put in nearly a million hours on the gargantuan job of integrating the two companies, planning every possible aspect of the deal. They thought of everything—how to merge two divergent cultures, how to make sure every employee got an HP paycheck—and every big customer had a new sales liaison assigned from the day the merger closed. Of course, that didn't mean the merger would pay off financially. Several believed top brass had convinced business managers to sign up for unrealistic growth and earnings targets. "The phrase you hear is 'dead woman walking' about Fiorina, said one clean-team member. This person attended a meeting to discuss a photo shoot for a newspaper ad, which ran in March. At the meeting, many clean-team staffers wanted to be assured that the ad would not be used to attack Walter

Hewlett. "It was clear people didn't want to be part of the smear campaign."

Nonetheless, some critics of the deal supported the merger because they didn't want to see months of round-the-clock work wasted—and they wanted to collect their hefty retention bonuses. Many of these integration-team members were among the 6,000 who had been given bonuses of roughly $50,000 per person. "I'm going to vote for [the merger]," said one clean-team manager. "I'm giving up on the stock, and taking the cash. The bribe worked."

Tanking morale could be partly attributed to HP's own lack of confidence. Many managers simply believed the job of managing an $80-billion behemoth was beyond them. Others, led by Fiorina and Hackborn, argued that there was no choice but to take a shot. "I literally don't know if it can be done," said former HP Labs chief Joel Birnbaum. "But I'd rather go for it, and say 'So what if no one has ever been successful with something like this before?' Why not us?"

The most divisive flap in the entire proxy fight broke out in late February.

Fiorina and HP's top executives were preparing to make their final pitch to Wall Street with an all-day presentation at a Manhattan hotel. For months, Hewlett had been stewing over the pay packages the board had discussed giving Fiorina and Capellas. As a member of HP's compensation committee, he'd helped to craft postmerger contracts that would pay Capellas and Fiorina roughly $115 million, including salary, bonuses, and options.

A few key details were not set in stone, such as the vesting scheduling for the options. Although HP's government filings confirmed that the executives would get a raise, Hewlett said he began demanding in December that HP divulge the existing details to investors.

If there was ever a time when the proxy fight resembled a dirty political campaign, this was it. At first, HP planned to announce the executive pay packages *before* the shareholder vote. When a January filing said that they would be negotiated *after* the vote, *BusinessWeek* wrote a short story suggesting investors might cry foul. "It's clearly material information, and the SEC ought to make them make it public," Neal was quoted in the article.[4] At a board meeting January 18, Sonsini and Fiorina demanded that Hewlett stop using their pay packages as a tool in his proxy fight, according to Hewlett. That day, HP's compensation committee agreed that "no new employment contracts exist," meaning all prior conversations were null and void.

It didn't end there, however. Hewlett knew that HP's lawyers had written "side letter" agreements to Compaq's lawyers, reiterating terms of the pay packages. So far as he was concerned, the $115 million compensation for both executives that the board had discussed before the shareholder vote would in all likelihood stand.

Hewlett saved his powder for when it would have ultimate impact: the day before HP's February 27 conference with Wall Street analysts, probably its last group pitch. That day, his team issued a press release that shared details of the $115-million packages. Outraged, HP's board put out a letter castigating him for playing with the facts. "Your words and actions in recent weeks are not the words and actions of the Walter Hewlett each of us has known for many years," the board wrote.[5] Fiorina was clearly furious when she broached the subject in her opening remarks at the analysts meeting the next day. "Let me be clear: Shareholders have every right to know the details of my compensation package. But we cannot disclose employment contracts that do not yet exist."

Still, Hewlett would not back down—instead, he took this dangerous game of chicken to unexpected heights. On February 28, he released copies of the actual term sheets, side letters, and board minutes. This was outright boardroom heresy, but Neal knew that HP would never dare sue Hewlett, for dread of once again making him a martyr. "He knew those pay packages were no longer on the table, and he leaked them to win a proxy contest—not to come to the aid of shareholders," says Wilson Sonsini's Korman. Maybe so, but most corporate governance experts think HP should have disclosed what it knew to shareholders. That would become especially clear when Michael Capellas resigned to become CEO of World-Com in November 2002—taking with him $14 million in a post-merger agreement he'd negotiated with Compaq's board in the months after the merger was announced.

On March 5, HP celebrated a huge victory, a near-death experience of sorts. After weeks of constant courting by both sides, ISS recommended that investors vote for the merger. If ISS had opposed the merger, HP would have surely lost the proxy fight. With ISS's blessing, it was going to be a fight to the finish.

Fiorina had worked hard to nail this one. After multiple visits and phone calls, she visited ISS by herself for one last meeting. Why did ISS agree to meet with her yet again? "I wanted to see the substance beyond the style," said ISS President Pat McGurn. "And we did see it. The caricature is that she's all pitch and no delivery. That's not what we found."

The deciding factor, however, was the detailed integration plan HP and Compaq presented. Product road maps had been decided on, so there would be none of the postmerger infighting that had plagued so many tech mergers. All managers would know the financial goals that would determine their compensation. Salespeople would all have "sales playbooks and toolkits" so they would know what products to sell, and how best to do it. And the companies had done "pioneering work" to figure out how to meld the best of Compaq's aggressive, confrontational corporate culture with HP's more deliberative, team-based approach "It is hard to remain unimpressed in the face of such enthusiastic attention paid to the integration effort," ISS concluded in its report.[6]

It was not a clean sweep. The moral victory went to Walter Hewlett, who was praised for his "sincere, courageous independence." "We view the conduct that management objects to—mounting a contest to publicly probe at management's compensation arrangements—as not only becoming but praiseworthy in many respects," the report said.[7] Still, the coast was clear for Fiorina to try to bring home the deal of her career.

It would not be easy. The day after ISS's decision, Hewlett got a couple of gifts. Standard & Poor's lowered its credit rating on HP, and CalPERS, a big California retirement fund, came out against the merger. In the days that followed, Hewlett and his road-show traveling companions were able to convince a host of other pension funds to publicly announce their intention to oppose the merger. This was a remarkable achievement, because investors almost never volunteer such information, Burch said. But if it made great head-lines, such small fry were not going to make much of a difference.

Still, both sides knew it was a dead heat. Hewlett was pulling slightly ahead with individual shareholders, and would clearly take the majority of the 5 percent of shares held by current and former employees. Both sides knew HP would win most of the top 10 investors, but just one or two defectors might be enough. People started to draw comparisons between the merger vote and the his-toric battle over the razor-close presidential election five months ear-lier, which led to bloodletting between the Bush and Gore camps.

"It's like the election: It's going to come down to a couple of votes in Florida," said former HP executive Daniel Warmenhoven, the CEO of Network Appliance, Inc.

Hewlett did finally sharpen his criticism of Fiorina in the final days before the shareholder vote. On February 23, he told *Business-Week* that "One of the big risks in this deal is that we've got a CEO who has a track record of being overoptimistic. That doesn't bode well for the management of one of the most difficult mergers that has ever been attempted." Finally, he admitted that he would try to oust her and get a new CEO if she lost the vote. "This time around, we do not want someone learning on the job," he sniped in a March 12 conference call with the press. He would later regret the comment. "A lot of investors felt Carly was the problem and wanted me to point it out," he said in an interview in June. "Eventually, I took them up on it. But in a way, I was pulled off base." Hewlett would show integrity of a different kind in the final days.

Prior to the shareholder vote, Hewlett's advisors hatched a scheme whereby Hewlett would buy up to $500 million worth of HP stock from shareholders who favored the deal. His advisors believed this move might give Hewlett the shares he needed to win the day.

Hewlett refused to go through with it. On March 13, he broke the news. "I'm not going to do this," he explained. "If we won [by buying shares], how was I going to be able to walk into HP's board-room and say 'The shareholders have decided?' "

Of all the shareholders, it was clear that one big investor could make all the difference. Hewlett would come tantalizingly close to landing it. Starting in late February, Hewlett's advisors had been lobbying Deutsche Bank. Dean Barr, the chief investment officer of Deutsche Bank's global investment arm, told Fleischer that the bank's policy wasn't to meet with combatants in a proxy fight; its proxy committees would make the call based on publicly available information. However, on March 15, as Hewlett and his advisors were jetting between investor meetings, Barr told Fleischer that the proxy committee of the bank's U.S. Asset Management subsidiary and of its Europe-based investment arm had voted to oppose the merger. It was a huge victory.

Barr said the bank would probably put out an announcement that day, but he asked Fleischer not to mention it to anyone. According to a deposition from Fleischer, Barr said it was sensitive internally, because Deutsche Bank had a banking relationship with HP that might be put at risk by the decision. Barr later testified that the conversation with Fleischer never occurred.

When no announcement went out and with the shareholder vote just days away, Fleischer grew concerned. He reached Barr on the day before the shareholder vote. Barr confirmed that the bank still planned to vote against the merger—but that it would not put out a release.

On the same day Deutsche Bank told Hewlett it was voting his way, HP's proxy solicitor Alan Miller got wind of their decision. He warned Bob Wayman, stopping him in his tracks. He and Fiorina hadn't even bothered to visit with Deutsche Bank.

Wayman knew top executives with the bank's commercial banking unit, which for years had been trying to win more business from HP. Other than some yeoman's work providing basic credit facilities, it had been shot down in efforts to win lucrative assignments, such as taking Agilent public. Even when almost every other Wall Street analyst was trashing the stock in the early months, Deutsche Bank's George Elling had been one of the most enthusiastic supporters. Later, HP handed the bank a $1-million contract to investigate how other institutions were voting—including an extra $1 million if HP won the proxy fight. What's more, Deutsche Bank vice chairman Benjamin Griswold and Robert Thornton had promised Wayman that the company would vote according to the ISS recommendation.

As such, there was nothing to worry about. Even on March 15, they reassured Wayman "that everything is fine, that Deutsche Bank is supporting the merger," according to the trial transcript.[8]

At that point, the so-called Chinese Wall was holding firm at Deutsche Bank. That wall separated Deutsche Bank's investment managers, who have a legal obligation to their shareholders, and its dealmakers, who provide financial advice to corporations. The bankers are not supposed to have any influence over the investment gurus.

However, that Chinese Wall was about to crumble. The trouble started on Sunday, March 17, when Miller told Fiorina that the rumor about Deutsche Bank. That night, Fiorina called Wayman at his home and left a voice mail: "Hi Bob. It's Carly. It's Sunday night. Call the guy at Deutsche Bank again first thing in the morning. And if you don't get the right answer from him then you and I need to demand a conference call, an audience, et cetera, to make sure we get them in the right place. You need a definitive answer. You need a definite answer from the vice chairman and, if it's the wrong one, we have to swing into action." The message ends with this now famous line: "See what we can get, but we may have to do something extraordinary to bring them over the line here."[9]

On Monday, Wayman did what Fiorina asked and called his sources to search for the truth. Embarrassed, and no doubt worried about their banking contracts, one of the bank executives called Wayman back with the bad news. Wayman insisted that HP, having been misled, at least be given the opportunity to make its pitch before a decision was made. At that point, Griswold slipped through the Chinese Wall and asked Barr on the investment side to set up a meeting with HP. They decided that to maintain the appearance of fairness, they should meet with Hewlett as well.

The bank called Fleischer at 5:30 A.M. on the day of the shareholder vote. They wanted to speak with Hewlett for 15 minutes at 7:45, just fifteen minutes before the shareholder vote was to begin. Hewlett would have been en route, so they decided on a 6:30 A.M. meeting. It had to be quick, because they were going to speak to HP at 7:00. Fleischer tried to call and e-mail Barr to ask him about the meeting and what had happened since they last spoke, but he got no response. If the bank was going to change its vote, it needed to do it by 10:00 A.M. West Coast time, when the polls on the proxy vote were scheduled to close.

At 6:30, Hewlett and Fleischer made an abbreviated version of their pitch, knowing something was fishy. There were many people on the line from the bank. Fleischer wasn't sure who, but Barr and members of the bank's proxy committee were there. For the most part, it was the same old pitch, including a swipe at Fiorina. "There are problems that we have known about for two or three years and the current management, the CEO has not executed properly on these. . . . This is a very different company than it was nine months ago. Everybody knows that time has run out and we need to make the tough choices." The idea that HP's problems were a function of Fiorina's mismanagement were to an extent true, but the company had managed to squelch this line of thinking.

After Hewlett's 15 minutes were up, Barr had a quick chat with Klaus Kaldemorgen, a member of the bank's European Proxy Committee. According to a transcript of the conversation later filed in court, Barr explained why they were hosting the two conference calls that morning. "You may or may not be aware, that we have an enormous banking relationship with Hewlett-Packard," Barr told him. "I have some very grave concerns that—and this is why this is taking place—that we need to have very strong documentation in place as it relates to this vote."

"I'm going to ask everyone to reconsider their vote based on the information they hear today," Barr continued. "That does not mean they have to change their vote. It just means I want people to make sure that they have heard all the evidence and all the facts."

Bank officials in Europe and New York remained on the line until Wayman joined the call. Again, it was a fairly standard pitch. When Fiorina came in on the call, she dove right in, reiterating that HP's board had spent three years scouring all the alternatives to a merger. She again accused Hewlett of having never contributed much during that process. As usual, Fiorina's oratorical skills sparkled. Whereas Hewlett meandered and stammered at times, she was clear and persuasive, speaking in compelling sound bites. And she pulled no punches. When asked about Hewlett's alternative plan, she reminded the bankers that "You must bear in mind that Mr. Hewlett's advisors have a large success fee tied to whether or not they can kill this merger," not mentioning the fees her own advisors stood to gain.

Then she claimed that the integration of HP and Compaq was going swimmingly, that 900 dedicated workers were right on track with internal plans. Judging from the value capture updates, many of those 900 did not agree, but that wasn't mentioned. "We will hit the market running," she said. Then she called up the old chaos theory: If not Compaq, then what? "The cost of a failed deal is real," she warned. "It is highly disruptive to the business. There are no alternatives that yield 14 to 17 dollars a share in value, I can assure you. And there are, frankly, no other alternatives that yield five to nine dollars a share, which is what this does." Then, before hanging up, she uttered some words that would later come under a legal microscope: "This is obviously of great importance to us as a company. It is of great importance to our ongoing relationship. We very much would like to have your support here. We think this is a crucially important decision for the company."[10]

Then she left for the shareholder meeting.

With Fiorina off the telephone line, the five Deutsche Bank officials who remained on the call held a quick discussion about what they had just heard. Barr immediately brought up Fiorina's point about Hewlett's paid advisors who stood to get $12 million if Hewlett succeeded. "You've got to ask the question whether the dissident shareholder or advisors are in this really for the benefit of the shareholder or are they really trying to protect their own fee?" Barr said, according to the transcript of the call.

An unidentified speaker on the line then pointed out the obvious flip side of Barr's question, regarding the bank's role as an advisor to HP. "Do we know what the advisors for HP are getting now? I mean they—I didn't want to ask the question because I was afraid it might be us, but. . . ."

"I believe the answer is we are one of the advisors," Barr answered.

"Isn't there some sort of performance fee associated with that as well?" the unidentified speaker continued.

"I don't—I have no way of knowing and I'm not even going to ask the question," Barr answered.

As the five Deutsche Bank executives discussed what they'd heard, it was clear that Fiorina had won the bake-off. One executive grabbed the chaos theory theme: "What will the end result be if the deal goes down? I think it's disastrous, in a way." Another weighed in about Hewlett: "He is a music teacher at Stanford."

With that, they took another vote. This time, it was 4 to 1 in favor of HP. Barr, clearly concerned about appearances, said, "So there is a change. . . . I need this absolutely unequivocally documented very carefully as relates to what has just transpired." With that, he urged someone to get the vote changed as fast as "humanly possible."

Before they all hung up, Kaldemorgen, calling from Germany, got back on the line. Before he could get a word in, Barr explained that the U.S. unit had changed its vote. After "a very considerable discussion with Carly Fiorina and Bob Wayman," the group had become concerned about "what happens if the merger doesn't go through." Again, it was the fear, uncertainty, and doubt card. It worked.

Kaldemorgen, clearly not buying the change of heart, shot back. "Well, I firmly disagree with that," he said. He pointed to the fact that the stock rose whenever news occurred that put the deal in doubt.

The others quickly jumped in. One cited how impressive Fiorina and Wayman had been, and worried that "Not only would this company probably lose its chairman, but it would probably lose a considerable number of board members as well."

Kaldemorgen, surprised that they were discussing changing their vote, held his ground. But Barr broke in: "The group here has changed the vote. . . . Obviously if you don't want to change your vote, that's your call. I would suggest to you—and I'm not trying to put undue pressure, but make sure that you have a very strong documented rationale for why you voted the way you did as it relates to this merger. This is extremely sensitive to people like . . . Doctor Ackerman."

The mention of Josef Ackerman, the bank's powerful CEO, seemed to do the trick. Kaldemorgen immediately changed his defiant tune. "I don't want to be smarter than you people in New York. So if the majority of you come to the conclusion that it's better for our customers to vote in favor, I'll try to change our vote here."

A few days later, Fiorina called Griswold to thank him for arranging the meeting with the investment side of the house. "Thanks for going to bat for us," she said, according to trial proceedings. "You know, I'd like to thank you personally. Look forward to doing business with you in the future." Three days later, Thornton advised Griswold to erase the message, which he did.

In so many ways, it was a shining example of the difficulties a shareholder—even one with Hewlett's money and name—has in taking on the corporate world. Just days before, the same group of people had felt strongly enough to break from corporate policy and not follow ISS's recommendation. What was different? They'd heard a sales pitch, to be sure. But was it any wonder that a career salesperson and a veteran CFO would do a more compelling job in 45 minutes than an "academic and musician" would do in 15? Other than that, the only change was that some banking business might be at stake, and the company's top brass might not like it.

In the end, Deutsche Bank's flip-flop probably did not decide the proxy fight. HP would win by a larger margin than the bank's total holdings. But it was a fitting, final vote in a sordid affair, in which HP backed its way into victory. It seemed clear that the majority of shareholders probably wished this merger had never happened, but Fiorina had played her cards right. Her victory was not a testament to the deal, or to investor confidence in her. It was a testament to her ability to play the game, to win the fight. Whether it was good for anyone else remains to be seen.

By 7:30 A.M., Hewlett's team was heading from the Cupertino Hilton Garden Inn, where they had rented a block of rooms, to the Flint Center nearby. Located on the campus of De Anza College, the Flint Center had hosted many of Steve Jobs's historic Apple Computer product launches. Now, the auditorium, with its red cloth seats and multitiered balconies, would be the site of the shareholder meeting that would change the course of HP's history.

Some of Hewlett's team members gathered in a wood-paneled room across the plaza that was equipped with phones and fax machines. As the votes came in, Fleischer and Burch did their best to guess who was voting, judging by the number of shares the voter held. "You don't see the name of the investor, so it's a black art," Fleischer says. "We certainly didn't feel we had it in the bag. And I think that was probably true on the other side." At this point, Fleischer likened the vote to the painful period of waiting for scores after taking exams. "There's no more studying you can do." You just wait.

Outside the Flint Center, a large crowd was gathering. Although an estimated 99 percent of the votes have been cast via proxy cards that had been mailed out, hundreds of shareholders flocked to Cupertino to witness the Hewlett-Fiorina showdown.

Security was tight; Fiorina's people had insisted on metal detectors. It was clearly going to be a hostile crowd. A large percentage of the stockholders wore green, the color of Hewlett's proxy cards. Angry employees from Compaq's European operations carried placards with mottos such as "Fire Two, Not 15,000," bemoaning the coming layoffs. Scores of journalists filed past the long line of investors heading in the other direction, waiting to get into the building. Comments, for the most part, were not complimentary. "This is not the time or place for a smarty pants," said Diana Lang, who'd driven up from Southern California. Mary Lee, a 14-year HP veteran who'd moved on to Agilent, said, "I supported Carly when she first came in. Now, it's just a sad state of affairs." When Hewlett arrived, he was given a hero's welcome. The crowd parted, as well-wishers approached to shake his hand and congratulate him.

Inside, Hewlett's camp took the 40 seats that had been reserved for them. More important was the question of whether Hewlett would be allowed to say anything. At first, Fiorina did not want to allow it, says Sonsini, who convinced her otherwise

As the scheduled 8:00 A.M. starting time came and went, reporters sitting in a tent set up outside began to wonder. Talk swirled that HP, fearing it didn't have the votes, might cancel the vote for another day. The company bylaws allowed it to do so.

By 8:30, the shareholder's meeting had finally begun. Fiorina, 30 minutes late to the podium, took the stage in a purple suit, white blouse, and pearl earrings. There were circles ringing her eyes; she looked like she'd been up all night. "There is one item on the agenda," she said. Chief Counsel Ann Baskins sat next to her, with Assistant Counsel Charles Charnas. The company claimed the delay was to give people stuck in the parking lot time to get to their seats; but the place, which had a Saint Patrick's Day flair due to all the green clothing, was by no means packed. That added to the faint air of suspicion.

After some opening remarks, Fiorina invited Hewlett to speak. No one knew what he would say, including Fiorina. Approaching a microphone toward the back of the room, he sheepishly raised his hand so the audience could find him. The crowd got on its feet and roared. Hewlett was their hero.

"Thank you very much," he said. "You need to turn up the sound. . . . Good morning. I am Walter Hewlett," he began stiffly. He didn't speak for long, but graciously thanked HP's investors, both supporters and otherwise, for hearing him out. He thanked HP's employees for suffering through the proxy fight. "For many decades, HP has represented a unique vision of the best an American corporation could be. The very public, very spirited debate over this merger has also been a debate about the soul of HP, and what it means for America. The HP Way is not a relic of another time, and it's not a piece of trivia relevant only to Hewlett and Packard family members."

The audience, again, clapped wildly, and Hewlett closed on a conciliatory note. "I've known and worked side by side with the HP directors for many years. We share a common interest in stability and stockholder value. My interest in this matter has been as a stockholder like you. We have tried to shine a bright light on the details. I truly believe this has made us a stronger company."

After Hewlett finished his speech, the audience rose to its feet again. Fiorina, too, clapped—relieved at his words. "Thank you very much, Walter," she said.

Then Fiorina opened the floor for questions from shareholders, who were not kind. There were complaints over the expense of the proxy fight, by a man who lugged a thick folder of mailings with him to the microphone. Others wanted to know if she would agree to renominate Hewlett, or if she would disclose her compensation. Asked about future relations with the families, she promised to work to find common ground. She answered a question about the impending 15,000 layoffs by pointing out that 36,000 people worked in businesses that were losing money; on balance, it was best for everyone to get those businesses healthy to prevent even more job loss. She was as polished and competent as ever, even in the face of hostility.

There was one question she was unable to escape so easily, however. It occurred when Al Knoll, an HP retiree, asked her about morale. When Fiorina responded that "The majority of employees of this company support this merger," a groan—half boos of outrage, half disbelieving laughter—echoed through the room.

"That's a fact," she reiterated. An even bigger groan.

As the question-and-answer session wound down, Baskins handed Fiorina a note onstage. After quickly unfolding the note and reading it, Fiorina made a move to end the meeting. At 10:10 A.M., she told the audience "The results of the vote will be announced when they are available."

In the audience, Hewlett's advisors watched these events with intense interest. They were already thinking about Deutsche Bank when Burch got an e-mail on his Blackberry pager confirming their fears. Deutsche Bank had voted for the merger. It was only seconds later that Fiorina took the note from Baskins and closed the polls. From their perspective, this was beginning to look very suspicious.

After the meeting, Fiorina rushed backstage, to a dressing room where her media and investor relations teams had gathered. It had come down to the wire—not only for the merger, but for Fiorina. Many of HP's board members, some of whom had grown even more loyal during the proxy fight, wanted her to stay on regardless. That would be difficult, however. Most likely, she'd be forced to resign. If she won, she would have pulled off one of the great comebacks in business history—the tech industry equivalent of Truman versus Dewey.

All eyes turned to HP's proxy solicitor, a stone-faced Alan Miller. "Be extremely conservative," Fiorina urged. "Where is the vote coming out?"

Three press releases had been prepared for this moment: one to announce victory, one to say it was too close to call, and one to graciously admit defeat. "Alan, which release do we put out?" Fiorina asked.

Miller, an unflappable numbers guy, was known for his straight talk. "You can put out release number one," he replied.

After the group broke up, lawyer Korman approached the proxy solicitor. "Are you sure, Alan?" one of Fiorina's advisors asked.

"It's mathematically impossible for them to have won," Miller responded.

Attorney Sonsini advised Fiorina to describe the margin of victory as "slim but sufficient," and the conversation briefly turned to what they should do about Hewlett. Should they quickly move to make amends or brush him off? Previously, Fiorina had decided that she did not want him back on the board, but after his remarks during the meeting, she was thinking that an olive branch might be a better alternative.

"Let's try to put this behind us," Fiorina said. It was decided that board member Sam Ginn, the only outside director other than Hewlett who had attended the day's meeting, should go talk to Hewlett to sound him out on the decision.

With that, Fiorina walked back to the stage for a press conference. Happy but exhausted, she announced the news. "Based on preliminary estimates we believe we have achieved sufficient votes," she said. Asked to elaborate, she used the "slim but sufficient" phrase.

Walter Hewlett hadn't conceded. It was too close to call, said his press release. Still, for as many crazy twists as there had been, the press conference he held back at the Hilton seemed more like that of a politician who had lost, but who had fought the good fight. Throngs of reporters packed the room for the meeting. Eleven TV cameras caught the action as Hewlett, as was typical in his public performances, stiffly reread the comments he'd made at the Flint Center.

He did not behave as if he'd lost. His advisors said they believed the vote was within 1 percent, and they began to float the salacious story of the Deutsche Bank flip-flop. Hewlett seemed contentedly above the fray. Clearly the crowd favorite, he calmly took questions. Asked what he would do going forward, he said he looked forward to getting back to his former life. "I do not expect to be holding another press conference anytime soon. While I fully expect to stay active in HP, I will resume my life as a musician and an academic."

Laughter spread through the room. Few people who'd met Hewlett ever doubted his motives or character; even Carly Fiorina had called him a "good and decent man." It seemed a fitting, hopeful end to what had been a sad, painful six months.

However, the story wasn't over.

After a quick lunch of cold cuts and cake, Hewlett and his advisors headed back to Cooley Godward's offices. Waiting for them there was Sam Ginn, Fiorina's assigned peacemaker. A warm man with a smooth Southern accent, he wanted to get a sense of Hewlett's feelings about everything that had happened. Now that it was done, was he willing to work with the board to make the deal a success? Hewlett said he was. But Ginn also asked whether he was going to forego any more challenges to the merger. Given the slim decision, the votes would have to be counted by an independent firm. Eighteen-wheelers full of proxy cards were already en route. Was he ready to concede, and forego other challenges? Hewlett didn't have to pause to consider the offer. He rejected it, saying he intended to let the process play out to the end, come what may.

"That's not what I wanted to hear," Ginn said.

When the group left Cooley Godward, nothing had been

resolved. Driving down scenic Route 280 toward home that night, Spencer Fleischer was looking forward to taking his family on vacation to Mexico. He was also wistful. "When it's over, you feel slightly at a loss," he said. But it wasn't over for Fleischer—or for any of the members of the Hewlett team.

People were already talking about a recount or litigation.

12

THE LAWSUIT

Are you aware that your complaint accuses Hewlett-Packard of lying?

—WILSON SONSINI LAWYER STEVE SCHATZ TO
WALTER HEWLETT

By the time Carly Fiorina declared victory on March 19, much of the world was downright sick of the HP story. Press coverage had been extensive. Shareholders had spent weeks unloading stuffed mailboxes and erasing proxy battle messages from their voice mail. They just wanted to move on. So did many HP employees, even those who loathed the deal. It was one thing to rally while there was a chance of victory, but now the deal was done. If you cared to keep your job, it was time to get with Fiorina's new program. "It was kind of like somebody died on March 19," said one manager in Boise. "It's a cloudy day, but I'm sure the sun is up there somewhere."

Fiorina's "slim but sufficient" victory wasn't enough to bring closure to the soap opera, however. Too many fishy details and too much intrigue remained. The rumors about Deutsche Bank's secret vote lingered. The bank's refusal to comment shrouded its vote in even more mystery.

Rumors that all was not well with Fiorina's merger effort continued to trickle in to the Hewlett team. It had started before the shareholder vote. In February, the wife of an HP employee e-mailed what appeared to be minutes of an internal HP meeting that suggested HP's various businesses were far from hitting the earnings goals that management had promised Wall Street. Another time, someone dropped off a one-page letter. Addressed to SEC chairman Harvey Pitt, it alleged "fraud and misinformation" in HP's S-4 filing with the government.[1] The letter claimed that Fiorina and Michael Capellas knew that the new HP would lose 10 to 15 percent in revenue during the integration process, rather than the 5 percent they publicly claimed. The cost savings would be far more than $2.5 billion, and the layoffs would be upward of 24,000 rather than 15,000. "Fiorina and Capellas have created an atmosphere of fear within the company, placing no priority on telling the truth and all priority on getting the merger to pass," the letter stated. "After Enron, they are aware of the implications of this fraud, and have instructed everyone to not talk about the true internal plans. Even now they are destroying records that demonstrate and document this fraud." Though thrilling, the letter was unsigned—and therefore useless in court.

In the days before the shareholder vote, this sort of activity had increased. A handful of HP managers frequently contacted Hewlett's advisors. One man who claimed to be a member of the integration team called repeatedly to dish dirt in the week before the shareholder vote, but wouldn't leave his name. Joele Frank and Dan Burch called him "Joe Stone." There were more cryptic calls from disgruntled employees who may have watched *All the President's Men* a few too many times. Like Deep Throat, they refused to even leave their names or phone numbers. Unlike Deep Throat, they weren't providing any great leads, and the only thing at stake was their jobs—not national security.

All of this uncertainty left Walter Hewlett in a very unsatisfying limbo. There was still an outside chance that he had actually won. The independent election inspector had not completed its vote count. Even after the preliminary count came out, both HP and Team Hewlett would be able to challenge the tally through a special appeal process. And there was still another option: to sue HP. Although Hewlett lacked any hard proof of illegal maneuvering, there were so many disturbing leads that going to court might be the only way to resolve them.

Victory would be a long shot, to be sure. To prove that Fiorina had bought Deutsche Bank's votes, Hewlett would need hard evidence—a written contract, a taped conversation, or an e-mail from Wayman or Fiorina referring to some tit-for-tat arrangement with the bank. It was unlikely he would find it.

More promising for Hewlett was the possibility HP was covering up problems within the integration effort—problems that would cause the merged company to come up short of what it had promised investors. Thousands of people were creating a vast paper trail as they brought the two companies together. Perhaps Hewlett could gather enough facts from those papers to prove that the company had improperly failed to disclose the truth to Wall Street.

Neal had a legal route for pressing the charges: the Chancery Court in Delaware. Shareholder class action suits had been thrown out of California state and federal courts, but Chancery was all but obligated by the Delaware corporate code to hear cases on disputed proxy votes. The court could probably hear and rule on the case in a matter of weeks—even before the vote counting had been finalized.

In the week after the shareholder vote, Hewlett had learned little about his future as an HP board member. Indeed, the board was split. Most of the members didn't want to renominate a traitor, especially after he'd told Sam Ginn he wasn't prepared to give up the fight. Others, including Fiorina, weren't so sure. Would Hewlett be included or not? On March 27, Fiorina abruptly called a board meeting so Hewlett could answer one crucial question: "Why should we put you on the board?"

During the phone meeting, Hewlett made his pitch. "I think I can still be useful," he said, "and now that the deed is done, I'll be supportive." But he was not ready to take a loyalty oath to management. He agreed to make a public statement to employees and sign a press release, but on his own terms, says Steve Neal. He warned that he was under no obligation to sit quietly. During the meeting, nobody mentioned the elephant in the room: the rumors in news articles that Hewlett might sue the company over the Deutsche Bank controversy. Steve Neal had told Hewlett not to mention that this was a possibility, because he was concerned that HP would bring some kind of quick legal action against Hewlett. "When you are in an adversarial relationship, you do not tell people what you think you might do," he said under deposition. However, if Hewlett was going to sue, it had to be soon if the court was to hear the case before the deal closed. Otherwise, the company would be left in limbo—merged but unmerged, waiting for a ruling.

A few hours after the board meeting, Hewlett made his decision. He gave Neal the nod to file the suit. He claimed a high-minded reason for this quick decision: He knew the board was considering renominating him, so he needed to file the suit before the board made that decision public. "He didn't want the board to feel bushwhacked," Neal claims.

HP's board didn't buy that for a second. As Sonsini puts it, "That lawsuit was on automatic." When the news of the suit broke the next morning, HP's board members were livid. Even then, Wilson Sonsini was drafting a press release inviting Hewlett to rejoin the board. Instead, the directors convened that day and decided not to renominate him. HP fired off a press release calling Hewlett's litigation "spurious." Walter Hewlett, HP's last link to the founding families, was off the board.

In the eyes of many, Hewlett's lawsuit seemed like a last-ditch effort that could only hurt the company. So long as the merger was in doubt, the company couldn't move on. It couldn't kill product lines or deal with morale problems. Customers might bolt rather than deal with the uncertainty. Hewlett, they believed, had gone over the line. "Even I, who was always in favor of spirited discussion in the boardroom, [didn't] think he could stay on the board," said governance expert Nell Minow, an outspoken HP critic. "You simply can't be in litigation with someone one day and in collegial discussions with them the next day."

It was worth the risk for Hewlett. He didn't care much about his folk-hero image, but did think he might win. Even if he didn't, the trial could at least put to rest his fears of wrongdoing once and for all. It might clear the decks, in a way, and clear management's name so everyone could move forward.

The lawsuit was a gripping read. It claimed that HP had coerced Deutsche Bank to vote most of its shares for the merger. It accused Fiorina of delaying the shareholders meeting so she could lobby Deutsche Bank and of keeping the polls open until the bank's votes were tallied. It also accused HP of hiding integration problems that might have caused investors, particularly ISS, to oppose the merger. All told, Hewlett asked the court to rule that the merger had been defeated at the shareholder vote.

Within days, Chancellor William B. Chandler, 51, agreed to take the case. When HP filed a motion to dismiss, he scheduled a rare weekend session to rule on the subject. By the time he rejected HP's motion on April 7, both sides were already gearing up for an expedited trial. Normally, such a complex suit would take a year or two to be heard, but this merger couldn't be held up indefinitely. Chandler would hear all of it in a three-day trial.

Both legal teams were already moving at warp speed. An hour after the lawsuit hit the news wires, Wilson Sonsini partner Boris Feldman had rushed from his office to HP headquarters to powwow with HP CFO Wayman and others. His firm, better known for processing IPOs and handling mergers than for litigating showy trials, put the full weight of its litigation department behind the effort. At the same time, Hewlett's lawyers set out on a scorched-earth raid for evidence. Neal cast a wide net. He asked the court for access to internal HP material—from minutes of board meetings to e-mails to personal journals. After tough negotiations, Chandler decided Cooley Godward could get its hands on any such material from 2002, but none before. Over the next few weeks, Wilson Sonsini reviewed 175,000 pages of material, and passed 45,000 pages on to Cooley.

HP's executives and lawyers were furious. Besides the damage done by extending the war for HP's soul a few more weeks, the lawsuit threatened to force Fiorina to unveil reams of sensitive proprietary information in court. That could help rivals and limit HP's ability to manage its financial plans.

Despite all the searching, Hewlett's lawyers found no smoking guns—but some of them felt warm. The most compelling evidence involved integration team issues. There were the e-mails from Compaq CFO Jeffrey Clarke, expressing grave concern over the merger. There was the study by HP executive Ken Wach that suggested the company could not hit its financial goals in high-end computers. There was the page from Michael Capellas's personal journal, in which the Compaq CEO wrote: "At the current course and speed we will fail." Most promising of all were the value capture updates, which suggested that many top managers on the integration clean team felt the company's chances of hitting Fiorina's goals were fading fast.

However, it was the Deutsche Bank allegation that grabbed the public's attention, especially after Fiorina's voice mail to Wayman was leaked to the *San Jose Mercury News* on April 10. It might mean nothing, but it sure raised questions—and generated fodder for many column inches. Mike Cassidy of the *Mercury News* came up with this parody:[2]

To: HP Staff

From: Carly

Subject: Voice Mail

You know how we've always said that HP is a voice mail culture? Uh, not anymore. From now on: Morse code, carrier pigeon, Etch A Sketch, even face-to-face if you have to. Anything but voice mail.

Read this memo. Memorize. Then eat it.

Hope you had a great weekend.
C.F.

Funny stuff, but the leak was a tragic example of just how broken HP's culture was. At HP, where loyalty to Bill Hewlett and Dave Packard had always been taken for granted, someone from the rank and file had turned on the CEO. This would have been shocking at many companies. At HP it was unthinkable. That special bond between HP's management and its employees seemed shattered.

Wayman sent an e-mail to employees in Fiorina's defense, noting that he felt personally violated by the voice-mail tap and insulted by the inference that he and Fiorina had plotted to do something illegal. "Frankly, I find these allegations both insulting and infuriating," he wrote. "Neither Carly nor I would ever act improperly in any business matter—much less use business assets to secure votes. . . . I'm convinced there is no harder-working CEO at any company. . . . It's time that we . . . give our leadership our full support.

Yet that voice mail had much scarier implications than HP might have believed. In the days that followed, both the SEC and the Department of Justice launched separate investigations, looking into HP's relationships with both Deutsche Bank's money management division and Northern Trust. On April 10, the U.S. Attorney's office sent HP a request for information about the votes of both investment banks.

Although not obligated to go public about these investigations, HP's lawyers advised the company to do so before Hewlett's side did.

"It deprived Walter of a bombshell," says Feldman.

Until now, Walter Hewlett had been able to wage his proxy fight from a distance. Other than an occasional board meeting, his fight wasn't hand-to-hand. It was a war of press releases and investor pitches. That changed on the morning of April 17, when Hewlett and Neal arrived at the offices of Wilson Sonsini to meet with HP's lawyers.

He was there to be deposed. Steve Schatz, a former government prosecutor, wanted to prove that Hewlett wasn't the Jimmy Stewart character the press had made him out to be. Schatz had earned a reputation within the firm as an ace cross-examiner. Now, he set his sights on proving not only that Hewlett had a spurious lawsuit, but that he was not nearly as informed, honest, or credible as Carly Fiorina.

Schatz let Hewlett know how he felt about him immediately, apologizing that the deposition was starting a few minutes late. "I hope you won't think that I had some nefarious rationale for it starting a few minutes late," he said, a clear reference to Hewlett's claim that HP delayed the start of the shareholder vote so it could lean on Deutsche Bank. From there, Schatz didn't hold back.

At one point, his face inches from Hewlett and his finger jabbing the air, Schatz asked: "Are you aware that your complaint accuses Hewlett-Packard of lying?" according to Hewlett and Steve Neal. The session was rife with mutual disdain, disrespect, and rudeness. Schatz fired away, and reloaded every few seconds. Schatz denies he did anything inappropriate.

Hewlett was not the patsy Schatz might have expected. He did not hold back when asked about the HP executives' motivations.

"I believe that Ms. Fiorina misrepresented to investors what was going on in the clean room." He felt the same way about Wayman. Later, when Schatz asked whether Hewlett thought it was okay to be disingenuous in an adversarial relationship, as he was when he failed to tell the board he was planning to bring the lawsuit, he responded: "The Nazis come to a door in Holland and they knock on the door and they say, do you have any Jewish people stored in the attic, and there are Jewish people stored in the attic. What's the right answer?"

"So it is your belief that the Hewlett-Packard board were the Nazis and I guess you are the individual protecting the [Jews] in the attic?" Schatz retorted.

"I am not drawing any kind of analogy between myself and the [family of Anne Frank]. I'm merely saying that when you talk about truth and truthfulness, you need to talk about also the context."

Angered with the proceedings, Neal repeatedly considered calling off the session, and even e-mailed lawyers in Delaware to request Chandler's okay to do so, but the two men continued their aggressive volley. Even the lawyers were bickering. When Schatz finally accepted one of Neal's countless objections at 2:00 P.M., Schatz sarcastically added, "There's a first time for everything, Mr. Neal."

Later, when Schatz asked Neal to stop objecting to the form of almost every question he asked, Hewlett looked at his lawyer and translated: "He wants you to shut up."

Roughing up Hewlett a little further, Schatz took a dig at

Hewlett's trust-fund existence. Asking him why he missed a board meeting in late July, Hewlett answered that he was on vacation.

"Vacation from what?" Schatz asked, loving the line even as it rolled off his tongue.

By the time Schatz finished, it was 6:55 P.M.—eight hours of testimony. Schatz was more than satisfied. "I wanted to establish that he wasn't forthright," says Schatz. "He justified it, but you had to really dig to get an answer."

Indeed, Hewlett made some comments during his deposition that supported HP's claim that he was an uninformed business dabbler. Asked about annual sales of the Vermont Telephone Company, of which he was chair, he could only guess at the answer. He said he had not read some of his own proxy filings, and he couldn't recall whether he'd read ISS's crucial report.

I f Hewlett's session was a marathon, Fiorina's was a 100-yard dash. It kicked off at 9:00 A.M. at Cooley Godward's offices. Neal began baiting her almost before he said hello.

"Not a very flattering picture of you in the paper this morning, was it?" he mocked as he began the deposition.

Fiorina just smiled. The lawyer who accompanied her, Feldman, had figured they were in for a long day. He had warned his wife not to expect him for supper. But at just after 11:00 A.M., Feldman phoned his office to let them know he'd return in a few minutes. Neal was through and en route to the airport for a flight. "I was stunned when Carly's deposition only lasted 90 minutes," says Feldman. "Carly basically wasn't deposed." Feldman could make it to lunch, never mind dinner.

Explaining why the meeting was so short, Neal said he didn't think he would hear anything new from Fiorina, so there was no point in giving her too much of a taste of his court strategy. "I wanted to take her temperature, to see what kind of witness she was going to be," Neal says. He also wanted to show her documents that he planned to use as evidence in court, in part so she might provide information about what refuting documents she had. For weeks, his team had been concerned that HP had another set of reports that put the value capture updates in context—and proved management's claim that the companies were on track to hit their financial goals.

Fiorina and her team arrived in Wilmington on Sunday, setting up pretrial shop in a war room in the swanky Hotel du Pont. The hotel even broke down a wall, so HP's lawyers could easily move between their rooms. "It was a war wing, not a war room," says one lawyer.

During the trial, which started the next morning—just a month after the suit was filed—six witnesses would testify, with lawyers submitting more than 500 trial exhibits.

Although Hewlett's case got off to a good start with Neal's textbook opening, that would be the high-water mark. Fiorina made sure of that. Neal's priority on the first day was to pin Fiorina down and get her to agree that HP had promised investors some absolute numbers: $81 billion in sales and $6.9 billion in operating profits. Fiorina wouldn't give in, but said all HP had promised was savings of $2.5 billion by 2004 and no less than 4.9 percent revenue loss related to the merger. However, if there were no absolute numbers, that percentage drop was meaningless. She could always say that declines were due to the economy, rather than to the merger.

Fiorina also had compelling answers for other tough questions. When Neal asked Fiorina to explain the famous voice mail and what she had meant by "doing something extraordinary," she coolly cleared away the intrigue.

"Well, I wasn't sure precisely," she responded. "I was trying to convey a sense of urgency and a sense of priority. This was new and significant news. So, it certainly included, in my mind, maybe we had to get on an airplane, maybe we had to ask a board member to talk to them. . . . I knew we couldn't simply leave it—that we never had an opportunity to present our case, but they were going to vote against us."

Getting out of the limousine after breakfast on Day 2 of the trial, Fiorina again appeared to be in top form.

"Today, I'm going for it. I'm ratcheting this up, counselor," she told Sonsini. "You have any problem with that?'

"Nope," he answered.

The longer Fiorina was on the stand, Sonsini figured, the more the judge could see how passionately she believed in the deal.

Neal again tried to embarrass her, this time by asking about her education. "I believe you said you had gotten a bachelor's degree and I didn't hear what you said you got it in?"

"Medieval history and art," she answered. Any masters? "Other than two in business administration, no," she shot back.

It remained ugly as Neal sunk his teeth into the Deutsche Bank allegations.

"I suppose it doesn't take a beautiful mind to infer that somebody who is simultaneously trying to maintain and expand a relationship with the Hewlett-Packard Company would have concluded that it is not helpful in this effort to have Hewlett-Packard's CEO and CFO unhappy with them. Would you agree with that?"

"Mr. Neal, it was crystal clear after six months of waging a proxy contest that we felt strongly that this was the best alternative," Fiorina said, continuing along that train of thought. "Of course they knew we wanted them to vote for this deal. That wasn't news to them on March 18th. It was crystal clear from the moment we announced this merger and worked tirelessly to present the merits of our case. That's not news."

Throughout her appearance, she turned every simple question into an advantage. Wayman, Compaq CFO Clarke, and HP board member Phil Condit followed up, all leaving very little room for doubt.

If Fiorina was the picture of poise and confidence, Hewlett, uncomfortable in the spotlight, choked on basic details when he took the stand. Just as during his deposition, he forgot details and dates. Then again, Hewlett's testimony actually had little to do with the case. He did not have any knowledge about the clean team, or about the Deutsche Bank discussions, per se. HP's lawyers wanted him on the stand largely for theatrics. Hewlett served one purpose: "I wanted there to be a sharp contrast between Carly and Walter," Schatz says. "It was clear that Carly had a much better grasp of the facts."

In that, Schatz was successful. Hewlett couldn't recall the

background of fellow board member Sam Ginn, the former CEO of AirTouch Communications. He failed to mention that he was on the board of Harvard's overseers when asked about his activities. Despite Hewlett's steady performances in investor meetings over the months, he seemed to fall apart during questioning. Overwhelmed by Schatz's assault, he asked that questions be repeated.

"I'm sorry," he told the lawyer. "I flipped out while you were asking that question. Can you ask it again?"

Instead of backing off, Schatz got even tougher.

One key moment came when he got Hewlett to admit that many of his concerns about HP's integration team were based on rumors. How could Hewlett base a lawsuit on rumors? It was a tough admission for his supporters to hear.

As people filed from the courtroom after Hewlett's testimony, one spectator muttered "That was painful to watch."[3] There was some mixed opinion about his performance. In a way, his brutal honesty was proof that he was willing to tell the truth, even if it hurt his cause. But all in all, Schatz had succeeded. "You saw him in court," said Sonsini lawyer Marty Korman of Hewlett. "And that's just the trailer."

After three days of testimony, Judge Chandler was ready to rule. Six months had boiled down to this, and it wasn't close. His decision was a landslide in favor of HP, clearing the company on both of Hewlett's accusations. First, he tossed aside the idea that HP "knowingly misrepresented material facts about integration in an effort to persuade ISS and possibly others to approve of the merger," as Hewlett had alleged.[4] Clarke's testimony during the trial helped deflate Hewlett's charge that HP lied. Although he said in an e-mail to Capellas that the results of HP's value capture efforts were ugly, he insisted on the stand that he had written the e-mail out of frustration because he couldn't get conservative business managers to commit to more aggressive revenue goals. Board member Condit also deflated Hewlett's argument by testifying that business units always submit low sales targets so they'll be easy to hit.[5]

In addition, the judge wasn't buying Hewlett's allegation that HP overstated merger progress the company had made in its communications with investors: "Nothing in the record indicates that HP lied to or deliberately misled ISS or the HP shareholders about its integration efforts." Further, the judge slapped down the charge that HP coerced bankers, stating he was convinced that Fiorina's voice mail message represented "reasonable actions taken by an executive faced with unexpected adverse information."[6]

Hewlett had a much higher burden with the vote-buying count. In the end, he couldn't prove that HP had used its business relationship with the bank as a weapon to earn its votes. Deutsche Bank may have decided on its own to support the merger to safeguard its banking business with HP, but HP had done nothing untoward itself. If anyone had done anything wrong, it was Deutsche Bank. The fact that the commercial bankers set up the March 19 call with Fiorina and Wayman "raises clear questions about the integrity of the internal ethical wall that purportedly separates Deutsche Bank's asset management division from its commercial division."

The judge also scoffed at one more point—that Fiorina was threatening to pull HP's future business from the bank when she signed off on the conference call by saying: "It is of great importance to our ongoing relationship. We very much would like to have your support here. We think this is a crucially important decision for this company."[7] Hewlett considered the statement evidence that the bank was coerced; the judge accepted Fiorina's explanation that the statement was "the typical way she ended similar calls."

The win was a huge relief for Fiorina, and a major victory. Her rock-solid testimony gained her new admirers. She'd won by being credible and through understanding her business. Fiorina, the ultimate marketer, left the trial with a new reputation intact: that of a CEO who could speak credibly about the business and move past a proxy battle to get the job done.

Yet some questions lingered about Chandler's decision. Neal, for one, believed Chandler had to write a strongly worded opinion—either for or against—because he wanted to avoid an appeal. That way, the merger could continue. All told, Neal thought there was no clear way for Chandler to say where HP crossed the legal line. Still, several niggling questions persisted. HP said most of its sales losses would be in low-margin businesses, taking a small toll on profits. However, the value capture reports showed that the company expected big gaps from its enterprise computing business. HP also publicly said it was feeling confident at times when the evaluations in the value capture reports were bleak. If Fiorina believed these reports were so bogus, why didn't she put out a memo that said so, Neal asked. Where were the documents to prove they were on course? Sales executives like Fiorina surely knew that closing gaps in a business plan is a two-way compromise. In this case, HP's top brass had simply written off the dour value capture updates as so much sandbagging. The stated goals were right, and the findings of the team were wrong. End of story.

Of course, HP's lawyer was singing a different tune. "That judge's opinion is almost as if I'd written it myself," Sonsini quipped.

On May 7, the day the HP–Compaq merger officially closed, HP and Compaq finally got to celebrate their marriage publicly. It was a beautiful, chilly spring day in Silicon Valley. A big banner hung across the customer visitor center at its Cupertino campus: "HP + Compaq: The New Power of Innovation."

There were some signs that perceptions were changing. Suddenly, the Wall Street analysts were putting out bullish reports on HP. With its stock so low, it couldn't help but go north.

Some of the disdain for Fiorina that had torn the company apart had ebbed. Employees had a newfound appreciation for the fight she had waged to keep HP moving forward. She might not be their perfect CEO, but she had fought for HP in court and told the world untold times how much she loved the company. Maybe it was time to believe her and give her a chance.

As she and Capellas prepared to host a big pep rally near HP headquarters, Fiorina was completely prepared to deliver her remarks to a quiet audience. She was in for something different, however. The buzz started a half-hour before she took the stage. Capellas, in a blue suit and tie, peeked out from behind a curtain and saw about a third of the company's workforce cheering. By the time he and Fiorina arrived onstage, the audience was on its feet. "It was like a rock concert before the Rolling Stones come on stage," says human resources chief Susan Bowick. "This crowd whipped itself into a frenzy," adds Keith Yamashita, the consultant who helped stage the day's events.

Not everyone felt jubilant, however. Some employees watching at other HP sites remained depressed with the deal and unimpressed with Fiorina. In one room, where some gathered to watch the event on screen, there was silence. "It's going to take a while" for everyone to come around, remarked one Boise-based business manager. "I'm more of a whore. I'm back on board . . . I'm ready to make this work. Hopefully, I'm a leading indicator." But, he added, "There is some real deep hurt that's going to take a while."

Later in May, HP and Compaq held a closing dinner to celebrate their victory, for about 150 people at the historic Fairmont Hotel in San Francisco. "There was lots to celebrate," Wilson Sonsini's Korman said. There were skits and prizes. One employee sang a song called "Can't I Have a Saturday Off?" a joke about the long hours they all worked. They conducted "Shareholders' Choice Awards." Best Screenplay went to the judge's decision, the S-4, and the December 19 report. Best Thriller went to ISS, the Packard Foundation, and Judge Chandler's decision. Best Supporting Actor went to Fiorina's husband, Frank. It was a warm evening, with many laughs. "She made it clear she knew it was not a one-man operation," said Brad Finkelstein, another Wilson Sonsini lawyer.

That night, Boris Feldman, who'd coached Fiorina so well for the trial, told his wife something many others had thought before him, after watching her perform under such intense pressure: "She could be the first woman president of the U.S."

Sometime after the HP victory party, Hewlett retreated to San Felipe to reconnect with a small group of close friends and try to make sense of the decision. Now a public figure, but out of the media frenzy, Hewlett finally had time to reflect in a place he had loved since childhood. On June 22, Hewlett invited about 70 people who'd been involved in his fight to the ranch. The group ate hot dogs and burgers, as people took turns sharing memories. Hewlett had been depressed after the judge's decision, disappointed that the judge had given HP such a clean sweep. Now, any sadness had been replaced with a strange satisfaction. He reviewed the events of his time in the "alternative universe," and what he thought the lessons were. All in all, he'd been able to give shareholders an alternative. He'd had a fair hearing from investors. Although he'd lost, the scrutiny the proxy fight had brought to the deal probably improved its chances of success. "My goal here was to shine a light on this transaction, and I think we did that," he said. "And my goal was to do it in a moral and principled way."

EPILOGUE

After the merger closed, the furor quickly began to settle down at HP, as everyone knew it would. People went back to work, and focused less on the epic battle for HP's soul and more on keeping their jobs amid the political upheaval. The HP Way—with its focus on pragmatism and loyalty—worked in management's favor. Even Fiorina's critics began looking for reasons to forgive, forget, and move on.

The outside world also simmered down. Wall Street analysts who had ridiculed the deal reset the bar. They advised investors that it would be years before success or failure of the merger could be accurately judged. Barring an overall execution fiasco, the huge savings from the layoffs and other cutbacks would help prop up the company until the economy recovered. As of late 2002, the new HP was off to a great start in that regard. The company was a full year ahead of schedule on its cost-cutting plans, and had cut losses in its PC and high-end computing units in half in the quarter that ended October 31. Revenues were holding up better than many expected, and the stock had jumped approximately 65 percent in the weeks that followed. "Our strategy is working, we're executing and we're picking up momentum," she told analysts in announcing the quarterly numbers in November. She was even back doing coffee talks, to buck up the troops. "It was Carly as her best," said one employee after attending one of these events. "Every time you want to count her out, she does something to make you think 'dammit, she's one tough lady.'"

However, much has been lost. Internally, a widespread sense of resignation has taken over. Many employees feel HP is now just another company. They once felt obliged to speak their mind to management, but they are now distrustful or even fearful. The sense of company pride is greatly diminished. Assuming the job market recovers, many insiders expect a major exodus of talent after May 2003, when thousands of executives and managers are to receive the second half of lucrative retention bonuses granted to get them to stay through the merger. Says Hewlett, "I'm very sad that HP has been transformed. It's a different kind of company now. And it was all unnecessary."

Fiorina and her supporters on the board argue that the changes were necessary. They are undoubtedly correct on that score. For more than a decade, arguably, HP had stopped building new markets and had lost its aggressiveness. Fiorina and the board weren't the only ones who wanted change—so did almost every HP employee, as did Hewlett. Even Lew Platt, who gallantly stepped down when it became clear his brand of leadership did not cut it in an age of celebrity CEOs, knew it.

The critical question is whether Fiorina's changes will work in the long term. In the first two years of her tenure, they did not. Perhaps the Compaq merger will reverse the outcome. On paper, it's conceivable. By dint of its sheer size, HP will have great influence in the industries where it does business. If Fiorina's goal to be a soup-to-nuts provider pans out, the company could emerge as a meaningful rival to IBM. In some parts of the new company, say some employees, decision making is faster. That's particularly true in the computer divisions, where there has been something of a reverse takeover, say many insiders, with Compaq people taking many of the important jobs and taking the reins on future direction. "We're a much more decisive organization," says an HP executive. "Things aren't how they were, but they never are."

Realistically, it will be impossible to know how the merger is doing until the economic downturn that began in 2001 ends. So long as tech spending remains depressed, there's little new business for HP to lose. Still, there are plenty of danger signs. Wall Street analysts had thought HP would maintain the big market-share lead in PCs it got as a result of the merger, but Dell closed the gap in less than six months. While computer losses have dropped, the company remains dangerously dependent on the printer business. In fiscal 2002, which ended on October 31 of that year, 85 percent of operating profits came from inkjet supplies such as cartridges. Now, Dell has targeted the printer market. "Dell is going to nuke them," predicts longtime Silicon Valley investor Roger McNamee. "If Dell sells only $100 million of printer supplies, they can put a world of hurt on HP."

Going forward, it's hard to imagine how HP can recapture its old form. Even if it executes the merger without a glitch, it's in a difficult strategic spot. The new HP is a market leader in almost every market, except the most profitable, strategically important one: software. Although Fiorina says the merger sets the company up to create new markets, size rarely helps in that regard. Now, with its massive Windows-based computer business, it's doubtful any new businesses could become big enough to matter. Fiorina and Capellas predicted the company would be able to grow at 10 percent per year, but that will be a stretch. "It's much easier to grow at 10 percent if you're a $40-billion than if you're an $80-billion company," says former CEO John Young, the man who oversaw HP's initial thrust into the computer business. "How are they going to come up with $8 billion in new growth each year? It doesn't happen just because you want it to. They have a fundamental boat anchor, and I don't think it's moveable."

If there are many questions about HP's future, it's clear the company has already lost much of its old value. The unique bond between management and employees has been largely severed. Few doubt the company once known for its lifetime employment record will hesitate to pull the trigger; as of November 2002, for example, it tacked on an extra 2,900 people to the expected 15,000 cuts. Indeed, on the night before the merger was announced in September 2001, an HP press person told the author—with pride, no less—that the companies might be able to slash 30,000 jobs. "I no longer feel any allegiance to HP as a company," says one 23-year veteran who expects to look for a new job soon. "The HP Way still exists among the employees, but it's being maintained from the bottom up."

The company's reputation for integrity has also taken a hit. Even when it was beginning to struggle in the late 1990s, HP remained the corporate gold standard in that regard. Now, that's been badly damaged. "Bill and Dave would be troubled by the loss of credibility at HP," says Lew Platt. "There's a lot of duck and cover going on in the place. It's all about spin these days, and not enough truth. It's lost that special place in business that it used to hold."

The proxy fight didn't enhance the company's reputation for integrity. Though it could have been far worse—proxy-fight experts say it was actually a fairly clean fight, all in all—HP did not live up to the company's old standards. Many corporate governance experts think Fiorina should have earned Hewlett's support, or not risked opening the company up to the divisive fight, and question the personal nature of the attack from HP on Hewlett's qualifications. "To bludgeon a guy that represents at least 50 percent of the owners showed a tremendous lack of respect for corporate governance," says Jeffrey Sonnenfeld, associate dean of the Yale School of Management. "She drove him into a corporate crusade, to which he was fully entitled."

Fiorina and her supporters deny they acted improperly in any way, and say the decision in Delaware Chancery Court was a total vindication. However, though the company did nothing illegal, its ethical standards can be called into question. Michael Capellas is a case in point. During the proxy fight, the companies went out of their way to assure investors that the operations-minded Capellas would remain at the company to provide the perfect complement to Fiorina. Instead, Capellas left in November 2002 to become CEO of WorldCom. It's common for the CEO of an acquired company to jump ship rather than play second fiddle, and the company used that as the explanation.

Other ethical questions have been raised. During the proxy fight, Fiorina and her advisors were outraged when Hewlett disclosed details of postmerger contracts the company had drawn up but never finalized for top executives. In February, Fiorina stood on a stage in front of analysts, expressed her indignation, and insisted that no such deals existed. But there was at least one. In December, Capellas had worked out changes to his contract with the Compaq board that gave him huge incentives to leave before September 2003. When he left, he walked off with more than $14.4 million. Coincidentally, that's the size of the retention bonus he gallantly agreed to forego in November 2001—ostensibly as a sign to investors that he was in it for the long haul.

Fiorina's proxy-fight victory itself was as much a victory of spin as of substance. To be sure, the company communicated a reasonable, well-conceived strategy for the merger, one that some investors found convincing. Still, most investors wish the merger had never been attempted—and they certainly didn't appreciate being placed at the center of a nasty proxy fight. If it hadn't been for fears of the chaos that might result if HP had to replace its CEO, or maybe even its board, Hewlett would have been able to come up with the extra 3 percent he needed to win. Tellingly, chaos was a central reason that Deutsche Bank cited before voting its 17 million or so shares for the merger, moments after speaking with Fiorina and Wayman. Indeed, if the proxy fight had been held just a few months later, after corporate scandals had become the leading story in the country, Fiorina might not have been able to pull it off at all.

Is there one person to blame? Certainly, there's enough fault to go around. HP's board deserves some attention. After years of doing nothing while HP's performance slipped, the board succumbed to pressure just as the internet bubble was about to burst— and brought in a person whose resume and personality almost guaranteed major moves toward Net-style management. "This is a story of a misguided board getting caught up in the Net frenzy at the end, and got caught up in a search for a false messiah," says Jeff Sonnenfeld. Says Harvard professor Rakesh Khurana, author of *Searching for a Corporate Savior,* "They bet on the fleeting over the timeless."

As of November 2002, the board was in full support of Fiorina. Evidently, she was doing exactly what the board hoped she would. At a time when many insiders were convinced that her ambitious reforms were creating chaos, the board made her chair in September 2000. During the Compaq talks, the board never insisted on having even one meeting to discuss the deal outside of her presence, says Hewlett—much less deal effectively with Hewlett's concerns about the transaction. In late 2001, even after a year in which she'd plunged the company into controversy, the board sweetened her pay package further, expanding her potential bonus from $3 million to $9 million. "That's mind boggling, especially when she's considerably overpaid already," says corporate governance watchdog Nell Minow. Indeed, on two occasions during her HP tenure Fiorina had to voluntarily give up huge bonuses contractually due to her, to avoid public criticism. To compensation experts, the need for such acts is less a sign of selflessness than of a poorly conceived pay package. "From the start, it was pay for attendance, not pay for performance. With $70 million in restricted stock, it was always going to be hard for her to say to the employees, 'We're all in this together,'" said Matt Ward, president of WestWard Pay Strategies in San Francisco.

And what of Fiorina? Undoubtedly, she is a better CEO now than she was when she arrived. She is wary of overpromising, is far more operationally minded, and has proven to be more adept at cost cutting than many predicted. She's survived a trial by fire and shown no signs of cracking. Those who work closely with her are more admiring than ever. "I think she has gained tremendous experience and judgment," says Larry Sonsini. "She's learned a tremendous amount about the strength of her own convictions." Indeed, she remains confident as ever that HP can buck the odds and prove the skeptics wrong. In November 2002, Fiorina introduced a new ad campaign titled "Everything is Possible" at the Comdex trade show. She explained the campaign in a speech at the conference. "It is an affirmation of our belief that progress is not made by the cynics and the doubters. It is made by those who believe everything is possible."

Everything isn't probable, however, and much will depend on Fiorina herself. In the months after the merger, she went largely underground, leaving the job of healing the wounds of the proxy fight to Capellas. When Capellas resigned, she decided not to replace him. Instead, she intends to run the company by herself, and execute a sweeping strategy designed to take on everyone from Dell to IBM. It's a "be-everything-to-everyone" plan, the likes of which has never before worked. Few think it will work this time, either. Already, many investors think HP will ultimately be broken up, to unlock the value of the printer business that is now propping up HP's other businesses.

The timing of all this is unfortunate. HP appears to have lost its way just when the world was hankering for the HP that was—a company that erred on the side of fiscal conservatism, had a deep commitment to its employees, and increased its stock price by delivering real results, year in year out, rather than through deal making or hype. Says Harvard professor and Intel Corporation board member David Yoffie, "The historic strength of HP is in basic engineering. But Carly tried to build the business the easy way," through marketing and acquisitions. "The right answer was to go back to engineering and innovation."

That's what Hewlett wanted to happen. After the merger was finalized, he disappeared back into his former, nonpublic life as a philanthropist, musician, and academic, but he continues to watch the situation. As of late 2002, he had resolved to stay on the sidelines until at least 2004, to give Fiorina and the board an opportunity to make the merger work. He said he did not intend to seek a spot on the board in 2003. If the family interests wanted to get a seat, "The leadership for that needs to come from the Packards," he said, given the enmity between the board and himself. Still, he said, "I don't think I'm out of the picture forever." He remains in touch with attorney Steve Neal. If the Compaq merger ends up going the way of so many failed tech mergers of the past, one wonders if he will take on the board again—this time to try to take control of the company.

How will Walter Hewlett be remembered? Most likely he will go down in history as an unlikely, somewhat flawed, champion of investors' rights. It's clear from the facts that he should have been more engaged as the Compaq deal was being negotiated. By his own admission, he should have done more to stop the deal before it was announced. However, most experts feel his fight against the board was a courageous act. Almost all involved in the fight were surprised by his fortitude, and the way in which he fought the fight. His efforts may have lasting impact. Not all dissidents have his money or his family name, so it's unlikely that there will be a wave of high-profile proxy fights, but "He's made the path of dissent in the boardroom much easier," says Charles Elson, director of the Center for Corporate Governance at the University of Delaware. "He's made it more likely that other directors will say 'I'm not going to let you do to me what they did to Walter Hewlett. I'm going to say no, and I'm going to say it loudly.' "

As a result, Carly Fiorina has won the biggest victory of her career. She has landed on her feet, with the support of her board for the most part, although many people close to Dick Hackborn say he is saddened by the breakdown of HP's culture, and frustrated with her unwillingness to listen to criticism. Now, perhaps for the first time in her career, she'll have to show she can grow a business for the long haul. If she's successful, it seems likely that her success will be based on an approach that bears only passing resemblance to the HP Way. Though the company logo says "Invent," most people think the focus will continue to shift to marketing and sales. "HP has gone from substance to appearance, and I find that a terrible loss," says Jobst Brandt, who joined HP in 1968 and now consults with HP Labs. "She's reconstructing the company in her image."

One way or another, HP will move forward. The HP Way is not the only way to run a company, as just a quick glance around the computer business will show. From IBM's command-and-control excellence to Microsoft's ruthlessness to the aesthetic perfectionism of Steve Jobs's Apple, there are many approaches. The old HP Way was an approach that was admirable, and benefited and improved all who came in touch with it—customers, employees, investors, and society at large—but maybe its time had come. Maybe nothing is truly timeless.

Notes

PROLOGUE

1. "The 2002 Fortune 500," *Fortune,* 15 April 2001, 193; www .fortune.com/lists/F500.
2. HP commissioned Goldman to do a study regarding Hewlett's concern about the relationship between corporate size and stock performance. The results were presented to the board before the merger was okayed.

CHAPTER 1

1. Proceedings of *Walter B. Hewlett v. Hewlett-Packard Company,* 25 Delaware Chancery Court 19513 (2002).
2. Michelle Quinn and Tracy Seipel, "Fiorina Voice Mail Reveals Late Scramble," *San Jose Mercury News,* 10 April 2002, p. 1.
3. The author attended the trial. Much of the physical detail of the courtroom described in this chapter comes directly from his notes. Dialogue comes from a transcript of the proceedings of *Hewlett v. Hewlett-Packard Co.*
4. A copy of the summary pages of the value capture updates was described in court and shown to the author by a source who requested anonymity.

CHAPTER 2

1. Peter Burrows, "The Boss," *BusinessWeek,* 2 August 1999, 80.
2. "Sneed, Joseph Perkins," *Handbook of Texas Online,* www.tsha.utexas .edu/handbook/online/articles/view/SS/fsn10.html.
3. Sunny Nash, "Calvert, Texas: Preserving a Town's Heritage," *Ancestry Magazine,* www.ancestry.com/library/view/ancmag/777.asp.
4. Clara Sneed, "Because This Is Texas," *Panhandle Plains Historical Review* 72 (1999): 6.
5. Ibid., 19, 29, 60.
6. Ibid., 42, 65. Sneed notes in the article that Beal Sneed spent nine months in jail in 1924, for bribing a juror in a land dispute, after appealing for aid from power brokers including President Herbert Hoover.

7. Stuart L. Gastwirth, "Professional Portrait, Joseph T. Sneed," *Cornell Law Forum,* 13 May 1960.

8. Carly Fiorina, "Making the Best of a Mess," *New York Times,* 29 September 1999, Management section, p. 8.

9. "Sneed Resigns from Faculty; Cites Offer and Dusty Foot," *Cornell Law Forum,* 18 May 1962.

10. *Leonardo Andrade, Petitioner-Appelant, v. Attorney General of the State of California,* 270 F.3d 743 (9th Cir. 2001). Sneed wrote, "Two consecutive sentences of 25 years to life—with parole eligibility only after the minimum 50 years—is obviously severe. Nonetheless, it is the sentence mandated by the citizens of California and legislated by their elected representatives."

11. Patricia Sellers, "The Fifty Most Powerful Women in American Business," *Fortune,* 12 October 1998, 81.

12. Sylvia Tiersten, "Lucent Technologies' Carly Fiorina: How a Philosophy Major Came to Drive Lucent's Biggest Engine," *Investor's Business Daily,* 4 March 1999.

13. Information from the Objectivist Center, a Web site dedicated to Ayn Rand and her philosophy and writings, www.objectivistcenter.org.

14. Carly Fiorina, "The Process of Distillation: Getting to the Essence of Things," commencement address, Stanford University, Palo Alto, California, 7 June 2001.

15. Carleton Bartlem and Edwin Locke, "The Coch and French Study: A Critique and Reinterpretation," *Human Relations* 34(7):555–566.

CHAPTER 3

1. David Packard, *The HP Way* (Boston: HarperBusiness, 1995), 23.

2. Hewlett made this comment to former Hewlett-Packard archivist Karen Lewis.

3. Packard, *The HP Way,* 32–33.

4. Ibid., 35.

5. Ibid., 42, 43.

6. William Hewlett, interview by A. Michael McMahon, Institute of Electrical and Electronics Engineers, Inc., History Center Oral History Program, 27 November 1984.

7. Packard, *The HP Way,* 47–48.

8. James C. Collins and Jerry I. Porras, *Built to Last* (New York: HarperBusiness, 1994), 56.

9. Ward Winslow, "David Packard, Doer Extraordinary," *A Palo Alto Editor's Scrapbook,* 1994, p. 175. Self-published.

10. Agilent Technologies corporate timeline, www.agilent.com.

11. David Packard, "Corporate Objectives of the Hewlett-Packard Company," internal memo, January 1959.
12. Packard, *The HP Way*, 6.
13. Hewlett, interview by McMahon.
14. Collins and Porras, *Built to Last*, p. 212.
15. *Self Made in California*, promotional video for the state of California, produced by PBS and United Airlines, October 1997.

CHAPTER 4

1. DEC was later purchased by Compaq, and is now part of HP.
2. "Human Resources at Hewlett-Packard," Harvard Business School Case Study 9-495-051, 1 November 1995, p. 12.
3. Peter Burrows, "Why Fiorina Convinced an Icon to Become Chairman," *BusinessWeek Online*, www.businessweek.com/1999/99_31/b3640010.htm.
4. Michael Moritz, *The Little Kingdom* (New York: William Morrow and Co., 1984), 126.
5. Oliver Wendell Holmes, "The Deacon's Masterpiece," in *The Complete Poetical Works of Oliver Wendell Holmes*, ed. H.E.S. (Boston: Houghton, Mifflin, 1895), 158–160.

CHAPTER 5

1. Carly Fiorina, "Making the Best of a Mess," *New York Times*, 29 September 1999, p. 8.
2. Ibid.
3. Computer Science and Telecommunications Board, "FTS2000 Case Study," in Beyond FTS2000: A Program for Change (National Academy Press, 1989), Appendix A.
4. Opinion regarding protest of AT&T Communications Inc. to the General Services Administration Board of Contract Appeals, GSBCA No. 9252-P, Solicitation No. ETN-87-0001, 17 May 1988.
5. Ibid.
6. Carleton S. Fiorina, "The Education Crisis: Business and Government's Role in Reform," thesis paper, Massachusetts Institute of Technology, Cambridge, 1989.
7. "Creating a Corporate Identity for a $20 Billion Start-up: Lucent Technologies," Design Management Institute Case Study (Boston: Design Management Institute Press, January 1999), 6–9.
8. Details and the quotation from Fiorina from Judith H. Dobrzynski, "A Season of Opening Days: Companies Make New Issues a Big Event on Wall St.," *New York Times*, 19 April 1996, p. D1.

9. "Philips Electronics N.V. and Lucent Technologies Plan Joint Venture to Create World Leader in Consumer Communications Products," Lucent Technologies Web site, 17 June 1997.
10. Ibid.
11. Peter Elstrom, "Lucent's Ascent," *BusinessWeek,* 8 February 1999; www.businessweek.com/1999/99_06/b3615110.htm.
12. John J. Keller, "Unlikely Team: An AT&T Outsider and a Veteran Join to Run New Spinoff," *Wall Street Journal,* 14 October 1996.
13. Carly Fiorina, "Making the Best of a Mess."
14. Winstar could draw down only $500 million at a time, and it couldn't get more until the previous $500 million was repaid. Some Lucent sources insist that the company began losing money on the deal only when McGinn renewed it on easier terms after Fiorina had departed for HP. "The deal I did was paid off 100 percent," says Rogers. "[Winstar] paid us back in full."
15. Patricia Sellers, "The Fifty Most Powerful Women in American Business, *Fortune,* 12 October 1998, 76.
16. Steve Rosenbush and Brian Grow, "Rolling Blackouts at Lucent," *BusinessWeek,* 16 July 2001.
17. Jonathan Weil, "SEC Probe of Lucent Is Broader," *Wall Street Journal,* 1 November 2002, c1.

CHAPTER 6

1. Platt disputes this account. He says HP had cooled on Lane as interest in Fiorina rose, and says "If we put on a full-court press, I think we could have gotten him."
2. Details of Fiorina's pay come from her employment agreement with HP, which is posted on a corporate governance Web site called the Corporate Library. The URL is http://files.thecorporatelibrary.net/contract/CEO_hwp.htm.
3. Carly Fiorina, "The Process of Distillation: Getting to the Essence of Things," commencement address, Stanford University, Palo Alto, California, 7 June 2001.

CHAPTER 7

1. "Glass Ceiling Still Exists," Associated Press, 6 January 2000; abcnews.go.com/sections/business/DailyNews/glassceiling000106.html.
2. "Forbes Best Paid CEOs," *Forbes Online,* www.forbes.com/2002/04/25/ceos.html.

3. HP's Schedule 14A proxy filing for its 2002 annual meeting, filed 4 April 2002.
4. Peter Burrows, "The Radical," *Business Week,* 19 February, 2001, 70.
5. Peter Burrows, "The Boss," *Business Week,* 2 August 1999, 76.
6. Interview with author, 18 August 2000.
7. Quentin Hardy, "The Cult of Carly," *Forbes,* 13 December 1999, 138.
8. "Rules of the Garage," HP Web site, www.hp.com/hpinfo/newsroom/hpads/1999/rules.html.
9. Philip Meza and Robert A. Burgelman, "The New HP Way," Stanford University Graduate School of Business Case Study SM-72, 5 May 2000.
10. Interview with author, 20 July 1999.
11. Steven Berglas, "Those Were the Days," Inc.com, 1 April 2000, www.inc.com/magazine/20000401/18105.html.
12. David Price, "Apparently Not," 30 May 2000. Column on HP Web site, provided to author by an anonymous source.

CHAPTER 8

1. Interview with the author, 26 July 2000. All subsequent quoted statements by Fiorina in this chapter are taken from interviews with the author, from her public statements at analysts meetings, or from internal speeches provided to the author by HP public relations before March 2002.
2. Vicky Ward, "The Battle for Hewlett Packard," *Vanity Fair,* 11 June 2002, 84.
3. Peter Burrows, "Doubts About HP—Compaq's Financial Goal," *BusinessWeek Online,* 18 March 2002; www.businessweek.com/bwdaily/dnflash/mar2002/nf20020318_6628.htm.
4. Toni Sacconaghi, "HP Downgraded to Market Perform: Too Much Too Soon in Light of Quarterly Challenges, *Bernstein Research Call,* 13 June 2000, p. 2.
5. Critics weren't impressed. The board had given her a $1,141,250 bonus for the first half of HP's fiscal year, the most she was eligible to get.

CHAPTER 9

1. Board member Jay Keyworth says Hewlett did not object to Fiorina being named chairperson, but confirms that Hewlett did ask that a lead outside director be named. The board rejected the idea.
2. Proceedings of *Walter B. Hewlett v. Hewlett-Packard Company,* 25 Delaware Chancery Court 19513 (2002) 220.

3. Steve Hamm, "Compaq's Rockin' Boss," *BusinessWeek,* 4 September 2000; www.businessweek.com/2000/00_36/b3697001.htm.
4. Keyworth says Hewlett told Hackborn he would advise the Hewlett Foundation to sell shares of HP. "It was his suggestion to share this information outside the board that had us, and Carly, disturbed," Keyworth wrote in an e-mail, 4 December 2002.
5. Peter Burrows, "HP—Compaq: Where's the Upside?" *BusinessWeek,* 17 September 2001; http://www.businessweek.com/magazine/content/01_38/b3749042.htm.
6. Steve Shepard, "A Talk with Scott McNealy," *BusinessWeek Online,* 1 April 2002; www.businessweek.com/magazine/content/02_13/b3776087.htm.

CHAPTER 10

1. HP's Schedule 14A proxy filing for its 2001 annual meeting, filed 25 January 2001.
2. Woodley Packard resigned from the Packard Foundation in 1999, ostensibly due to philosophical differences with the rest of the board.
3. In late November, after Hewlett had publicly opposed the deal, FFL was given a $3.5-million contract, with a $12 million success fee if the deal was voted down.
4. Tracy Siepel, "Packard Says He's Displeased with the Direction of HP," *San Jose Mercury News,* 7 November 2001, p. 15A.
5. Interview with Rob Hof of *BusinessWeek,* 6 November 2001.
6. Interview with editorial board of *BusinessWeek,* January 2002.
7. Remarks by Jack Welch at a *BusinessWeek* conference, San Francisco, 6 December 2001.
8. Note posted to a Yahoo! message board, 10 November 2000. Archive has since been removed.
9. Ian Fried, "Employees Stump for HP Merger," CNET News.com, 14 December 2001, news.com.com/2100-1001-277037.html?legacy=cnet.
10. "Walter Hewlett Opposes Merger, or Does He?" Reuters, www.usatoday.com/life/cyber/invest/2001/11/16/hewlett-undecided.htm.
11. "Walter Hewlett Responds to Packard Foundation Decision," press release for Walter Hewlett, 7 December 2001.
12. Interview with author, 7 December 2001.

CHAPTER 11

1. Andrew Park, "Can Compaq Survive as a Solo Act," *BusinessWeek.* 24 December 2001, 71.

2. In interviews for a December 31 *BusinessWeek* story, "Walter Hewlett: Behind His Big Switcheroo," Hewlett said he had assumed HP would have to pay a higher price for Compaq if he publicly opposed the deal. However, in the SEC filing, he claimed he had been told the price would go up. After HP complained, Hewlett's subsequent filings reflected the fact that Hewlett had assumed the price would be higher.
3. The editors, Open Letter, *Red Herring*, 15 January 2002; www .redherring.com/insider/2002/0124/1476.htm.
4. Peter Burrows, "Hewlett: Show Me Carly's Money," 28 January 2002, www.businessweek.com/magazine/content/02_04/c3767003.htm.
5. "An Open Letter to Walter Hewlett," HP Web site, 26 February 2002; www.hp.com/hpinfo/newsroom/feature_stories/openletter.pdf.
6. Ram Kumar, "Proxy Analysis: Hewlett-Packard Co.," Institutional Shareholder Services, Rockville, MD, 5 March 2002, 17.
7. Ibid., 18.
8. Quotes and dialogue in this chapter are from a transcript of the proceedings of *Walter B. Hewlett v. Hewlett-Packard Company*, 25 Delaware Chancery Court 19513 (2002), 43, 44, 47.
9. Michelle Quinn and Tracy Seipel, "Fiorina Voice Mail Reveals Late Scramble," *San Jose Mercury News*, 10 April 2002, p 1.
10. Conference call dialogue in this chapter from *Hewlett v. Hewlett-Packard Co.*, Transcript of March 19th Deutsche Bank Teleconference, 5, 13, 43, 61, 64, 75.

CHAPTER 12

1. A copy of the letter was left at the Silicon Valley bureau of *Business-Week*. When contacted an SEC spokesman could not confirm whether the SEC had received the letter.
2. Mike Cassidy, "Deep Ear Adds New Act to HP Drama," 11 April 2002, *San Jose Mercury News*, 1A.
3. Peter Burrows, "Walter Hewlett's Last Stand," *BusinessWeek Online*, 25 April 2002, www.businessweek.can/technology/content/apr2002/ tc20020425_6992.htm.
4. *Walter B. Hewlett v. Hewlett-Packard Company*, Del. Ch. 27-28, Chandler C. (April 8, 2002).
5. Burrows, "Walter Hewlett's Last Stand."
6. *Walter B. Hewlett v. Hewlett-Packard Company*, opinion, p. 29 Chandler C. April 30, 2002.
7. *Hewlett v. Hewlett-Packard Co.*, Transcript of March 19th Deutsche Bank Teleconference.

Sources

While covering HP for *BusinessWeek* magazine from 1995 to 2002, the author had access to many top company executives, including Lew Platt, Joel Birnbaum, Ann Livermore, Webb McKinney, Antonio Perez, Carolyn Ticknor, Bob Wayman, and Duane Zitzner, as well as directors Sam Ginn, Dick Hackborn, and Bob Knowling. He had five extensive interviews with Carly Fiorina between July 1999 and December 2001, in the course of writing three cover stories about HP during that time ("The Boss," 2 August 1999; "The Radical," 19 February 2001; and "Carly's Last Stand?" 24 December 2001). All quotes from Fiorina and other current HP executives and directors, with the exception of Jay Keyworth, were taken from interviews done before the Compaq merger closed, unless otherwise noted.

The author has had no on-the-record access to HP executives since March 2002. An effort was made to let those sources who declined to speak with him, both at HP and elsewhere, know about the material he intended to use, to give them an opportunity to respond or clarify their perspectives. Some of them responded, although most did not, including Carly Fiorina, Bob Wayman, Sam Ginn, and Dick Hackborn.

The author had extensive interviews with Walter Hewlett and his advisors. He also had interviews with some of HP's advisors. These include Wilson Sonsini Goodrich & Rosati lawyers Larry Sonsini, Marty Korman, Steve Schatz, and Boris Feldman. He also spoke with HP board member Jay Keyworth, Keith Yamashita of Stone & Yamashita, and George Sard and Drew Brown of Citigate Sard Verbinnen, an investor relations firm that worked with HP. Many other sources requested anonymity.

The heart of several chapters of the book is the proxy battle and the trial. Much of the source material for these sections was drawn from transcripts of the trial in the Chancery Court in Delaware, as well as depositions from some of the witnesses, including Walter Hewlett and some of his advisors. HP refused to provide depositions from its executives, and did not clear its advisors to do so, either. Throughout the book, the author also relied on financial filings with the SEC, legal opinions, newspaper accounts, and the many reports and other filings issued by HP and by Walter Hewlett during the proxy fight.

Legal documents used in the book include:

Transcript of *Walter B. Hewlett v. Hewlett-Packard Company*, 25 Delaware Chancery Court 19513 (2002).

Deposition of Walter B. Hewlett, Palo Alto, CA, 17 April 2002. 19513.

Deposition of Tully Friedman, San Francisco, CA, 18 April 2002. 19513.

Deposition of Spencer Fleischer, San Francisco, CA, 18 August 2002. 19513.

Deposition of Joele Frank, New York, NY, 20 April 2002.

PROLOGUE

Information about HP's August 31 board meeting at Wilson Sonsini's offices is drawn primarily from interviews with Walter Hewlett, Cooley Godward CEO Steve Neal, and Larry Sonsini and Marty Korman of Wilson Sonsini Goodrich & Rosati, as well as reporting by other anonymous HP insiders.

CHAPTER 1

The author attended the trial at the Chancery Court in Delaware. Much of the physical detail comes directly from his notes. Most of the dialogue was taken directly from the trial transcript. Information from the value capture updates was gleaned from the proceedings. Also, a source who requested anonymity showed the author selected pages of the value capture updates late in 2002.

CHAPTER 2

The author drew much of the information about the Sneed family and John Beal Sneed from an article written by Carly Fiorina's sister,

Clara Sneed, titled "Because This Is Texas" (*Panhandle Plains Historical Review* 72[1999]: 6). Another useful source was the *Handbook of Texas Online* (www.tsha.utexas.edu/handbook/online/articles/view/SS/fsn10.html). Some of Fiorina's childhood and college friends, family acquaintances, and professors at the University of Maryland's Robert H. Smith School of Business were also interviewed, as were colleagues and former colleagues of her father, Senior Judge Joseph T. Sneed of the U.S. Court of Appeals for the Ninth Circuit. One of the sources was Todd Bartlem, Fiorina's ex-husband. HP declined requests to speak with Frank Fiorina or other members of Carly Fiorina's family.

CHAPTER 3

Walter Hewlett, and to a lesser extent Eleanor Hewlett Gimon and David Woodley Packard, provided background on their families. Karen Lewis and many former HP employees provided most of the material in this chapter. The author also relied on a number of books, particularly David Packard's *The HP Way* (Boston: HarperBusiness, 1995). *Built to Last,* by James C. Collins and Jerry I. Porras (New York: HarperBusiness, 1994), helped the author describe Hewlett and Packard's business philosophies. An interview by A. Michael McMahon with Bill Hewlett for the Institute of Electrical and Electronics Engineers, Inc., History Center Oral History Program (27 November 1984) was also helpful.

CHAPTER 4

Interviews with many former HP employees rounded out the picture of how HP got into the computer and calculator businesses. Michael Maccoby's 1976 book, *The Gamesman* (New York: Simon & Schuster)—a cult classic among HP old-timers—helped shape the author's description of Dick Hackborn. Although Hackborn is not mentioned by name, Maccoby confirms press reports that the character Jack Wakefield was modeled directly on him. A spokesperson for Microsoft confirms that Bill Gates once offered Hackborn a top position with the software company. Rick Belluzzo, Lew Platt, and

Willem Roelandts, among others, provided their perspectives on some of the debates about the future of HP's computer business in the mid-1990s. Karen Lewis told the author about Dave Packard's reading of Oliver Wendell Holmes's "The Deacon's Masterpiece." Information about HP's intellectual property agreement with Microsoft was provided by Rick Belluzzo and other HP executives who were involved in the negotiations. George Bodway and James Mackey, the lead managers of the study of $40-billion-plus companies, provided information about that effort.

CHAPTER 5

A column Fiorina wrote for the *New York Times* ("Making the Best of a Mess," 29 September 1999) was helpful in describing her first job at AT&T. Colleagues during the FTS2000 negotiations, including Lew Golm, Tony Bardo, Harry Carr, and Paul Goulding were helpful, as was reporter Calvin Sims, who is on sabbatical from the *New York Times*. Many sources contacted to discuss her days at Lucent, including the PCC joint venture, requested anonymity. Of those that were on record, interviews with Nina Aversano, Marc Schweig, Dick Sadai, and Bob Allen were particularly helpful. The incident with Pacific Bell was confirmed by a high-ranking Lucent official and a Pacific Bell executive who was in the room. Both requested anonymity. The author also referred to Aversano's lawsuit against Lucent (*Nina Aversano v. Lucent Technologies*, Middlesex County, Superior Court of New Jersey, Mid-L-10004-00), as well as a shareholder lawsuit against Winstar (*Winstar Securities Litigation*, U.S. District Court, Southern District of New York, 01 Civ. 3014.) Lehman Brothers analyst Steve Levy was extremely helpful in analyzing Lucent's financials for this chapter.

CHAPTER 6

Much of the information gathered about HP's CEO search was collected for the 2 August 1999 *BusinessWeek* cover story, "The Boss." Jeff Christian provided much additional detail, as did Lew Platt, George Keyworth, Rich Hagberg, and candidates including Ray Lane, Ed Zander, and Gary Daichendt.

CHAPTER 7

The author relied on his interviews with Fiorina for the *BusinessWeek* story "The Radical" (19 February 2001), as well as interviews with current and former HP employees, for much of the information regarding her first months at HP. George Sard, an investor relations consultant, also provided helpful details.

CHAPTER 8

Reporting regarding the Cult of Carly came from many sources, both former and current employees. The *BusinessWeek* story that ran the day before the vote (Peter Burrows, "Doubts About HP–Compaq's Financial Goal," *BusinessWeek Online,* 18 March 2002; www.businessweek.com/bwdaily/dnflash/mar2002/nf20020318_ 6628.htm) cited two members of the clean team and five former HP executives who had talked with other clean-team members. All were anonymous sources. One of the clean-team members, a high-ranking manager who had access to the financial progress of the deal, said revenue loss related to the merger could be 10 to 15 percent, rather than the public claim of 4.9 percent. In the course of reporting this story, the author was given the name of HP executive Ken Wach. He declined to comment on the record, and the author did not cite his name in the article. During the trial between HP and Walter Hewlett, it was disclosed that Wach had done a study and made comments claiming that the new HP's high-end computer business was not likely to meet management's public projections for that business. Fiorina's comments from her "Welcome to the New HP" speech were from the author's notes, as he watched a video of the speech provided by HP public relations. Details on channel stuffing in this chapter came primarily from interviews with six former HP executives, four of whom had direct knowledge of the activity.

CHAPTER 9

Much of the reporting regarding Walter Hewlett's missed board meetings came from Hewlett and HP board member Jay Keyworth, as well as Larry Sonsini, Marty Korman, and other anonymous HP advisors. The same is true for the dialogue at board meetings. As for Capellas's talks with Michael Dell, sources included an investment banker involved in the HP–Compaq merger, as well as a top-ranking Dell insider. Dell Computer declined comment. Reporting regarding Goldman analyst Laura Conigliaro's comments in the days before the merger was announced came from HP advisors close to Goldman, as well as HP insiders.

Regarding Bluestone Software, the author spoke with three former executives of that company, an investment banker who helped with the transaction, and former HP software managers, as well as executives from other HP software partners.

CHAPTER 10

A main goal of the author's reporting in this chapter was to examine the process that Walter Hewlett and the foundations used to determine what, if anything, they would do in light of the Compaq merger. Many people provided descriptions of this process in painstaking detail. These include Walter Hewlett, Hewlett Foundation chief investment officer Laurie Hoagland, and Hewlett Foundation trustee Jim Gaither, as well as Steve Neal, and Keith Flaum from Cooley Godward; Tully Friedman and Spencer Fleischer of Friedman Fleischer & Lowe; John Coughlin of the Parthenon Group; and Joele Frank, Dan Katcher, and Todd Glass of Joele Frank, Wilkinson Brimmer Katcher. Also interviewed on this topic were David and Lucile Packard Foundation president Richard Schlossberg and foundation trustees Dean Morton and Lew Platt, as well as David Woodley Packard. Susan Packard Orr and her sisters refused requests for interviews.

CHAPTER 11

Information on Hewlett's aborted plan to buy $500 million in shares in the final days of the proxy fight come from Hewlett and three of his advisors, who requested anonymity. Details of Deutsche Bank's decision to switch its vote comes primarily from Spencer

Fleischer's deposition, the trial transcript, and the transcript of the bank's call with Hewlett and with HP management on the day of the shareholder vote. Deutsche Bank officials did not respond to requests for information.

CHAPTER 12

A copy of the unsigned letter to Harvey Pitt, which was also sent to Hewlett's advisors, was delivered as well to *Business Week*'s Silicon Valley bureau. Details of the HP board meeting to consider inviting Hewlett back on the board come from Walter Hewlett, Steve Neal, Larry Sonsini, and another HP insider. Dialogue from Walter Hewlett's deposition comes directly from that deposition. The phrase "Vacation from what?" does not appear in the transcript, but Steve Schatz recalls saying the phrase, and Steve Neal recalls hearing it. It might have been said during an interchange when the deposition was not being recorded, possibly during an off-record exchange. Dialogue from the trial comes from the transcript of the proceedings.

A Note about Sourcing

Much of the reporting for this book was done with Hewlett-Packard's assistance. The author had many interviews with numerous top executives and board members between 1995 and March 2002. These included extensive interviews with Carly Fiorina. Where she and other HP executives and directors are quoted directly in the book, it is from interviews held during that time.

Since the shareholder vote on the Compaq merger on March 19, 2002, the author has had no further access to HP executives. HP warned me this would occur as I was preparing an article that appeared on *BusinessWeek*'s Web site on March 18, citing concerns some insiders had about the long-term prospects for the merger. As such, I want to make it clear that none of HP's top executives have talked on the record with me since that time, nor have any of its directors other than George Keyworth. Other than one brief e-mail from Ann Livermore, HP chose not to respond to e-mails seeking their response to material in this book. Allison Johnson, senior vice president of global brand and communications, said in an e-mail that my queries were "filled with inaccuracies, false claims, and mischaracterizations." She continued, "We cannot invest the time required to do the point-by-point clarifications that would be required to help you rewrite your book. Based on experience, we have no confidence that such efforts would yield an accurate portrayal of HP and its management team." The author stands by his reporting and articles for *BusinessWeek*.

This book was completed at a difficult time and under difficult circumstances for a reporter. Besides choosing not to participate, the company instructed other potential sources not to speak with me. Many other sources requested anonymity for a variety of reasons. Some former HP executives have lucrative severance packages that require that they not discuss the company publicly. Given the state of the economy and the high-tech job market in 2002, many other HP insiders did not want to speak on the record for fear of losing their jobs. Pending lawsuits and SEC investigations made others, particularly those who work or worked for Lucent, request anonymity.

Although the book depends heavily on these anonymous sources in parts, I have used only material that has been confirmed by multiple sources. Similarly, quotes attributed to anonymous sources reflect views that are held by multiple people, to reflect a more broadly held view.

Index

Index

DEMCO